ADVANCE

Cracks of Destruction

"... Sherrie Lancaster recounts her abandonment by her mother and a life-long quest to find the love and acceptance she lost. Skillfully written, the story flows smoothly, and readers will sympathize with Lancaster's emotional pain ... those in similar situations will relate to Lancaster's struggles, heartfully detailed in the pages."

—BlueInk Review

"Sherrie Lancaster writes with raw emotion in this honest work that fully explores the devastating effects of trauma that can stay with a person for the rest of their life. There's a tremendous amount of sympathy and empathy to be found in the work ... using an adult perspective to explore the confusion she felt as a young child. Overall, *Cracks of Destruction* is recommended for fans of emotive memoirs dealing with profound family dynamics."

—K.C. Finn, Reader's Favorite

"As one of the estimated 7,000+ abandoned children in the US each year, author Sherrie Lancaster shows us that generational trauma continues to impact lives. Sherrie narrates her journey with day by day, year by year attention to detail. Her relationships, both disastrous and heartwarming, are written with uninhibited candor and raw emotion. Sherrie's story will make you cry, feel completely heartbroken, and laugh out loud as you follow her search for a family unit and personal identity. *Cracks of Destruction* is at once a history, a memoir, an autobiography, and a life lesson on how to be strong and just keep going."

—Kathleen Perreault, MS, CCC-Sp

"... an unflinching portrayal of a life plagued by fractured relationships, yearning for love, and the enduring resilience of the human spirit. Through Lancaster's introspective prose, she invites readers to bear witness to her struggles, painting a vivid picture of a life marked by profound longing, heartbreaking disappointment, and the unyielding pursuit of healing. *Cracks of Destruction* is not an easy book to read but it is a worthy one. It will resonate with people who appreciate intimate testaments to the power of resilience and the unbreakable bonds that we often have to create ourselves in the family we build in our adulthood ..."

—Asher Syed, Readers' Favorite

"*Cracks of Destruction: A Daughter's Search for Home* is a story of how a woman deals with the demons of her past. This emotional read will call out to your heart ... The heartfelt emotions this book showcases is a remarkable story ... the perfect example of what it takes to survive."

—Midwest Book Review

"*Cracks of Destruction* by Sherrie Lancaster is the account of events, people, places, problems, and solutions the author has experienced throughout her life. Her survival is nothing short of inspiring. I recommend this memoir to anyone who enjoys autobiographies that reflect a personal view of the world from someone who endured so much controversy and adversity.

—Amy Raines, Readers' Favorite

"Bittersweet as it accepts past pains for the sake of personal growth ... Narrated with a sense of immediacy, the book conveys Lancaster's feelings of fear, desperation, and confusion with clarity ... a heartfelt memoir about finding home ..."

—*Foreword* Clarion Reviews

Cracks of Destruction

A DAUGHTER'S SEARCH FOR HOME

Cracks of Destruction

A DAUGHTER'S SEARCH FOR HOME

Sherrie Lancaster

MERRY DISSONANCE PRESS   CASTLE ROCK, COLORADO

Cracks of Destruction: A Daughter's Search for Home

Published by Merry Dissonance Press, LLC
Castle Rock, CO

FIRST EDITION
2023

Publisher's Cataloging-in-Publication
(Provided by Cassidy Cataloguing Services, Inc.)

Names: Lancaster, Sherrie, author.

Title: Cracks of destruction : a daughter's search for home / Sherrie Lancaster.
Description: First edition. | Castle Rock, Colorado : Merry Dissonance Press, [2023]
Identifiers: ISBN: 978-1-939919-68-7
Subjects: LCSH: Lancaster, Sherrie. | Dysfunctional families--Personal narratives. | Desertion and non-support--Personal narratives. | Child abuse--Personal narratives. | Psychological child abuse--Personal narratives. | Mother and child. | Parent and child. | Children of divorced parents--Relocation. | Adult children of dysfunctional families. | Popular music--Psycho- logical aspects. | BISAC: BIOGRAPHY & AUTOBIOGRAPHY / Survival. | BIOGRAPHY & AUTOBIOGRAPHY / Women. Classification: LCC: RC455.4.F3 L36 2023 | DDC: 616.89--dc23

ISBN 978-1-939919-68-7

Book Interior and Cover Design © 2023
Cover Design by Victoria Wolf, wolfdesignandmarketing.com
Book Design by Victoria Wolf, wolfdesignandmarketing.com
Editing by Donna Mazzitelli, writingwithdonna.com
All Rights Reserved by Sherrie Lancaster and Merry Dissonance Press, LLC

This book reflects the author's present recollections of experiences over time. Some names have been changed, some events have been compressed, and some dialogue has been recreated.

For Dorothy, Dorothy and Harold

(Front cover image: Our New House in Heyburn, Idaho.
The outside fireplace wall shows Dad's beautiful brick and rock work.
The "7Ls" on the chimney isn't seen from this angle.)

Trouble hunts indifference, and it's particularly satisfied with the indifferent, selfish one. Regardless of ethnicity or class, trouble always tracks the children of that one. Eventually, those children will be consigned to trouble's damage with only the fortunate few rescued.

—Sherrie Lancaster

PROLOGUE

"Blue Eyes Crying in the Rain"

SONS OF THE PIONEERS

LAS VEGAS, NEVADA

The old lady fixes up nice. With just the right touch of paint and accessories, she's altogether respectable. Not fashionable—respectable. She lives in the Las Vegas Valley between the dazzling Strip and the rugged Spring Mountains, where the most beautiful sunsets on the planet perform just off her porch. The old lady's been my home now for more than two dozen years. My oldest has always been a little ashamed of her, while my youngest is too little to know if he is or not. I'm not. I traveled endless miles through many years before I could claim this prize.

Songs accompanied me throughout those years, and I count on them to remind me where I've been. Like comfortable old friends, they're still with me now to revive the pure excitement only kids can truly live, taking me back to the many homes my brothers and I nicknamed just to keep track of them all. We crammed kid-perfect adventures into a scrap of time at whichever was the current kids' paradise until Mom put everyone back on the road again, roaming to the next place.

Which move was the straw that broke the family's back? It wasn't the last of seventeen moves with her in six years across half of the country. No, it started long before the boys and I were born. But the seventeenth move was my end and ragged struggle to begin, so I'll take you there with me for a minute or two.

There—yesterday—I'm ten.

EL DORADO SPRINGS, MISSOURI

I've tramped a million miles behind my brother Dean, exploring creeks, natural springs, woods, and fields surrounding the little farmhouse we currently call home. I tramp behind him now along a narrow, gravel road to town. Dean, two years older, was the baby in a family of four boys until a girl—me—came along.

We're friends, Dean and me—the best kind. We've killed each other in gladiator battles, shot each other with pop guns loaded with hard Russian olives, sword-fought to the death, and fed our chickens chewed bubble gum mixed with toothpaste when Mom wasn't looking. Chickens love us. But we're not playing today; we're on a mission, and we're dead serious.

It's a pretty autumn October day, and no one's around to say we can't walk to town. Dad's still at work, and the two oldest boys, Ronnie and Carson, left home before this latest move. Craig, two years older than Dean, didn't bother coming home after school, so why can't we head to town if we want? Besides, we have to because we need to find our mom. We haven't seen her in days since she moved out when Dad was at work and we were in school. When I couldn't find her anywhere that day, I found her bedroom dresser empty. And I found a pain I'd never known.

Dad loves Mom. I know because I've always seen it. Arriving home from work to learn she left us sent Dad wandering through the house, looking at all of her that was gone. When he folded his tall, lean frame to sit on a kitchen chair, Dean and I each put a hand on Dad's shoulders as he broke then covered his eyes and quietly cried. We'd never seen him do that. It seemed the house was dark as we stood by him; we all knew the light was gone.

When Dad decided to move back to Tucson, Arizona, because he couldn't stay here anymore without her, Dean and I realized we wouldn't be just a couple of miles from her; we'd be halfway across the country. We knew she'd want to keep us when she found out. That's why we have to walk to town and find her before it's too late. Dean figures it won't be hard with only one tavern in town. If she isn't there, we'll just wait around until *he* shows up, and she'll be with *him*.

Dean marches straight through the tavern doorway with me right on his heels. We stop only a second in the dark room before we see her, and she isn't alone. They're curled up in a booth right in front of us.

"Dad's moving us back to Tucson," Dean tells her. "We're leaving Saturday after he gets home from work."

We wait for words we know she'll say, leaning in together, holding our breaths … waiting … waiting.

"Ya wanna coke?" *he* asks, shattering the tangible hope in the air.

"Meet me in the park Saturday at two," Mom says. "Now you kids go back home and be good."

Craig, Dean, and I are early, so we sit in the grass at Spring Park to wait. I see her walking toward us, always so pretty with her hair just right, makeup perfect, and sparkling-blue eyes. My world revolves around her.

Mom gives us a quick hug and kiss and hands each of us a keepsake, as though things can replace her. She gives me the Bible Dad gave her before our roaming started. She gives Dean her gold cross necklace and Craig her Kodak camera—the same camera that took scores of pictures of my family: Mom, Dad, four boys, and me.

She tells us to be good and mind Dad. She says she'll write then gives us another hug and kiss, only to turn and walk away crying. I've always hated watching her cry and the helpless feeling I drown in from her tears. The three of us didn't say a word except "thank you" when she handed us that stuff. I can't believe she's walking away without looking back.

Watching until she's out of sight, we turn from the park, each of us lost in our own way: Craig's red with anger and tears, Dean's whiter than a ghost, and I'm numb, confused, empty. Not one of us thought to ask for her address, and she didn't offer it. We don't know what our address will be in Tucson, so how can she write anyway?

I'm glad I won't be going to school in town anymore. I used to like it because it's the same school Dad went to when he was little, but it's hard now when every crummy kid knows what happened. Their eyes follow me because Mom left us to go with *him*. The four kids *he* left behind probably aren't doing any better, but I still hate them all, even though I don't know them. Can't they keep their *dad* at home so *he'll* leave my mother alone? I can't imagine life without her.

Roaming with Mom is over, but my endless years of wandering begin when we leave hours later in the middle of the night, only taking what the little car can hold. We packed our clothes and very few personal things. I take some dolls, the Bible, a diary Mom gave me, a gray basket, and a wooden, mirrored Whitman's Chocolate box—gifts Gramma received when Mom was born. Gramma gave them to me when I was seven. Dad leaves all his bills, and I leave almost everything else, including my childhood and mother.

It's a rotten night—dark, gloomy, raining. Headlights from the few oncoming cars viciously smear raindrops on the windshield then throw them away to the dark. The radio is on, crackly and low. Through static, I hear "Blue Eyes Crying in the Rain" as I fight not to cry. Dad silently drives into the darkness with three miserable, surly kids.

Where It Began

1

"To Each His Own"

FRANKIE LAINE

Boyd's Lounge below the Oregon Trail Café in downtown Burley, Idaho, was busy most Friday and Saturday nights, but with WWII over, the bar's jumping practically every night. Dad landed a job at Boyd's. A steady job and toe-tapping jukebox music made life good—much better than the army life he recently left behind.

Mom liked to tell me about the fuss she caused in Boyd's when she tried getting a handsome new bartender's attention. When nothing worked, she decided to accuse him of shortchanging her. The song "To Each His Own" travels through my mind when I hear the clamor in Boyd's Lounge, smell cigarette smoke, and hear honky-tonk music. I see Dad working behind the bar as Mom laughs from far away and tells the story again.

"Excuse me," Mom says with her voice lost in the blare of music and several boisterous conversations.

"Say, bartender!" Mom's voice finds its target.

Dad turns from the cash register after ringing up a purchase. "Yes?" he asks, pushing the cash drawer shut with a clang.

"You didn't give me the right change for this," Mom says, toying with her glass.

"Yes, I did," Dad replies with a hint of a smile before turning to another customer.

"No, you didn't," Mom presses.

"Well, guess I'll just have to mix you another one on the house." Dad sets the drink in front of Mom and says, "Now we're even."

"Thank you." Mom smiles and tips her glass to him. "But you still owe me twenty-five cents."

Dad's broad shoulders settle easily as he leans on the bar with his strong hands in front of Mom. A straight, masculine nose complements his smooth face, strong jaw, and long neck. A smile plays around a full mouth while he gazes from two handsome, melancholy, dark-blue eyes into her mischievous, sparkling-blue ones.

"Listen, Miss," Dad begins as a man interrupts, asking Mom to dance.

"I'll be back for my money!" Mom tosses over her shoulder.

"I don't owe you any!"

But the smile she throws him, along with those blue eyes, keeps his attention for a minute.

"She dances circles around that clod," Dad says to no one in particular as he watches Mom and finds himself wishing he were dancing with her. Instead, he two-steps down the length of the bar to continue working. After the dance, Mom's back, demanding her change.

"You don't dance too bad," Dad says.

"Oh? You can do it better?" Mom spars.

"On my worst night."

"Would you care to prove it?"

The conversation leads to a dance after Dad's shift is over, and the dance leads to a date. Dates are spent anywhere they can dance because they both love polkas, waltzes, and country-western. Early on, they start developing their dance that's poetry in motion on any dance floor. It blends Dad's easygoing, rhythmic, Missouri-smooth steps and Mom's jitterbug country two-step. Mom never did get her quarter, but the dates lead to fifteen years of bantering about who taught who how to dance. And the fate of Mom and Dad's unborn kids is sealed.

Standing just inside Boyd's Lounge, looking at the bar across a smoke-filled room, I'm on vacation, trying to capture remnants of my family. A country-western song is playing on the jukebox while a few couples manage to obliterate the song's beat on the dance floor. I order a beer and sit at a small table away from the crowd. My long-ago neighbors warned me that Boyd's is rougher than it used to be, and it's not a good idea for me to be here alone.

I'm not worried. I'd spent a couple of formative years growing up in a bar, so I sip my beer and see Mom and Dad through smoke and time on the dance floor, doing what they do so well together. They meld as one when they dance, but everything else is completely opposite. Other than obvious differences between males and females, Dad, at six foot four, is tall and lean. Mom is five foot two with a rounded, womanly figure. Dad's quiet, easygoing, and unflappable; Mom's talkative, lively, and easily annoyed.

How did that handsome man and pretty woman both happen to be in a little town in southern Idaho at Boyd's Lounge on the same night of the same week, month, and year? Sitting here, I think about it again. Although there were similarities in their early years—poor and roaming around the country—they developed very different personalities. Maybe that's what attracted them to each other in the beginning.

As an adolescent, Dad had been shuffled from pillar to post after his mother died of tuberculosis and his dad gave him to anyone needing some work done. Dad managed to survive his childhood and the Great Depression then married a woman from a wealthy family and had a son. When he realized he couldn't stomach how he was expected to live with daily orders that came with money he didn't want, he divorced and struck out on his own again. He soon found himself in the middle of WWII's terrible battles in Europe.

Mom had a lousy childhood that turned appalling after her parents divorced when she was four years old. During the next decade, her mother's choice of men drove Mom to leave an intolerable situation. After two failed marriages and two baby boys before she was twenty, Mom went to Burley, Idaho, where her mother—Gramma—lived.

Dad mustered out of the army in Fort Lewis, Washington, with one hundred dollars in cash from the US government, a Veterans of Foreign Wars service pin, and a Bronze Star medal. After heading to Burley, where his brother lived, he found a bartending job at Boyd's Lounge. He soon found himself being harassed by a pretty woman he decided to get to know better.

Abandon or forsake? The dictionary states that abandon implies a complete rejection of one's responsibilities, and forsake stresses renouncing a person or thing formerly dear to one. To me, they both mean that someone—usually a kid—dies inside because of someone's—usually an adult's—actions. Those two words are the curse that's plagued my family tree for generations. So, you see, the curse didn't start with me, but it will end with me.

Finishing my drink in Boyd's as the last refrains of "To Each His Own" drift through my mind, Mom and Dad finish their dance and fall in love. They married the following spring in Elko, Nevada.

Although I'm mature well beyond my twenty-two years, it'll still take more years of living before I begin to come to terms with the miles, years, and songs I had absolutely no control over as a kid, but as an adult, I have to navigate. I leave Boyd's with no more understanding than I had when I arrived.

2

"This Old House"

STUART HAMBLEN

When the US government sold surplus army barracks after the war, Dad bought one and moved it to a lot on Malta Avenue across railroad sidings from Burley. He built a basement, sat the barracks on top, and added all the final touches Mom wanted. After two more boys were born, I came along, and the barracks was my first home. When I arrived in the middle of a winter blizzard, my house didn't look like a barracks anymore. It was a lovely, small white home filled with a family of seven.

❧

After seeing Boyd's Lounge, the next day's stop has to be that little house on Malta Avenue.

The first time I slowly drive by, my heart nearly stops when I see a little girl sitting on the front-door landing, inspecting a skinned knee like I'd done a million times. Or was she me, and I didn't have to leave? I do belong somewhere … but no, it can't be. *Breathe, damnit, steer the car.* The little girl has long, brown hair, not blond. My heart nearly stops again when I see a dog in the yard looking like our family dog Zip.

The second time I slowly drive by, the little girl's gone and a woman's looking out the picture window in the front room. The third time, I decide to stop before she calls the cops on me.

Staring across the street after I parked, I felt my heart pounding. It still looks like my Barracks Home, but it's not a kids' paradise outside anymore. The yard isn't fenced by shrubs with red currant berries, and the flowers, rock garden, and sandbox are gone. The boys' mysterious tar-papered clubhouse, where I couldn't stick even a toe inside, is gone too. Craig sneaked me in once but first swore me to secrecy. I had to cross my heart, hope to die, and spit to promise I wouldn't tell the other boys. I kept my word but still complained to anyone who'd listen that I couldn't go inside. Finally, Mom gave the boys an ultimatum: let me play with them in the clubhouse or attend a tea party hosted by me. The tea party was voted the least of two evils, mostly because Mom's cookies would be involved. I hate to see the clubhouse gone.

The woman answers the door when I knock, and after introducing myself and explaining why I want to come in, she smiles.

"Two of your brothers have been here to see the house too!" she says, waving me inside.

I know without asking which two brothers that would be: the same two I followed home from our last walk to town. I think we've been homeless in our minds since.

The so-very-familiar inside briefly paralyzes me. Stepping into my Barracks Home, I can't breathe. The woman must think I'm crazy, but I can't help it. I'm lightheaded and can't think. I wish she'd just stop talking. I can faintly hear music. I have an overwhelming urge to sit down on the floor and cry. Trying to keep myself together and buy some time, I look around from just inside the front door to see the house is neat and clean but not like when it was Mom's.

Mom was miserably, immaculately clean. When Gramma visited, she flicked cigarette ashes in her hand rather than dirty one of Mom's ashtrays. Dad gave up smoking pipes after Mom washed them in hot, soapy water and scraped the cake out of each bowl to thoroughly clean and unknowingly ruin them. Kids couldn't step on throw rugs in the front room because that would mash the pile or walk on the polished wood floor because that would ruin the shine. Kids weren't allowed to sit on furniture or touch almost anything. Mom ironed our pajamas and starched our pillowcases. She was constantly cleaning someone or something. But there was always music playing on Mom's radio with a chance to be swirled around in a quick dance before she passed me on her way to clean something else.

Dirty, abandoned shacks and bedbugs from the Depression had left their mark on Mom. She was nine years old when she started roaming with her little sister, Ruth, Gramma, and stepdad Del from state to state, looking for work. They lived out of a car and found jobs as field hands, thinning and topping beets and onions. Sometimes they found a shack to live in for a while. When Gramma lit candles, the shack's walls and floor usually started crawling with bedbugs. Mom gathered big red ants in a jar for Gramma to shake out in the shack and on the bedclothes. The ants ate the bedbugs but not before the bedbugs tried to eat each person as they slept. Gramma could never entirely get rid of them. When she packed up to move on, the bedbugs moved with them in the seams of their blankets and clothes.

"Sleep tight and don't let the bedbugs bite," Mom said when she tucked me in at night.

Still frozen near the doorway, I see a play table where mine used to sit. Kids are sitting there, and the least-of-two-evils tea party is underway. The boys—my brothers—are my main adversaries, my partners-in-crime, my playmates, and my protectors. But if they could help it, they wouldn't be caught dead sitting at my play table. And yet, here they are with hands folded and every hair in place.

Ronnie sits across from me. Being the oldest, he seems like an adult to me. His freckled, rascal face favors Mom with a boy version of her pug nose, and his slim frame is topped with Mom's thick, brown hair. He's our ringleader and peacemaker.

Next to Ronnie in age and at the table, Carson's almost sitting still. He's constantly just getting out of trouble and always smiling. He lives to tease us and does until Mom threatens him with his life if he doesn't stop. He's slim like Ronnie but has reddish-brown hair that will grow curly. His freckled face and straight, narrow nose aren't like Mom's at all, but his eyes are. They're a much lighter blue than Mom's but have the look of her eyes.

Next is Mom and Dad's first kid together, Craig. He's blond and husky with Mom's face and temperament. He tries to keep up with Ronnie and Carson, but he's stuck between them and the younger boy and girl. He'd fit okay if he didn't try so hard, but he's not comfortable with the older ones and doesn't want to be comfortable with the younger ones.

Dean sits closest to me. He's a miniature Dad with his straight nose and melancholy, dark-blue eyes. His brown hair will grow into Dad's black hair. He's next in age to me, so we play together at the same speed, although we can still fight with the best of them. He's been my buddy from the beginning, and I adore him.

Even though the boys look completely miserable, I'm happy out of my mind because they can't escape. Yet, Carson tries his best to do just that.

"Sit down, Carson," Mom barks.

Many times, I've watched Carson talk Mom into something. With his arms hugging her waist, Mom's resolve weakens when he kisses her arm then bolts for the door and his latest adventure.

"I said sit down!" Mom barks again. It didn't work this time. "If you boys don't sit still, you can all do this again tomorrow," Mom warns. The second she turns back to the stove, they stick out their tongues at me.

"Mama! They're doin' it again!"

"Okay, I'm almost done," Mom says.

She finishes heating canned milk with water and sugar in a pot on the stove and pours the delicious concoction into my teapot.

"Sherrie's the host, so she'll pour tea and serve cookies. You boys mind your manners and make proper conversation."

Mom stays close to make sure they behave themselves, but Craig still angrily stares at me the entire time. I'm never invited into the clubhouse again.

Leaning against the front doorjamb now for support, I'm looking where Mom's first telephone sat in a place of honor in the front room close to the radio we listened to every night after dinner. Kids were forbidden to touch the radio or the fascinating black phone. I loved the ratchety noise it made when Mom turned the dial with her finger. It took forever before the phone rang the first time, but Mom didn't pick it up.

"Mama! Get it!"

She said something about "a party line and it isn't the right ring so I can't answer it because it's for someone else and we have to listen for the right ring so be quiet and don't yell and scare me to death anymore."

Another forever passed before the phone rang the right ring. It was exciting to watch Mom pick up the handle with a curly black rope and say hello. I wondered why she was crying because I thought she liked the phone. I learned the caller, her oldest sister, told her that their dad had just died. It was a long time before I watched her answer it again.

I can't hold the front door up forever, but now I'm looking at their TV sitting where ours had been. Gramma had a TV before us, but Mom refused to put up with Del's pouting because we were there to watch it, so it wasn't long until Dad and the boys carried one into my Barracks Home. I'm that little girl jumping up and down with excitement, watching Dad set it up and turn it on. When I have to tear to the TV and touch the people in it, Mom whacks my butt then wipes off my fingerprints as I watch through hot tears my very first TV commercial about a Chevrolet. The TV's big and boxy with dials beside the screen. Oh! I want to turn those dials.

Supported by the door, I still want to turn them. With the radio and phone off-limits, it's a wonder kids are allowed to sit in the same room to watch TV. We can, but only if we're sitting quietly on the floor. Commercials showing families rushing to a bomb shelter in a nuclear attack petrify me. I want the grownups to talk as they usually do during commercials so I can't hear the part about knowing where the closest shelter is located. I don't have a clue where it's at. Mom says, "Don't be silly." But if I'm being silly, why aren't they talking?

I come to know those commercials are a result of the post-WWII Cold War era that casts a cloud over everything with a fear that grows as I grow. Fallout shelters and stockpiling food and water are common subjects. The Iron Curtain, an imaginary line between democracy and communism, separates Europe and spreads the bomb's fear everywhere, even over my Barracks Home.

When Dad is at work and the boys are in school, Mom and I watch *The Millionaire* and plan how we'll spend a million dollars after Michael Anthony shows up with it. We watch housewives crowned as *Queen for a Day*, *Make Room for Daddy* with Danny Thomas, and *My Little Margie* with Gale Storm. I love cowboy shows. *Hopalong Cassidy* is my favorite, but *The Lone Ranger* and *The Cisco Kid* are close seconds. I watch any cowboy show I can and practice with my brothers' six-shooters so I'll grow up cowboy.

Muttering "I'm sorry" and taking one more step inside, I scan for a safe place to look—one that won't overwhelm me. But I'm looking at the kitchen cupboard where my favorite aunt, Aunt Ruth, laughed and called for Mom to watch as she propped me against the cupboard then coaxed me into walking a few steps before falling on her stomach and, in the process, learning to walk.

The woman quietly takes my hand for a tour of the house—as if I need a tour. Maybe she's just afraid I'm going to faint. I'm still not breathing very well. My eyes are wet ... and that music ... then the house up close: the front room, the bedroom across the way, the kitchen, the back door, and the basement stairs. I know each room, each nook and cranny, and every step and stair. I know the boys will be home any minute from school. I see Gramma from the kitchen window, wearing her furry coat with candy hidden in the pockets as she walks down the alley for a visit. Dad's finally home from work because Zip's barking in the yard.

I'm following the woman down the basement stairs, the same stairs that, as a child, seemed only a narrow channel cut through cement. I can feel the footsteps of that little girl and crave to be her again as I walk the stairs where my first black eye was the result of navigating them. The stair wall is still lined with shelves that stored Mom's quart jars filled with home-canned fruits and vegetables. Once down the stairs for the night, there was no going back up until morning. A bucket was kept downstairs for nighttime emergencies, usually in the boys' room, but it was always too dark and cold to even think about getting up to find it. Sometimes, I yelled until one of the boys brought it to me, and other times, I wet the bed in my sleep to face the wrath of Mom in the morning.

The woman patiently waits while I stand in the doorway to my first little bedroom. But I can't step in. Turning to the boys' room, I see their bunkbed with the two youngest on the bottom bunk and the two oldest on the top, except when I was thrown up there during wintertime Saturday evenings. I'm the two-year-old yelling for the boys to help me get down, but they won't.

In the wintertime, after Dad takes Mom downtown to dance, Ronnie and Carson drape a thin blanket over the TV then turn off the volume and all the lights. The blanket casts spooky shadows, creating the stage for our game. The rule is everyone crawls on all fours while trying to scare someone to death. When you touch someone first, they're out. Trouble is, I never get to play. As soon as we start, one of the boys throws a blanket over me and lugs me downstairs to chuck me up on the top bunk in the boys' room, where I scream for help because I'm scared to climb down in the total dark. Even if I did manage it, I'd never make it alive back up the dark stairs.

After the boys straighten up and put the blankets away, they finally retrieve me. Together, we raid the kitchen and eat anything Ronnie thinks we can without getting in trouble. I get the first bite sitting on the kitchen counter in their efforts to keep me quiet about what they've been up to. Then it's time to hit the stairs again for bed.

Nodding "yes" when the woman touches my arm, asking if I'm ready, I follow her back upstairs.

"Do you mind if I go outside for a minute?" I ask, standing by the back door.

"Not at all. Just knock when you're ready to come back in."

The woman is kind, giving me space to keep it together, but I need to be alone for a few minutes. I'm looking at the yard where my first years were happily spent playing with Dean. I'm standing on the back step where Mom taught us how to make mud pies with the rich, black dirt by the step. Because I dressed like Dean—in shorts, no shirt, and barefoot—Mom slathered us with suntan oil to avoid us being burnt to a crisp. Later, Dean and I conjured up on demand the oil scent to remind us of her.

Having to sit down, I take a little hop to the top of the cinderblock wall Dad built between our yard and the alley. I'm immediately flying down basement stairs again, slung over a brother's shoulder.

During summertime Saturday nights after we're in bed, Mom, Dad, and our neighbors Paul and Blanche Coffey go out dancing. We're out of bed heading outdoors the second they leave. The boys sit me on top of the cinderblock wall, where I'm the lookout for the grownups' return. My brothers and the Coffey boys play up and down the street, occasionally checking if I'm still on the wall. I scream for the boys when I see headlights, and one of them snatches me then tumbles down the stairs to our beds. Mom always sends Dad to check on us when they get home, and Dad never says anything to Mom about us being heavy breathing, sweaty kids lying in our beds.

Mom's up early on Sunday morning, no matter how late they stayed out dancing, because there are five hungry kids to feed. She lets Dad sleep, but her patience is wearing thin when the record volume is turned up on "Under the Double Eagle" or "Beer Barrel Polka," filling the house with music. It isn't long until Dad sleepily dances out of the bedroom, looking for Mom. He dances her around the front room and to the kitchen to find his coffee.

Still sitting on the cinderblock wall, I'm staring at the tree where Carson swung once. Although Ronnie was the patient one, Carson the tease could get on his last nerve. When Ronnie and Craig decided to stop his constant teasing, they tackled Carson, tied a rope around him, hoisted him up the tree, and left him dangling there. Kid-like, Ronnie and Craig didn't intend to kill Carson—they just wanted him out of commission for a while. Luckily, Dad saw Carson clutching the rope around his neck, swinging from the tree, and saved him.

A horn honks somewhere, and I'm really tired. The woman opens the back door after I tap, and I thank her for allowing me inside.

"I'll probably be back tomorrow, but I'll walk the alley and not bother you anymore."

"You were no bother," the woman says.

I head back to the only motel in Burley, where I'd spent the previous night. On the way, I stop for something to eat and a Pepsi. In bed, I'm not drifting to sleep but back to those times again. They were the best times I'd spent with my family, so why not? Didn't I come here to try and figure it all out—to heal the hole in my heart? I'm drifting back again, as if I could stop myself ....

Everyone thinks I'm Craig's dwarf twin because I'm blond, too, with Mom's face, but I won't grow into their temperament—maybe because I have Dad's and Dean's melancholy, dark-blue eyes. In the mornings, Mom gathers my hair into a ponytail or two braids. I hate braids because she pulls them so tight the skin on my temples stretches both eyes sideways. I have to cry before Mom loosens them to let my eyelids snap back into place.

I'm stuck with braids even when Mom gives the boys mohawk haircuts after the school year is over. She shaves each boy's head except for a shaped strip of hair from their foreheads to the napes of their necks. Now they look like wild Indians instead of just acting like them. It only takes a couple of days before Mom realizes she has trouble when four sunburned heads come inside for lunch. Even though she coats each head with suntan oil, soon blisters, peeling scalps, and scabs sit at her kitchen table.

I want a mohawk, too, because I'm a tomboy. I have to be to keep up with the boys. I can blow Ronnie's Boy Scout bugle louder than any of them can, which doesn't help because I'm only a girl. Even so, they usually let me play with them. I have no choice playing Dog Pile, finding myself on the bottom of a pile of tangled boys smelling like Zip when he's wet. When I wiggle out, they let me climb on top of the heap to yell, "I'm king of the hill!" But more often than not, they cheat. And when they do, I start slugging with my fingers clenched over my thumbs. Craig catches my fists to pull my thumbs out where they should be over my clenched fingers then holds them up for me to see.

"This is how you slug! If you keep doing it the other way, you'll break your thumbs. So, do it right!" he tells me. Now I know how to slug boys properly.

About the time I learn to slug, I'm realizing the boys are different from me, and I'm as interested in the difference as they are. They dare me to show them the difference, so I double-dog-dare them to show me first. They triple-dog-dare me, so I hafta show'um. I give a quick pull-down peek and wait for them to show me. But they won't.

"You hafta show me!" I yell.

"Make us!" they yell back.

"You're already made but too dumb to know it!" I scream, but they still run away laughing.

I stomp through the back door to tell Mom on them. Very quickly, all hell breaks loose. She finds her stick, rounds up the boys, and makes them lean over the back of the couch and drop their Levi's and underwear. With me watching, she whacks each boy a few times before moving on to the next one. I'm almost sorry I told on them, watching angry red welts spread over white butt cheeks. When Mom's finished, the boys pull up their pants, wipe their tears, and throw me looks that could kill a lesser little girl. Then they head back outside.

I'm poison. The boys won't talk to me or let me play with them. And what's worse, they pretend I don't exist. This is killing me. I can't even get a good stomp going walking into the kitchen.

"Mama, the boys say I'm poison and won't play with me."

For the first time, Mom treats my boy complaint seriously.

"Yes, I suppose you'll be poison for a while. The boys are ashamed and embarrassed, and they need time to work that out. So you need to leave them alone. They'll play with you again, I promise, but you have to wait for them," Mom says. "Now go play with your dolls."

Crud! Now I hafta play with dolls. Who wants to do that when you have boys? But Mom's right. It isn't long before they let me play again, and I'm treated as just another rambunctious little kid.

We're regularly whipped with one hand and loved with the other for any infraction of Mom's rules. Her whippings with the stick, a switch from a tree, or a piece of lath are murder. And it's worse if you try to run away. My most vivid whipping is earned at two years old from methodically stomping down every square inch of pile on a front room rug. I don't know Mom's watching every stomp, and when I see her, I run in the opposite direction. Out of nowhere, she grabs my fleeing arm and whacks my butt, sending me flying around in a circle. Each time my feet hit the floor, the stick hits my butt, and I'm airborne again. When she's finished, my butt's flaming mush and my arm's rubbed worse than when Carson gives me a wrist burn.

If one of the boys gets himself into dire trouble and Mom's tired, she makes him sit still—which is murder in itself—until Dad gets home. When he arrives, Dad obliges Mom by taking the guilty one around back to beat the tar out of him. The kids who aren't in trouble—at least not caught yet—gather silently by Mom, where we flinch with each wail while Mom wipes tears from her eyes. Finally, Dad and the beaten boy, acting very sorry, walk back into the house.

I learned years later that Dad never beat the boy; instead, after giving him a good talking to, Dad whacked his own leg while the kid provided sound effects. I got the short end of the stick on that because Mom always whipped me herself.

The next morning in my motel room, there's a half-eaten sandwich next to an unfinished Pepsi on the nightstand. Not having changed into pajamas, I quickly shower and put on fresh clothes. Reenergized and excited again, I head for the alley by my Barracks Home. My eyes are red and puffy, but isn't that what sunglasses are for?

Walking down the alley to Gramma's back gate, I recall how I loved it when I walked there with Mom because she was happy, and when Mom was happy, everyone was happy. When we arrived at the gate, Mom reached over the top to flip something so it would open up and let us in. Then she got mad all over again when we passed the outhouse just inside the gate because her stepdad Del still hadn't built Gramma an indoor bathroom.

The fence, gate, and outhouse are gone now. And so is the mass of beautifully colored flowers in Gramma's backyard, where sunflowers were much taller than her. The huge round blooms were so heavy with seeds they had to be propped up with poles. But the long, narrow sidewalk leading to the back door is still here.

I feel the warmth of Mom's hand again as she holds mine, following the sidewalk to the back steps and through the screen door Gramma holds open for us. Mom and Gramma are the same height and build, and they hug and kiss as we walk into the lovely, warm kitchen.

"There'll be plenty of dirt cleaned when I'm dead and gone," Gramma laughingly says if she's watching TV instead of finishing her housework when

Mom and I arrive for a visit. Gramma's hooked on soap operas and loves *The Edge of Night*. She's also a vigorous wrestling fan and never misses a Gorgeous George match.

Occasionally, Gramma invites us for Sunday dinner, and we have to bathe early and dress in our Sunday best. Everyone's on their best behavior, too, except Del, who usually pouts and ignores us all. Mom's hated Del since she was nine years old, but Dad's always polite to him. Sometimes they walk outside to stand with hands in their pockets while rocking on their heels to toes while they talk.

While Gramma cooks, I beg Mom to retell one of my favorite stories: the chopped-off-thumb-in-the-pan story.

When Mom was little, she watched Gramma open a can of corn and pour it into a pan to heat. Mom shrieked when she saw a thumb bobbing in the pan with the corn. Apparently, the thumb—fingernail, knuckle, and all—had been canned right along with the corn. Mom and Gramma laugh again when they both agree the thumbnail was neatly trimmed.

Having been broke myself as an adult, I understand Gramma toying with the idea of picking out the offensive thumb to salvage the corn. Heat from the canning process surely killed any germs. But Gramma decided they weren't that poor and she could fry an extra spud instead.

Gramma's chicken is sputtering and popping in hot lard, and spuds are ready for mashing. After the chicken's done, she'll make gravy from the drippings. A homemade apple pie just out of the oven is cooling on the counter. Dad's favorite meal is almost ready.

Kids sit on grass in Gramma's front yard under a huge shade tree in the warm sunshine to eat while adults sit at the kitchen table. Dad comes outside to referee dessert so I can eat my pie without one of the boys stealing it. Four pairs of eyes never stray from my plate, waiting to see how much is left after I'm full. Even when I spit on the last of the pie, the boys still fight over it.

Standing in front of Gramma's house so many years later, I'm sad to see the huge tree gone. Remembering the mysterious place across the street from Gramma, I turn to look at it.

The first and last time until first grade, I played with a little girl who was in the basement house across the street from Gramma. I'd always wanted to explore the mysterious place but found it like our basement, only bigger and not at all mysterious—just weird with no windows. We played with pop-apart beads, the current rage for little girls, but soon I was ready for the boys. Girls just weren't as much fun.

Oblivious to the world beyond, I walk the alley back to my car parked across the street from my Barracks Home.

3

"Let the Rest of the World Go By"

SLIM WHITMAN

Sitting in my car after walking to Gramma's, I'm wondering again why I can't just let all this die and be happy with the life I've been trying to build for almost half of my twenty-two years. Well, because the first years of my life were happy, stable, even normal, and filled with kids' pure excitement … until everything began to change.

Fighting with myself for the umpteenth time, I hear cars arriving across the street at my Barracks Home. My head finds a headrest as I close my eyes to see Mom talking about her sisters.

Mom says the meanness in her family comes from her dad, with her oldest sister inheriting most of it while her only brother suffered most from it. Good or bad, aunts with uncles in tow are always coming or going. They arrive in a happy mood, but very often, someone leaves mad. And heaven help the sister who breaks the ice first by talking to the mad sister because there'll be hell to pay from the wronged sister when she finds out.

Most of Mom's older sisters' visits are stressful, even for the kids. If a kid forgets to say Aunt or Uncle so-and-so, someone jumps down the kid's throat. And never try to listen in.

"Oh! Go outside and play. If we let a fart, we'll put it in a bottle and save it for you!" the aunts say if a kid gets caught hanging around.

I don't like it when the oldest, Aunt Anna, visits. I haven't liked her from the start. She tries to make me sit on her lap or hold her hand and makes jokes when I won't. Mom comes to the rescue by sending me outside to play with the boys. I know Mom doesn't always like her either.

Aunt Mary's sweet and happy. She's a cowgirl who loves Western magazines, clothes, and music. I love listening to her yodel during a song because it's so pretty. She doesn't have any children, causing Mom and Gramma to say she needs some kids to forget her own aches and pains. I know she likes the boys and me—she just doesn't know what to do with us.

When Anna or Mary visit, Gramma always asks if they've heard from the third older sister, Aunt Leota. Gramma's sad because they never know where she is or how she's doing. When Gramma isn't there, the whispers say Leota's a prostitute in Nevada. I don't know what that means, but I guess she's very busy or she'd visit more often like the other aunts.

The only brother, and closest in age to Mom, Uncle Louie, swings me around laughing when he comes over to see his sisters. He's always smiling while avoiding their feuds.

The best times are when the little sister visits. Aunt Ruth had a different dad who was one-third Cherokee Indian, and she's tall, unlike the others. We call her our gorgeous Ant Root.

Starting the car to force myself back to the present, I head to the motel. Instead, I find myself walking in the park near downtown Burley, where the boys and I walked many times to play.

I'm standing near play equipment in an expanse of green grass so I can hear the boys yell and play on the monkey bars, merry-go-round, and teeter-totter. When I walk to the swing set to sit down a minute, my feet first unexpectedly find the dipped area on the ground under the swing seat. I'm dizzy—almost falling, then floating because I remember that little patch of ground better than anything else I'll ever remember. My feet had helped keep it there when I jumped up and down, yelling for one of the boys to boost me up on the swing seat and push me higher and higher. That little patch of ground proves I've been here; I had been part of a family and belonged somewhere once.

Leaning against my car, looking at buildings on Burley's main street, I know it's still a small town with less than six thousand people. And everywhere I've looked, people still have gardens because the rich, black soil is perfect for growing nearly anything. I know Mexicans are still an important workforce in the fields surrounding Burley, and there's still a Basque community too. My favorite part of downtown, and what fascinated me more than anything else in my world, were the Indians. But they're gone now.

I always stared in awe at Blackfeet Indians when I saw them in town. The women wore full Indian garb with beads and trinkets on long dresses, while the men wore tunics with feathers and beads attached and leggings. They all had blanket shawls draped over their shoulders and beautiful, long, coal-black hair. The Indians gathered downtown, where they sat wrapped up in blankets, leaning against storefronts to watch everything up and down the street. As a little girl, I thought they were beautiful and scary too.

I walk across the street, remembering how everything looked back then. *The dime store doesn't seem to have changed*, I think as I enter. I see myself in Mom's old Buick, and she's driving to the dime store as I keep an eye out for the Indians because they like the dime store too. Mom parks then holds my hand, walking around the corner. Finally, I see the Indians! I'm fascinated and stare while Mom jerks me along, ordering, "Stop staring!"

I usually get in trouble in the store for wanting something or touching something. "Wish in one hand and crap in the other, then see which one gets full fastest." Mom's very ladylike and proper, but she does have a string of sayings that'll cause a sailor to blush.

Somehow, I wander away in the store without getting caught, so I know Mom's searching for me. When she finds me in the midst of a group of Indians, talking excitedly in their language, she excuses herself, poking her arm into their tight circle to fish for any handy little body part. The Indians finally break rank, allowing Mom to grab me, but they continue stroking my blond hair and chattering. I can't stop staring at all the black hair falling toward me. Mom holds my arm in a vise grip and flies out of the store before they can keep me for a good luck charm. I can't wait for the next dime store trip.

"Excuse me," I hear, suddenly brought back to the present. A woman's trying to walk around me while I stand in the center of a narrow aisle in the dime store where the Indians once captured me. After purchasing a pair of earrings for a keepsake and walking back to my car, I realize I'm starving and don't want another sandwich like last night.

I head for the Oregon Trail Café, where I order a large, hot meal. Sitting in the quiet café, waiting for my order, I'm missing Mom's kitchen table and her delicious food. Then I'm at her table—eating, listening, dodging the boys.

Mom tells us at every meal to eat all the food on our plates. "There are starving kids in China," she states, like that will give us more of an appetite. She reminds us that when Dad was little, his dad wouldn't let him eat until the adults finished. It was only then that Dad could forage through leftovers to eat what he wanted, but what he wanted was meat, and there was never any meat left over. Now Mom fills Dad up at every meal.

Mom's an excellent cook, and we devour nearly everything she makes. After cooking a pot of something smelling irresistible, she adds a little more salt, declaring, "Every little bit helps, the old woman said as she peed in the sea."

Baking soda biscuits are mixed, plumped, patted, and cut. Extra sugar's added if they're going to be the shortcake for a strawberries and shortcake dessert. Each biscuit is swiped in grease in the bottom of the biscuit pan, first one side then the other, before going in the oven to bake and fill the air with a delicious aroma.

Mom handles a huge Idaho potato with ease. She peels it in one continuous piece and slices it so the slices fall into sizzling lard in a skillet. She's finished several potatoes, it seems, before I finish asking what's for dinner besides fried spuds. Then she tells me about when she was little and babysat the littler girls, sister Ruth and three cousins, when the mothers went out. There was never anything to eat after they left, so Mom made do by peeling and slicing potatoes. She cooked a slice at a time speared on a fork over a wood fire as the rest hungrily waited for their treat. They all cried when a piece of nearly cooked spud fell from the fork and disappeared in the flames. Everyone then had to wait that much longer for her treat.

Attempting to eat with the boys is tough because they always try to get a loud reaction out of me so they can snicker when it's me, instead of them, in trouble with Mom. Even when I mind my own business, at least one finger is pointed at me when I look up from my plate. The sneaky finger might be sticking out from between a plate and the gravy bowl or peeking out from an armpit. The pointing finger belongs to the boy with the smirk, and the armpit belongs to another. It's a toss-up who'll be in trouble at each meal: the boys or me.

When we've finished eating, no one leaves the table without first kissing Mom to thank her and to say the meal was delicious. She smiles with each kiss.

"I'm glad you liked it, and even if you didn't, it'll make a turd," Mom says with a laugh, making another sailor blush.

After filling up at the café, I'm back in the motel room in PJs this time. But instead of sleeping, I'm remembering adventures when the boys let me tag along. Lying in bed, I'm scurrying to keep up with them.

On our adventures, we walk in the time-honored kid pecking order of oldest to youngest. I wonder if I were older than a brother, could I walk in front of him? I know that's dumber than dumb because the boys would change the rules to make me walk behind, no matter the age. I don't really mind as long as I get to tag along. They occasionally check, making sure I'm keeping up, especially when we get close to home. They know they'll get killed if they lose me.

The best adventure is to follow them looking for Gramma's wire because, kid-like, there're so many fascinating things to find in a pile of junk. Gramma collects copper wire to sell, and we scour the town looking for it. If it's a public dump, junkyard, or trash heap, we search until we're run out or find some wire for Gramma, along with numerous treasures for ourselves. We take the wire to Gramma's, where the boys strip off the rubber and toss the wire into a bucket. After the bucket's full, Gramma sells the wire and gives us a cut of the profit. Back home, the boys sneak their treasures into the clubhouse, but Mom usually confiscates mine because I'm still banned from the clubhouse and have nowhere to hide my loot.

We keep a sharp eye out for snakes on our excursions. It seems we're always running into one—usually just a garden or water snake. Mom told us a nest of rattlesnakes smells like cucumbers, so when the boys talk snakes, I sniff the air because I hate being surprised by one.

Picnics mean snakes. Mom has an iron ice chest that must weigh a thousand pounds empty. After she packs it full of fried chicken, potato salad, dessert, and snacks, we're on our way, looking for a good fishing spot that's usually down a steep bank at Minidoka Reservoir. The boys haul the gear down while Dad lugs the iron cooler. It's an unwritten law that no one tells Mom if a snake's sighted. We stomp around to scare off anything lurking, but many times, we've just set up camp when Mom spots one. As if on cue, everyone starts packing up to haul everything back to the pickup, then we're off to find a new site.

Still lying on the motel bed, I'm remembering how pretty Mom was and the times I saw Dad smiling his gentle smile while watching her.

Mom keeps herself looking pretty with a makeup bag that's serious business. No one's allowed to touch it, and no one talks while she uses it. Sitting on the floor, I watch her twirl a wet washrag then drape the cooled rag over a bare shoulder, adjust a small electric fan, and start putting on makeup.

"Hurry, Mama! We'll be late for the rodeo!"

"If I tell you one more time to be quiet, we won't go … hmm what caused these little marks in my compact?" Mom wonders.

I hold my breath, waiting, but she doesn't say anything more. Looks like we've dodged another whipping because the night before, after our parents went dancing, the boys sat me on the kitchen counter and covered my face with a sample of everything in the bag. Ronnie held up Mom's makeup mirror for me to admire the handiwork then scrubbed my face clean.

The rodeo at the Burley fairgrounds is the best adventure. The boys and I get close to the chutes so we can stick our arms through the wood rails to touch the horses' rumps as they shoot out the gate. When someone catches us, we run to the bleachers for cotton candy and pop.

Sitting up in bed now and not the least bit sleepy, I know it's a good thing I'm driving home in the morning. If I stay any longer, the ghosts will likely kill me. And if they don't kill me, I'll have to get mad again to endure them. Especially when I think of the last days at my Barracks Home ….

My world is perfect: adventurous and innocent. And even though the basement stairs still try to kill me, my home's perfect because my world fits here. But Mom doesn't want it anymore. She says the house is on the wrong side of the tracks. I wonder why our side's wrong? Why aren't *they* the ones on the wrong side?

"What's this wood thing, Mama?"

"It's a for-sale sign."

"What are we selling?"

"The house."

"My house? Noooo!"

I hug the signpost and cry. When I won't let go, Mom cries with me then staunchly walks back to the house, wiping tears and calling over her shoulder, "Come on, Sherrie!"

I bawl and wonder how I can live without my Barracks Home. I already have to live without Dean every day since he started first grade. Dad easily pries my fingers from the post and carries me, sobbing, against his chest back inside.

At four and a half years old, life soon becomes a cycle of packing our things and unpacking them.

4

"When You Wore a Tulip"

MOM

The roaming starts and doesn't stop.

Mom has tremendous influence over us because we love her. She's warm, playful, affectionate, tough, and unmovable. Her word is law. We abide by that law, as much as kids can, because we want her happy. When Mom's happy, everyone's happy. So when Mom says she wants to move, we move. Traveling to the next place becomes a normal way of life. At the end of the road, there's always a home waiting for us and a job waiting for Dad.

I never knew if Dad questioned what drove Mom to keep moving. He undoubtedly went along with it to keep her happy, even though he would have been content to stay in one place after his roaming years. Dad never talked much about his early life, or anything, for that matter, but he did tell me about Mildred, hard-dirt floors, and the trains.

Mildred Edwards was a schoolteacher living with her father in El Dorado Springs when Dad's mother died from tuberculosis. Dad was thirteen months old when Mildred took him to raise, and he would live with her for many years. Edward E. Edwards must have been a kind man because he allowed his daughter to care for the baby. He may have received payment; I don't know. But the fact is he allowed it to happen, and Mildred was good for my baby Dad.

When he could work, Dad had to move back to the country homestead with his stern, strict father. Whenever he came home late, even from work, his dad was hiding to jump out and beat the hell out of him all the way up the stairs. Dad was never asked any questions before or after the beatings.

Dad spent years being shuffled around to live with and work for various relatives or acquaintances. He stayed several times with his paternal grandparents, helping work their farm. They had lived and raised twelve kids in a farmhouse with a hard-dirt floor that was cleaner than any modern floor Dad had ever seen—except for Mom's. His grandmother never spoke her husband's first name; she referred to him only as Mr. Lancaster or Man. His grandfather hardly talked to his wife and rarely to his grandson.

"Grampa, why don't you talk to me," Dad once asked.

"Everything's okay. Don't need to say anything," the old man replied.

During the Great Depression when jobs were impossible to find, Dad illegally rode the rails like millions of others, hitching rides on freight trains back and forth across the country, looking for a better life. Dad had been a bindlestiff—a hobo, not a bum. A bum didn't want to work; a bindlestiff did. Bindlestiffs were hobos who carried a bundle containing all their belongings: change of underwear, socks, razor, comb.

Dad stayed in shacks in Tacoma's "Hollywood on the Tide Flats," Seattle's "Hooverville," and other "Hoovervilles" across the country. "Hooverville" was the name for shantytowns built by the poor and named for President Hoover, whose policies were blamed for millions of destitute Americans. The makeshift homes were made from cardboard boxes, crates, corrugated metal, tarpaper, and anything else that could offer shelter.

Dad saw people who were penniless and hungry and met others in hobo jungles—a community of hobos usually close to a railroad track—who shared their last bites of food with him. He once sat next to a tearful father shielding his children's eyes while their mother prostituted herself across the railroad car to earn money to feed her family. Dad saw many other things he never talked about.

Now Dad's roaming again, only in a pickup with a family of seven. We usually don't move far from Gramma, and there are regular trips back to see her when we do. I like coming back at night and seeing the friendly, twinkling lights of Burley from a distance.

"On the outskirts of Burley," Mom fondly says as she cries, and she cries whether we're coming or going. She says her bladder is between her eyes, and I believe her because she cries about something good or bad nearly every day. The barometer of my world is whether Mom's crying or not.

I knew even back then it wasn't Burley that made Mom cry; it's who's in Burley. Gramma and Burley are synonymous. I know now that the daughters—Mom and I—had a strong need to be close to our mothers, but the mothers—Mom and Gramma—didn't need that closeness for any continuous amount of time. Gramma loved Mom, and Mom loved me, but they turned their love on and off on a dime, so you really never knew where you stood with them. They pushed love away and pulled it back: an emotionally destructive tug-of-war. I wasn't the only one caught up in it—Dad and the boys were too.

Our early roaming is a never-ending adventure. As soon as we're on the road, we sing "When You Wore a Tulip," the song Mom designated as our good luck song. We follow her lead in "Three Little Fishes," "So Long Oolong," "Bimbo," and many other old or new songs she likes. I love when she sings because that means she's happy.

The first move from Burley takes us to an old farmhouse near Corvallis, Montana, in the Bitterroot Mountains. We'll stay here through part of the upcoming winter.

After our new place has a thorough cleaning, the first dinner cooked includes homemade light bread so the house will smell like our home. The recipe is Gramma's, and the ingredients are measured by the handful with the final result of two loaves and twenty-four buns. I watch Mom knead, punch, and pound the dough then wait for it to rise. She kneads, punches, and pounds once more for buns and twice more for loaves. The top of the dough is brushed with grease before going in the oven, and the smell of light bread baking drives us out of our minds with hunger. When the buns are done, Mom tosses one until it's cool enough to tear apart for a shared bite. There's nothing like warm, homemade bread melting in your mouth.

Mom tells me she was twelve the first time she tried to make bread. One day after Gramma and Del left for town, Mom decided to surprise her and have bread rising when they got back. She mixed up the dough and kneaded, punched, and pounded it before letting it rise, but nothing seemed to be happening. Mom didn't realize she hadn't waited long enough for it to rise and panicked because of the cost of the ingredients and the trouble it would cause for wasting them. So, she buried the dough in the chicken coop yard. After they returned, Mom anxiously watched chickens happily cluck, peck, and eat warm dough rising from the ground. She was relieved Gramma didn't notice what the chickens were eagerly eating.

We always have chickens, and even though they don't move with us, we soon have some because fried chicken is a favorite Sunday dinner. I've watched both Mom and Gramma select a hen from a group of ladies whose egg laying has slowed and explain to the hen how appreciative they are for the egg service and assure her that she'll make a fine Sunday dinner. It's here where their approach drastically differs.

Gramma stoops to pet the chicken then grabs its neck. She quickly stands, swinging the chicken around a few times before snapping its neck with a sudden flip of her wrist. The head's still in Gramma's fist as the body flies through the air, squirting blood.

Mom pets the chicken then stretches its neck over a stump. With her foot on the chicken's neck and trying to avoid the eye staring up at her, Mom severs the body with one blow from a small ax and jumps away from the squirting blood. After the hen's cleaned, she's dunked in boiling water, plucked, cut up, and fried. And she does make a fine Sunday dinner.

Not yet in school, I am constantly underfoot without Dean to play with, so Mom lets me help her. Mom won't let me gather eggs because I end up breaking too many, but I can turn a butter churn without any damage. I love watching Mom skim thick cream from fresh milk when Dad and the boys bring in the can after milking the cow. She ladles the cream with a wooden spoon and plops the spoonful into a glass bowl. I love the cream but hate churning it. I spend way too much time churning butter during these few months in Corvallis.

Each day, Mom has something delicious for dessert. Many times, a cake's baking during dinner, and we have warm cake with fresh butter on top for dessert. To ensure that everyone gets an equal piece, Mom says a pie must be carefully measured by counting each fluted crust tip. All eyes are on the pie and counting as Mom cuts it into seven exact pieces. We make sure they're exact, too, or a roar erupts, causing Mom to threaten us with the stick.

Shortly after moving in, the boys let me jump out of a hayloft door in an old, dilapidated barn after they show me how it's done. A gigantic pile of hay is on the ground directly below the hayloft door, which is near the barn's tapered roof. After watching each boy jump and listening to their yells of encouragement, I take the leap and fall *a million feet*.

"Shit! We forgot to move the pitchfork!" a brother yells as I'm plunging.

I land on the haystack and sink. The boys quickly dig me out and pound my back as I spit out dried alfalfa, cry, and look for blood from the pitchfork. They laugh at me then charge back to the loft to jump again.

Laugh at me, huh? I drag a scythe out of the barn to the haystack. Even though it's resting on the ground, it's all I can do to keep the curved blade upright because of its weight and the old, splintery, wooden handle. I manage it long enough to get yelled at several times, but I still threaten to kill the first boy who jumps.

"C'mon, chickens!"

Ronnie sneaks up behind to smack my butt and grab the scythe. He smacks with as much force as Mom when he doesn't approve of something.

In just a couple of months, the first snow of the season starts, and the boys and I bounce off the walls with excitement. We make snowmen, dig snow tunnels, and build snow wigwams, but the excitement fades after we're nearly snowed in for weeks. And even though they freeze solid, Mom insists on hanging bed sheets on the clothesline outside to smell country fresh. I help her carry the frozen sheets back inside to thaw out and dry.

"Be careful! Don't hit the sheet on the doorjamb. If you do, it'll break to pieces," Mom warns each washday.

I really want to whack the sheet and see it break with the ice, but knowing Mom's whacks holds me back.

The daily "it's time to get the stink blew off" means Mom's ready for some peace and quiet, so it's time for me to go outside before the boys come home from school. But going outside is a major undertaking. First and foremost, I'm told to go to the bathroom whether I have to or not. Then Mom begins the long, painful process of stuffing me into a snowsuit. With mittens and overshoes on, I'm finally ready, feeling like a stuffed mummy who definitely has to go to the bathroom. It ain't easy being little.

We celebrate Dean's seventh birthday early because, on his birthday in February, we leave Corvallis for Las Vegas, Nevada, to warm up, I suppose. The next adventure begins with Mom singing "When It's Nighttime in Nevada" about missing someone and because that's where we're headed. Mom's happy when she sings, so I'm happy too.

5

"When It's Nighttime in Nevada"

GENE AUTRY

Las Vegas in February seems like a tropical paradise to me. An occasional cold wind blows but doesn't last long, and it's nothing compared to a cold, snowy winter in Montana or a biting winter wind in southern Idaho. Little do we know what a Las Vegas spring and summer will bring when, at times, the wind's so strong it's nearly impossible to push open the front door. The heat begins in earnest in the summertime, bringing with it more wind, choking dust storms, and torrents of rain. But for now, it's still February.

The first thing Mom does when we move into someplace new is clean it until it sparkles. The first thing kids do is explore every nook and cranny inside and out. We hit a bonanza in the attic, finding a bag of pastel-colored casino chips in different colors for each denomination. We wonder if the chips are worth something and some gangsters will show up to take them. We'll live in this little two-story house on Dike Lane just east of Rancho and Bonanza for a few months. The area is miles from nothing, so the boys shoot rabbits in the desert on what's now a busy freeway interchange.

I celebrate my fifth birthday on Dike Lane, and Mom makes birthdays special. The birthday kid chooses dinner and the cake color, gets the biggest piece, and goes first. No one takes a bite until the birthday kid does, which starts the knuckle-bopping. Mom inserts toothpicks in the layer cake, hidden by the frosting, and you learn to be tricky when you get one: chew it up, hide it, or stick it unseen into someone else's cake. If you're caught with a toothpick, the other six will give you a head knuckle-bop, even if it's your party.

After one more move in Las Vegas and another month of intense heat and dust storms so thick you can't see across the street, we pack up and head back to Idaho. I'm too young to care about the mechanics of what gets packed up and how, but I know the bed of Dad's pickup is packed solid, extending higher than the sides with an empty spot for the boys and Zip to fit into. Because Mom's always happy during a move to someplace new, there's a holiday mood when we leave—especially during these first moves. At the move's end-of-road, the house is different, but our things in it aren't.

We stay in Kimberly for about a month before moving to Rock Creek Canyon, where we live in an old house with a widow's walk: a porch along the second story. The hills and canyons provide adventurous exploring because the trails are loaded with arrowheads, old wagons and wheels, and gorgeous rocks.

When we move to a new place, we plant a vegetable garden and flower-beds and arrange a rock garden with rocks that moved with us. Mom's never anywhere long before there's a rock garden and flowers outside, even though, at times, they are just blooming by the time we're packing up again. We all love searching the surrounding area for pretty-colored or unusual-shaped rocks because Mom loves it too. The new rocks will move with us when we leave. On one excursion in Rock Creek, we find a rock that's a foot and a half tall and shaped just like a sitting frog. Mom paints the rock frog's face and puts some markings on the body. We haul it everywhere before it's abandoned along with us in Missouri.

It's still summertime, and it's hot, so Dean leans against an ancient tree that shades the yard where we play. Standing completely still, he yells and talks so fast we can't understand a word he says. That gets Mom's attention.

"What's wrong, Dean?" Mom calls from the kitchen window.

"Mom!" Dean wails.

"What's wrong, I said!"

Dean raises both arms above his head, pointing both index fingers toward his feet. Mom runs to the yard while the rest of us watch in horror as a huge, five-foot-long blacksnake slowly slithers across Dean's bare feet. Mom's terrified of snakes, and this one's about as long as Mom is tall. She knows the snake isn't poisonous, so the best she can do is offer words of encouragement until it's finished with Dean's feet.

"You can do it, Dean. It won't hurt you!" Mom sounds confident though she's anything but.

As soon as the snake's tail clears Dean's last toe, he shoots like an arrow to her.

"Go wash your feet. Now!" Mom orders before he reaches her.

Because Dean's so pale, Mom wraps her arms around him, although she's careful not to get close to his feet.

Aunt Ruth would've grabbed a gun and shot the snake if she'd been here. Dean's lucky she wasn't because she isn't a very good shot. Once, when she went after a snake in her home with a rifle, she missed but kept right on trying. The snake escaped through the open front door without serious injury, but Aunt Ruth's walls and floors were mortally wounded.

When the boys are in school, Mom lets me watch *The Pinky Lee Show* on TV and eat a Twinkie. None of us went to kindergarten; it was either not mandatory or not offered, so Mom's preparing me for first grade next September. She teaches me how to play hopscotch and jacks and how to write my name on a little chalkboard. I practice while she reads. I hate when she reads and makes me be quiet. The white magazine pages have a million little black words on each one, and it seems it'll take the rest of my life for her to finish one page. I rock back and forth on my feet by her chair, hoping she'll stop. Mom does, long enough to sing a verse of a favorite song, "Little Playmate," then makes me practice some more.

After only a few months, we plan to move back to Kimberly again. Before we leave, the boys bury a tobacco can filled with their treasures so someday, someone will know we'd been here. Looking back now at the fact the boys buried the can tells me the older ones were probably getting sick of moving. But so far, I don't care because my family fits in a pickup packed solid with our things.

Mom sings "This Old House" on the way back to Kimberly, where Dad builds a rectangular-shaped cinderblock home in no time for us. We call it the Chicken Coop because that's what it'll be used for after we build our home. Mom hangs up sheets to divide the Chicken Coop into rooms after we're settled inside.

Zip had traveled with us during each move except when we left Rock Creek Canyon for the Chicken Coop. Mom left him, probably because he wasn't a puppy anymore and was becoming old and cantankerous. Carson cries himself to sleep every night, so Mom gives in and lets him and Dad go back to Rock Creek and bring Zip home.

I finally start first grade. At long last, I can go with Dean in the mornings. For the occasion, Mom makes a new shirt for each of the boys and a new dress for me. The boys are ordered to get me to school and home again in one piece. On the first day, I happily walk down the road, surrounded by the boys, with my hand firmly planted in Dean's. During each recess, at least one brother finds me to make sure I'm okay before running away to rejoin his friends.

"When they start school, you've lost them," Mom says to me after my first day at school.

I don't know what she meant by "lost them" because no matter our age, we still love her. Instead, it seems after I started school, something was set in motion that took only four years to complete before we lost her. Was this the beginning of Mom's leaving? Was she tired of us because we weren't babies anymore?

For now, Mom makes my school days special by buying the latest rage in girl's clothes: a poodle skirt, crinoline slip, bobby socks, and penny loafers. The boys wear button shirts and Levi's blue jeans with the belt loops cut off, the waistband riding just right on their hips, and cuffs turned up twice with an exact width on each.

It's always a relief to hear music in our home. It means Mom is happy. The best times are after school when Mom plays records and dances with us. She hooks the sheets up and out of the way and dances each of us up and down the length of the Chicken Coop to "If You've Got the Money I've Got the Time" by Lefty Frizzell, "Fraulein" by Bobby Helms, "Heartaches by the Number" by Guy Mitchell, and "Bummin' Around" by Hank Thompson. We listen and laugh to "The Flying Saucer" by Buchanan & Goodman, "Stranded in the Jungle" by The Cadets, and "What It Was, Was Football" by Andy Griffith.

Then there's a guy called Elvis. "One Night With You" and "I Want You, I Need You, I Love You" make Mom blush, but that doesn't stop us from listening to Elvis on the radio and loving him. Mom finally lets me stay up on Sunday night to watch him on *The Ed Sullivan Show*. The televised Elvis can be shown only from the waist up because of gyrations from the waist down as he sings. When I ask Mom why, she tells me to be quiet. I wish I could tell her to be quiet, but then I'd be running from a stick.

I share a small, curtained bedroom in the Chicken Coop with the boys. They still sleep in a bunkbed, with Ronnie and Carson on the top bunk and Craig and Dean on the bottom. I sleep on an army cot against the opposite wall. All hell breaks loose one night after Ronnie watches Carson climb down the ladder, pee in Ronnie's shoe, and climb back up. Carson swears he was asleep the whole time, and Ronnie says he's a dirty-rotten-lousy-liar. Dad empties the shoe as Mom threatens us with the stick unless we shut up and go back to sleep.

Ronnie gets even with him early one evening after Carson falls asleep snoring on the front room floor. Ronnie trickles hot sauce into Carson's open mouth while the rest of us kids stifle giggles. It takes an amazing amount of hot sauce before Carson chokes himself awake. By the time he's cooled off, we're nowhere to be found.

An old woman lives across a field from our Chicken Coop, and Mom tells us to stay away from her property. She wears her hair stuffed into a broken-down cowboy hat, a kerchief around her neck, shirt, pants, and worn-out cowboy boots. Best of all, the old woman has a six-shooter in a holster on her hip. The boys say the gun's loaded because they've seen her shoot at something or other. I'm sure I'll see her shoot someone someday: probably one of the boys. I'm careful sneaking around her place so I'm not the one shot.

Hiding in weeds, I watch her hoe the garden or clean the chicken coop. She catches me watching sometimes, but the only thing she shoots is menacing looks while taking a step toward me, at which time, I run like hell. Eventually, she only glances at me when she finds me watching. I think if we'd only lived there a little longer, she might have talked to me. I wish she had so she could tell me her stories.

The old woman is the first woman I've seen wearing pants. Mom, Gramma, and the aunts all wear housedresses and aprons for their chores. On hair day, they pin-curl hair with bobby pins, put on makeup, and wear a clean housedress. If they're going out to dance, they comb out the pin curls and put on a fancier dress. Pants and the six-shooter make the old woman all the more fascinating to me.

We walk to a canal near the Chicken Coop as often as we can. The boys are ordered not to swim near an open check-gate, where water rushes through the gate in the center of the canal, falling several feet to the lower level in the next section of canal. Because I can't swim yet, I find a ditch to play in while the boys roar through the check-gate. I love it when Dad comes, too, because he brings a rope to tie around my waist before throwing me into the canal and dragging me back to the bank, where I'm ready to be thrown in again and again.

Mom and I walk to the canal and nearby ponds to gather watercress and other greens to cook. We find tender, young asparagus shoots growing wild that Mom cuts with a paring knife she carries for that purpose. She bundles the shoots and greens together with string, then we walk home with armloads.

During potato harvest, high school kids are given two weeks off school to work in the fields picking spuds. Ronnie's seventeen and Carson's fourteen, so they jump at the chance to ditch school and make more money than Dad does on his construction job. They work hard for the money. After machinery digs up the potatoes, the boys walk doubled over up and down the rows with a gunnysack tied to their belts and a metal hook strapped to each knee, keeping the gunnysack spread open. They earn five cents a sack, averaging about ten dollars a day working from dawn to dusk. After working fourteen straight days and bagging around three thousand gunnysacks, they each earn about $150. Mom makes them buy school clothes with their earnings; the rest can be spent as they please—if she approves.

One evening at the Chicken Coop, Mom scoops me out of our galvanized bathtub, wraps me up in a towel, and carries me outside where Dad's standing. The boys are jumping around and pointing at a clear, cold sky that's blazing with stars so close we can nearly touch them. I snuggle up to Mom's warmth and try to see which light is Sputnik: the first artificial satellite launched by the Soviet Union.

It's October, and there hasn't been music playing at home for days, so Dad tells us kids it's time to cheer up Mom. He gives us some money and drops us off at a local dime store to buy birthday presents for her. The store's an adventure for me and a learning experience—the first of many my brothers shouldn't have given me. It's only after many more moves that I'll understand why we do what we do; we won't be living here very long, so why does it matter?

Price stickers aren't glued onto items very well, so we find what we want and peel off the price sticker to replace it with another from a less expensive item. Then we pool metal slugs we've saved up to see if there's enough to buy sodas. The metal slugs are exactly the size needed, and after some work, the pop machine usually exchanges a soda for the slugs.

Whatever we bought Mom apparently didn't help because a few days later, Mom drives me to Butte, Montana, to visit Aunt Anna and Uncle Ade. This is the first time we've gone somewhere without Dad and the boys, and I'm excited to have Mom all to myself. During the trip, she gives me saltine crackers and chewing gum to help me avoid getting carsick as I usually do on long trips. She tells me to watch the center white line, but I still turn green and throw up. I'm carsick most of the way and throw up out the window the length of downtown Butte. The town is so dark and dirty I don't think anyone will notice what I leave behind.

Anna and Ade live in a huge, forbidding-looking, multistory apartment building close to downtown. A woman friend of Anna's, Queenie, who's over six feet tall and weighs a lot, babysits me while Mom, Anna, and Ade go dancing. Later, I wake up to a screaming, knock-down-drag-out fight between Mom and Anna. I run to the front room, heading for the sisters to make them stop, when suddenly, Queenie's hand reaches out from nowhere to stop me. Ade's nowhere to be seen. I beg Queenie to stop them, but she only watches, holding me immobile. Mom and Anna each have a handful of the other's hair and punch, slap, and claw with their free hand. I can't believe my eyes. Mom shouldn't know how to fight like this or even want to. I cry and scream, but Queenie still does nothing.

They finally stop bleeding and crying. Mom throws our stuff together, and we leave in the middle of the night in the middle of a snowstorm. The snowflakes look like witches on brooms slugging the windshield. We make it back to the Chicken Coop after several hours with Mom still crying.

I don't know what Mom told Dad about the fight or why it happened because she never talks to me about it, but I'm momentarily important to the boys. I have information they want, so I tell them what I saw and heard, then they make me repeat the gorier details. The fight will become a point of reference for me in just a few years—a preview of what's to come.

Eventually, Anna and Ade start visiting again, but Anna doesn't make jokes anymore about me not liking her. She leaves me alone, and I like it that way.

"Kiss my foot and two joints higher. If that ain't my butt then I'm a liar," Gramma says.

That's the way I feel about Anna, but as an adult, I've often wondered what emptiness the older sisters lived in to elicit their behavior. Mom and her older sisters couldn't get along even when they tried. If one sister was mad at another sister, the rest were expected to be mad at her too. When Mom was mad at Aunt Mary during an Aunt Ruth visit, Aunt Ruth asked if she could call Aunt Mary. She secretly wanted to smooth things over between her two favorite sisters. After the call, Aunt Ruth asked if we could go visit Aunt Mary.

"Yes, but take your things with you when you go!" Mom replied.

I wanted to see Aunt Mary, too, because I liked her. But even as a little girl, I'd learned not to cross Mom in order to avoid a whipping or have to see her terrible tears. I just want her happy.

The main house won't be built as planned, and the Chicken Coop won't be used for chickens, because Mom decides to move again. I'm beginning to realize we'll always *move again soon*. I cry, hugging my first teacher goodbye; I want to stay in her class. I learn the only tears that count are Mom's because the house is already packed up when we get home from school. But for now, the excitement of another adventure takes over as soon as we're on the road. Mom's happy, and we all fit; that's all I need at six years old.

We sing "Let the Rest of the World Go By" on our way to Niagara Springs Ranch, nestled in a 350-foot-deep gorge in Snake River Canyon near Wendell, Idaho. The Rock House at the ranch is a large, two-story home made from lava rock with inside walls of wood and a screened porch. The backyard ends at the high river bank, and the ranch's land follows the Snake four miles downstream. A huge rock about ten feet high and twenty feet around sits by a walkway leading to the house, and I prefer to go over instead of around it. It's a magnificent old rock, and I wish it could tell me how it got here.

Local lore says a Mormon businessman from Salt Lake City, Utah, built the house as his summer home around 1920. During summer holiday, the man left his family in Salt Lake City and stayed at the Rock House with his other family. To have work time away from kids, the man had a huge treehouse built close to the house. A spiral staircase circles a massive tree trunk leading to the door of the treehouse. Ronnie and Carson climb up to explore while the rest of us wait below. It's still furnished with a desk, chair, table, and other rotting furniture. The spiral staircase is rotten in places, and we can see holes in the bottom of the house. Mom says it's too dangerous to play in, causing groans from us kids stuck on the ground.

On the other side of the Rock House, a poplar tree stands about a mile high, I think, with wood slats nailed evenly spaced all the way to the top, where a four-foot wood platform is attached. Many years before, this tree looked out over a peach orchard. The same local lore says the Mormon's summertime wife climbed the tree daily with her rifle to sit on the platform, taking potshots at fruit poachers.

The Rock House adventures are kid-perfect. Mom yells for Carson to get his rifle when a huge eagle swoops down to pick out a chicken for dinner. The eagle glides close to the chickens then soars away, banks, and comes in closer each time. The chickens are a mess, squawking and clustering together, when

Carson shoots the eagle just before it grabs a chicken—or me—in its massive talons. The eagle's dead when it hits the ground.

After a skunk takes up residence in the attic, Dad lets Ronnie crawl up there with him to shoot the beast. We feed several tiny, pink baby rabbits with my dolls' baby bottles after some varmint killed their mother. Zip moans from losing a porcupine fight, and Dad picks quills out of his muzzle with a pair of pliers. Carson tames a woodchuck, and Mom takes a picture of Dean with a horned owl sitting on his shoulder.

"Mom!" Dean says, squirming.

"Stand still!" Mom orders, snapping the picture.

"Now, what?" Mom asks, winding the film in her Kodak camera. Dean turns around so she can see the wet mess the owl made down the back of his shirt.

After a couple of months at the Rock House, I have what turns out to be German measles, and I'm so hot Mom calls a doctor. While Mom remakes my bed, Dad realizes that part of the bedspread's hot to his touch. As the doctor arrives, two fire trucks do, too, because Dad called them when he discovered the wall next to my bed is smoldering from the rock fireplace on the other side. To keep everyone calm, especially Mom, Dad didn't tell anyone until the fire trucks arrived. After a complete check, the doctor says I should survive, the firemen say the house is safe but not to use the fireplace anymore, and our days on this kid-perfect ranch are numbered.

The boys soon find Snake River Canyon is infested with rattlesnakes and sidewinders. A neighbor woman tells Mom she found a rattlesnake curled up in one of her kitchen drawers. The boys kill as many snakes as they can and keep the rattles as trophies. When we walk up a switchback gravel road to the top of the canyon to catch a school bus, there're plenty of sidewinder tracks on the road. But during our walks to and from the bus, the snakes avoid the hot sun.

We had resumed school in a two-room schoolhouse in Wendell. One room has six rows of desks with one row for each grade one through six. I'm in the first row, Dean's in the third, and Craig's in the fifth. The upstairs room, where Ronnie and Carson are, seats grades seven through twelve.

On the first day of May, we arrive at school dressed up to celebrate May Day. The playground has a tall pole with long, colorful streamers attached. After a picnic lunch, we skip around the May Pole, holding the streamers and weaving in and out, resulting in a beautifully colored, braided pole and happy kids. Long before I finish grade school, adults will ruin innocent fun by saying May Day shouldn't be celebrated because long ago, pagans started the holiday, and children shouldn't act like pagans. After I learn what pagan means, I think all kids mostly act like heathens. It's our job. And it seems adults' jobs are to ruin kids' fun.

When our teacher plans a Mother's Day ceremony, Craig, Dean, and I together make a corsage out of colored tissue paper. The teacher picks the oldest, Craig, to pin the corsage on Mom after the class sings "MOTHER." I'm mad because I want to do it. Craig comes down with the mumps, so now Dean's up, and I'm mad again. Then Dean comes down with the mumps, so the teacher finally picks me. I catch them the day after but not before I pin that corsage on Mom.

Carson's kicked out of school so many times the principal asks Dad and Mom to let him stay out for the short remainder of the school year after "the pie incident." Carson had climbed a tree during morning recess to reach pies cooling on the second-story kitchen windowsill next to his classroom and carefully dropped each pie into kids' waiting hands below. Dessert wasn't served at lunchtime that day, and Carson didn't return to the two-room schoolhouse. I finish first grade in that schoolhouse.

Our only neighbors at the Ranch, the Smeckpepper family, live just up the river, where they manage a fish hatchery. The older boys always wander up the river to visit the red-headed, freckled Smeckpepper girls. They won't let me go, so I play on the screened porch or rock in time to the McGuire Sisters' "Sugartime" on the radio or Mom singing "Don't Fence Me In." Mom says she feels fenced in living in a canyon with the Snake River on one side, the canyon wall on the other, and lots of snakes in between.

This time, rattlesnakes are why we have to move, or so Mom says. This is the first time I know Mom's reason for moving since the time we left my Barracks Home because we lived on the wrong side of the tracks. I'm seven years old now and beginning to see our life isn't like the lives of other kids in school. When kids ask where I'm from and I list the places I've lived, their surprised reaction confuses me at first. The idea begins to form that I'm not normal for moving so much. Eventually, I learn to only answer that I'm from Burley, Idaho.

We're leaving Niagara Springs Ranch after only about five months, and we're on our way to somewhere again—this time to Aunt Ruth's place in Lovelock, Nevada. The pickup is packed and parked near the school, with Zip chained to the bumper because today, Ronnie graduates from high school at the little two-room schoolhouse. After the ceremony, the boys and Zip occupy their empty space, with me in the cab. On our way to Aunt Ruth's, Mom sings "The Little Green Valley" about going back somewhere to find happiness.

6

"The Little Green Valley"

MARTY ROBBINS

Mom's happiest when we're on our way to somewhere. I think she wants to be happy because if I ask why she's crying, she always says, "Oh just let me get this out of my system, then I'll be okay." I walk around on eggshells until she stops, but in a little while, trouble's hanging over us again when she gets the blues, cries, and talks of moving. Her knack is making Dad want to go, too, and her tears help. I know because Dad doesn't like seeing girls cry. When it's me, Dad holds me tight on his lap, sopping up tears until I stop. With a kiss and a hug, he sets me on my way. When it's Mom, we move. The six of us, from me through the boys to Dad, enable her because life's heaven when Mom's happy and hell when she's crying. It's a relief when she starts packing, singing, and seeming happy again.

We stay in motels at night on those somewhere trips. Mom thinks they're handy and much better than camps alongside the road or the abandoned, bug-infested shacks of her childhood. Dad rarely talks about his childhood, but Mom needs to talk about hers and always tells me about those times and Gramma.

Gramma married Louie Parker and had four kids in Topeka, Kansas, before moving to Burke, Idaho. Burke is situated in narrow Burke Canyon with Canyon Creek flowing alongside in the Idaho Panhandle. During the late 1800s, Burke was a booming mining town with hundreds of miners living there. Less than four hundred people called it home when Mom was born there decades later. They lived in buildings that clung to the canyon wall, with steep, wood stairs leading down to the only narrow street that shared space with railroad tracks running through the cramped little town. Louie went to work at the mines in nearby Wallace then to the bars to drink, play cards, and pull penny slot machine handles.

The three older sisters had already left home at young ages when Mom was four years old and Gramma decided to leave the tyrant she'd been married to for twenty years. Her opportunity came when a neighbor woman befriended her and offered help. The woman's husband worked with Louie at the mines, and they'd seen the cruel way he treated his family.

Louie expected Louie Jr. and Mom to be seen and not heard and expected the same from his wife. Gramma couldn't talk unless Louie spoke first; otherwise, she was knocked across the room. Louie made a list of chores each morning that *better be complete* by the time he returned, or there'd be hell to pay. He told Gramma what to cook for his dinner each night, and she had to keep the meal fresh and warm without any idea when he'd finally come home after the inevitable beers and gambling.

One morning, Gramma stashed a small bag with the barest of necessities at the neighbor's house then took Mom with her but abandoned nine-year-old Louie Jr. when she slipped away in the middle of the night. The woman and her husband gave them a ride to Anna's, where Gramma would decide where to go from there.

Two years later, Gramma married a man who was one-third Cherokee Indian and had another baby girl, Ruth, in Firth near Blackfoot, Idaho. Three years later, Gramma took Mom and Ruth when she left the Indian. Gramma tried to make ends meet by waitressing in cafés in Grand Junction, Colorado, but the Depression was strangling the country, and she couldn't support herself, let alone two little girls.

Gramma's choice of men was lousy and held true again when she met Del in Grand Junction. The girls hated Del, who was surly and verbally abusive to Gramma and the little girls. After he called them every name in the book, he'd pout for days and treat them all like dogs. But Gramma stayed with him, probably because she was scared, knowing she couldn't make it alone. Putting up with Del's verbal abuse was better than being alone with no other prospect in sight.

For several years during the Depression, Del, Gramma, Mom, and Aunt Ruth lived from hand to mouth while they traveled the Western United States in Del's car, looking for work. They panned for gold in Arizona's Superstition Mountains and worked farms and ranches in Utah, Nevada, and Idaho. Del had a two-burner kerosene stove that Gramma cooked on. Mom scrubbed their clothes on a washboard with water hauled in a bucket from the nearest river. During fair weather, they spread blankets on the ground around a camp-fire to sleep. They peed behind bushes and pooped over logs, using vegetation for toilet paper. When they were lucky, they found a deserted shack to call home for a while. They were the luckiest when they ran into a CCC Camp, where they were never refused a food handout.

The Civilian Conservation Corps—better known as CCC Camps—was the most popular of the New Deal programs put in place by President Roosevelt during the Depression. Thousands of unemployed young men were recruited and sent to camps located in every state across the US, with many states having dozens or even more than a hundred camps in their state. At its height in the mid-1930s, there were over 2,600 camps housing over 505,000 men who were provided food, clothing, training, and the tools needed for the work at hand. The work they were enlisted to perform varied depending on their location. They planted more than three billion trees; built fire towers and roads; fought fires, floods, and soil erosion; and built small dams, parks, and drainage systems, to name just a few of the valuable jobs they performed. The CCC boys were paid thirty dollars a month, and each had to agree to a mandatory twenty-five-dollar allotment check to be sent back home to their families, leaving them with five dollars. This arrangement alone boosted the economy across the US. Another boost was literacy. An educational program was initiated at the camps where more than forty thousand young men were taught to read and write after work and on Sundays.[1]

There were five CCC Camps in the countryside around Burley. These CCC boys built most of the canal system and roads in the area and worked in the parks and forests.

As we travel, Mom's doing what she likes best, Dad loves Mom, and five kids still get caught up in a roaming adventure. *Something different* is still exciting, although the trips get boring at times.

To keep myself entertained, I imagine I'm hopping from telephone pole to telephone pole. The rhythm of hopping along with the drone of the engine always puts me to sleep. We're total vagabond kids, and pack-move-repeat is beginning to wear even though we don't realize it yet.

When I told Dean of my fantasy pole-hopping years later on a road trip, he said he'd done the same thing except his belongings were tied end-to-end on a length of rope he pulled along with him.

---

1   CCC Brief History. "Civilian Conservation Corps Legacy." Accessed Feb. 26, 2020, https://ccclegacy.org/CCC_Brief_History.html .

After being cramped up traveling, the excitement of watching for a motel's blinking "vacancy" sign with a reasonable room rate displayed puts everyone in a good mood. Dad rents one room with two beds: one for Mom and Dad, and one for Dean and me. The three older boys are sneaked in and out to save money and use sleeping bags on the motel room floor.

We eat food Mom packed for the trip and occasionally stop at a drive-in hamburger joint, where carhops on roller skates serve us in our car. Sometimes when we're all starving to death, we stop at a diner before looking for the blinking "vacancy" sign. I like the diners that have miniature jukeboxes at each booth. Mom drops a coin in a slot on the front of the jukebox then flips through pages of listed music by sliding metal tabs on top of the box from one side to the other. She pushes a brightly colored, numbered button, and "Lovesick Blues" swings out of the speakers.

Ronnie keeps us quiet on long trips by telling and retelling gruesome Clip Clop stories. Clip Clop got his name from terrible deformities: one causes him to take a short step with his right leg, ending with a clip sound as he pulls and drags his left leg, ending with a clop. You know when Clip Clop's after you because you can hear him coming a mile away. Slowly and steadily ever closer he comes. Clip Clop's passion is mutilating and devouring little kids. He's very tricky and can be hiding under your bed, waiting to grab a stray leg or arm hanging over the side. Once he gets hold of any part of you, it's certain death by devourment—a torturously slow and very loud dinner.

Burma-Shave signs advertising shaving cream capture us hook, line, and sinker. They're groups of six signs displaying one line of a rhyme: *Substitutes/ Can Let You Down/Quicker/Than A/ Strapless Gown/Burma-Shave*. The signs are everywhere on the roads we travel, and I think I learned how to read because of them.

Highway historical markers are great because Mom insists we stop to read them. Kids run around to stretch legs while someone reads the plaque that describes a historic event that took place on this spot or in the beautiful vista before us. Historic trails and events crisscross the roads we travel and the places we live in Idaho on the Snake River Plain. The Oregon Trail crosses southern Idaho following the Snake for more than three hundred miles, and it's not unusual to see ruts cut into trails by wagon wheels of those earlier travelers.

Shoshone Falls on the Snake are forty-five feet higher than Niagara Falls in upstate New York. The Snake River runs through Hells Canyon, where it's a half-mile deeper at its lowest point than the Grand Canyon. If I couldn't see the two-hundred-fifty-foot-wide Snake, I was never far from it. Rivers, reservoirs, waterfalls, canals, train trestles, hay derricks, Indian trails, rocks, and wood make up the Snake River Plain and me. I love Idaho—how it looks and everything in it—but in only a couple of years, I'll miss it the rest of my life because my family will never live here again.

We make our way to Aunt Ruth's, and a few days later, Dad buys a trailer house. But soon Mom's not satisfied again. We might have had a chance of staying put if Aunt Ruth stayed put near Gramma, but Aunt Ruth never stays in one place very long either, so there's no end in sight. It seems Mom's torn between living near Aunt Ruth or Gramma. She wants to be near Aunt Ruth, but Gramma always wins because Mom needs to be near Gramma. That is until Mom starts crying again.

After a few weeks, Dad has the trailer house moved back to Burley, where we live by a golf course for a month. The boys get jobs retrieving golf balls from the lake after hours, and I push my doll stroller on the green to watch the boys jump in the lake. I'm glad we're back in Idaho because there are more truckloads of baled hay to watch for than in Nevada. Mom assures me that when I make a wish looking at baled hay, it will come true if I look away and never look back.

After the trailer's sold after only a few weeks, we move into a house across the street from Gramma on Elba Avenue. We've come full circle with ten moves in three years, and we're living by Gramma again. This house is shabby compared to my Barracks Home, and we have an outhouse now, too, just like Gramma. But the boys don't have to use catalog pages for toilet paper because we have enough of the real deal. I'm really glad to be close to Gramma again, but Mom says this house is only temporary since Dad's looking for land somewhere close to build a new house. I'm excited to realize we're going to stay in Idaho!

The electricity goes out often during a storm. If it's dark out, Mom lights an oil lamp for us to huddle around at the kitchen table. She places a pan piled high with rubbing alcohol-soaked sugar in the center of the table and lights the sugar with a match. Then she tells spooky ghost stories as an eerie glow from the slow-burning sugar turns everyone's face a sickly green color. Other times, she teaches us how to play Solitaire and Crazy Eights. She helps make card houses, and Mom and I get mad when a draft flattens one. And time passes, as I wait to know where our new house will be built.

Ronnie's eighteen when he leaves home soon after we return from Nevada, and Mom cries a river. He has a job working for a surveying company and joins the Army Reserve as a tank driver. He's gone for about eighteen months before he comes back home to stay.

Several weeks after Ronnie leaves, we move to Heyburn, Idaho, across the Snake River from Burley, to rent an old house from an old man named Amos Miller, wearing old, patched coveralls. Amos Miller's house is only a mile or so from the land Dad bought to build our New House. The best part is that Amos Miller's house sits on an acre of land that's waiting for adventures to happen because the entire area is a junkyard filled with old farm equipment, stacked railroad ties, mountains of baling wire, old cars and engines, and more.

Kid-like, we find the junkyard is way more fun to play in than playing with toys. The long railroad ties are Robin Hood's bridge—the same bridge where Robin battled Little John to see who could cross first. Dean and I meet daily at the bridge to do battle. A broken-down tractor is Captain Hook's pirate ship with the Mermaids Lagoon in a galvanized tub riddled with holes. The

Lost Boys' home is hiding among the branches of a perfect climbing tree, and the Indian Village is just beyond a mountain of dirt and rocks.

Mom's kids never lacked imagination, but Dean and I explode with it here because of all the great junk to play in and Disney's *Peter Pan* movie. Dean and I had a *Peter Pan* picture book we wore out, but now we can play in the picture book at Amos Miller's.

We have to leave the junkyard behind during the day when school starts—with me in second grade, Dean in fourth, Craig in sixth, and Carson in tenth. Mom makes sure we all have the same kind of school supplies as the other kids. And she makes sure we have at least one new outfit to start off the school year. Being the only girl, I'm lucky when it comes to clothes, and the oldest boy at home is too. We get new clothes while the other boys deal with hand-me-downs.

Mom also makes us a sack lunch every morning with a surprise treat inside. When Mom was little and stayed in one place long enough for her and Ruth to go to school, their lunch was a leftover biscuit sandwich with butter if they had it and a slice of onion packed in an old lard can. Mom was ashamed to carry the dented can to school because it showed her classmates how poor she was. She was never dressed as well as the other girls and felt inferior, so she quit school before she finished the eighth grade. The shame those times caused Mom was the reason her kids went to school squeaky clean, with every hair in place, and carrying an appetizing sack lunch.

The boys gather at recess to play marbles, and Carson's the undisputed king. He lets me play with his winnings sometimes but never with the special marbles he keeps separate: aggies, commies, and glassies. I play jacks with other girls or play on the swings. When I struggle to gather momentum on the swing, someone gives me a gigantic push from behind. Looking back as I fly through the air, I know I'll see one of the boys galloping away.

Waiting for our New House to be built, we acquire a kitten that's roaming around Amos Miller's place. He's a cute little cider-colored guy we name Cider.

Not long after Cider moves in, the kids start breaking out with ringworms: nasty red patches with a circular raised area. Mom's mortified. We only go to a doctor if there's a danger of dying, so Mom treats the sores with douses of straight bleach tipped from the bottle. When that doesn't do the trick, we bathe in a galvanized tub with water and bleach. The ringworms lose. Cider's renamed Fungus Amongst Us, and he's bleached too.

Mom's remedies for our illnesses are few but effective. Perfume is warmed in a spoon over a stove burner and a drop or two is dripped into ears with earaches. Pure horseradish is dabbed on a tongue, then tears run and sinuses clear. Mentholatum is rubbed on a chest cold, and a flannel rag draped on the chest and around the neck is held in place by a safety pin. For general good health, a dose of cod liver oil is given each morning with a slice of orange to counteract the horrible taste. Any kid caught with a cut or scrape is subjected to the red-staining, burning terror of Merthiolate dripped from a glass post attached to the bottle cap. Dad rubs growing pains out of aching limbs with his hands in the middle of the night, and Mom gives peppermint oil mixed in water to upset stomachs. When all else fails, she holds a cold washrag on the forehead of the kid throwing up.

Craig taunts me, his favorite pastime, while we play outside at Amos Miller's. The older he gets, the more of a bully he becomes, and he infuriates me, calling me a half-breed. After I tell Mom on him, she comes out saying play nice or don't play at all. She tells Craig not to call me names. They're the same size and stand nose to nose. Craig says something smart-alecky, and she's right back at him, saying don't talk to her like that. He slugs her in the face. I try to run to her, but my feet won't move. In slow motion, her head rolls from side to side on the ground. I can't believe this happened, and I know it's my fault. If only I hadn't told on him. After an eternity, she stands up, holding her face and crying. Craig's nowhere to be seen.

There's no pretense about a whipping this time when Dad gets home from work. Mom and Craig's relationship turns into love-hate after that, and I never tell on him again, which works well to his advantage. That first slug will become another point of reference for me. Although it will no longer be Craig delivering the blows, I'll never forget their origins, making a silent, daily plea that the next beating she receives will be no worse than this one.

Every spare minute Dad isn't at work, we're on the land where our New House will soon stand. Dad and the boys clear sagebrush, level the ground, pour the foundation, and start building the house. They lay every brick and nail every nail except the ones Dad lets me attempt. He finishes several while I'm still hitting at one that's bent and messy. Dad straightens my nail, covers my hand on the hammer with his huge hand, and with one hit, drives my nail in.

Dad can build anything from stonework for beautiful fireplaces to houses and everything in between. He'd spent most of his life building something. Even WWII didn't interrupt Dad's building—just what he built.

As the country pulled itself out of the Depression and began preparing for a possible war, Dad found a steady job as a pile driver working for Raymond Concrete Pile Company. The company had been awarded a contract for cast-in-place concrete piles for a new building in Washington, DC. Dad was one of three shifts that worked twenty-four hours a day, seven days a week constructing the Pentagon. The building was supported by thousands of concrete piles—many of which Dad drove. The Pentagon was dedicated in January 1943, and two months later, Dad was drafted into the Army Corps of Engineers to build things for the Allies to use and blow up.

Dad can lay brick faster than the boys can mix cement, lime, and water with a hoe in a wheelbarrow then haul the concrete to him. Dad handles a trowel to smooth concrete—or mud, as he calls it—with the same precision Mom uses when frosting a cake. Instead of waiting for the boys to catch up,

Dad helps haul bricks and mixes cement and tips his cap at a jaunty angle to start laying brick again.

I usually play with my hula-hoop and pose for pictures Mom takes of the progress on the house. She works alongside Dad and the boys, which leaves little time for cooking, so we live on fried hamburgers and fried potatoes. We're all pretty sick of them—including Mom—by the time she cooks something different, but that's not until she finishes painting wood on the outside of the house a pretty shade of green. It's the same shade the bricks below the wood are speckled with and the same shade as the concrete. It all makes a very nice combination. As she paints, I beg Mom to tell Del's yellow-paint-story again.

Del left Chicago, Illinois, under some kind of threat. It was dark and raining while he hid out under a bridge until the men chasing him were long gone. As the sun rose the next morning, Del sat just feet away from a dead man hanging by the neck from a rope attached to the underside of the bridge. He headed west.

Del never learned how to read or write. Since Gramma read out loud to him and he could figure math in his head in an instant, Del had no desire to learn. But he was a good professional painter. Many times, Gramma helped Del on a job because that was the only way he'd give her money for anything extra, like a new dress. She wore a pair of Del's white overalls and painted alongside him all day, every day, until the job was finished. Of course, Gramma went home after work to cook, clean up, and do anything else necessary, but she was able to buy something special occasionally.

Del was known for his brilliant yellow house paint. He stirred an ordinary gallon of yellow paint, peed a stream into the paint can, and stirred some more. The result was a very pretty shade and much in demand, although his customers never knew how he came up with the vibrant color.

We move into our New House with half of the roof complete. Dad and the boys finish that up in no time, then we settle into the home where Mom says we'll always live. Happiness and excitement replace trouble hanging over us because I think we all believe her; I know I do. I love this house.

It's a split-level, ranch-style house on a road with only one other house in sight. And it's an accumulation of everything we all want. I have my own bedroom with a built-in doll shelf that I don't want, but Mom wants me to have, and the room's painted a beautiful light green I love. I have my own dresser, closet, and space. The boys' bedroom is huge with enough room to give each his own space. The large kitchen has raw wood beams and lots of free-hanging cupboards. A large rock flower box stands just inside the front door, and a beautiful rock fireplace with a full-length hearth covers one entire wall in the front room. The wall has the prettiest and most unusual rocks from Mom's collection. Outside, the chimney displays "7Ls" created by Carson from Mom's rock collection to represent the seven Lancasters. Mom tells me that I'll be married in front of the fireplace one day, with Dad, her, and all the boys present, but then she walks away crying. Did she already know that would never happen?

The property is framed by a white wood fence. Two ancient wagon wheels found over the years on our travels punctuate the sidewalk to the front door. Dad likes horses, so he builds a corral and buys Trix, a chestnut Arabian stallion with a blazing white star on his forehead, for Carson, and he buys Toy, a pretty gray mare Dad says is mine but she's really for Dean and Craig too. The boys had an Appaloosa before I was born, but Toy is my first and, unfortunately, only horse.

After Dad and Carson teach me how to ride Toy, sometimes Carson lets me follow as he rides Trix through the sagebrush to the bank of the Snake. He laughs and yells encouragement as I struggle to stay on Toy's bare back following Trix up and down a steep bank.

After some instruction from Dad, Carson instinctively took to riding. Watching him gallop Trix is poetry in motion because you can't tell where

Carson ends and Trix begins. I can manage a trot without too much trouble, but when the sagebrush's little purple flowers are blooming with their sweet smell in the air, I like to walk Toy through the greenish-silver brush.

I start third grade and quickly settle into a routine when Mom lets me get roller skates like the other girls. The metal, clamp-on skates are worthless unless you keep the skate key safe because it turns a device that makes the skates firmly clamp onto street shoes. After school, I put on my skates and hold the key tight, racing to the buses. I jump on the bottom step and loosen and remove the skates just as the bus driver yells at me for taking too long.

For occasional weekend entertainment, the Alfresco drive-in theater is just down the road from our New House. The admission price is cheaper if you walk in, so we kids hop out of the pickup a short distance from the entrance to walk down a long lane lined with light bulbs to a tall wood fence encircling the drive-in. Engaging in another experience the boys shouldn't have taught me, we gingerly unscrew the hot bulbs and toss them so they break as we walk. The loud pop when they hit the road sounds like a bomb.

Before the movie starts, we play in a playground below the enormous screen. The boys push me on a huge swing set until I nearly fly over the top support pole. It's exhilarating each time I float those few seconds with the hanging seat chains slack and clanging just before I fall far enough to make the chains taunt again with a huge bounce that lifts me off the swing seat. On the down-swing, the boys push me to do it all over again.

The projection finally starts with a *News Reel* followed by *Short Subjects*. When the cartoon begins, we tear back to the pickup. The *Snack Bar* advertisements make us starve to death, so Mom breaks out goodies she brought, then we munch our way through the coming attractions and settle in for the main feature. I'm asleep long before it's over, and I never see the beginning or end of the B movie.

One evening, too many cars arrive at the drive-in for us to break light bulbs, so the boys decide it's time to teach me another *something they shouldn't*. In very serious, hushed voices, they ask if I know the dirtiest word in the world.

"Sure do. Gook!" I reply.

I was born during the Korean War and heard that word a lot. When I get mad at the boys, it's one I throw at them. Seeing my ignorance, they proceed to educate me on the "F" word in all its tenses and variations. They warn me to never ever say it within hearing distance of Mom or I'll be beaten with the stick until I die. They go on to show me how to throw a proper bird by folding down my fingers leaving the middle one up. The "F" word doesn't bother me as much as my middle fingers. I have to watch out for them because forever after, they're on their way to sticking up.

We've been in the New House only a few months before Mom's crying again. Dean and I are constantly in trouble now because he's acquired a stutter and I regularly wet the bed—habits I'm sure were influenced by Mom's tears because a move inevitably will follow. Mom's mad, but it doesn't help either of us stop.

At eight years old, I know the dark, heavy trouble hanging over us when Mom cries. I see the worried look on Dad's face that's soon replaced with resignation. I see what I begin to realize is exasperation on the older boys' faces. My heart cracks in two when I see the anguish on Mom's crying face. I realize, too, that she's empty when she's like this and won't let us in to help her. Dean continues to stutter, and I continue to wet the bed.

One night, I find myself awake without knowing what woke me up or why I'm hugging the wall outside my bedroom door. Suddenly, Craig pokes me from behind and hisses "Go back to bed!" as he creeps toward the kitchen. My ears hurt. Is it because my fists are pushed hard against them or because of the crying and dishes crashing in the kitchen? I wish it all would just stop.

I can't open my eyes, and it's really hot. I need a drink of water, but I can't get out of bed. I can still hear crashing and crying as I roll in and out of sleep, fighting heat and thirst.

Someone shakes me awake. Mom's eyes are nearly swollen shut from crying—more so than I've ever seen. She tells me to get ready for school, but I can't. The bed's wet and blood's smeared over the pillowcase. Dad picks me out of bed and drives to the same doctor who delivered Craig, Dean, and me. He tells Dad mastoiditis caused my eardrum to burst as Dad holds my head still while the doctor tries to kill me by inserting a thin instrument with a small scoop to clean out debris.

When the doctor asks why Mom didn't bring me in, Dad says she had a bad night. "Was it a crying jag?" the doctor asks. Dad nods. The doctor says he's told Mom to stop them because they're bad for her. That comment surprised me, and I thought about it for a long time but never had the courage to ask Mom about it.

As an adult, I've wondered why the doctor didn't help Mom stop them instead of just telling her to stop. But maybe he did try. I now believe those crying jags relieved her enough to set aside selfishness and stay with us a while longer. I still struggle to understand why she was unhappy with a family who loved her so very much, and when she wasn't crying, she clearly loved us too.

After Dad drives me home, Mom cries when she tells me how the Indian, Ruth's dad, used an ice pick to puncture her eardrum when she was little, and she had an earache like mine. That made me mad inside, and I wonder why she cries for herself when I feel so bad. This is the first and last time I'm aware that she broke most of her dishes, but it won't be the last crying jag I experience.

In November, Gramma has a heart attack while visiting Aunt Ruth and her new baby in Sparks, Nevada. Mom goes to Sparks; Dad rents an ambulance. He drives it—with me along—to Sparks to bring Mom and Gramma home. The trip's exciting when Dad turns on the siren and flashing lights and runs stop signs in every little town. Sometimes Dad flips them on just to tease and wake me up. It's dark, and the lights bounce off the night back to me.

Gramma stays with us through the Christmas holiday so Mom can help while she recovers. I spend hours at the kitchen table while Gramma tells me her stories.

Gramma was born in Siloam Springs, Arkansas, in 1890. She was four years old when she traveled by covered wagon to Galena, Kansas, with her mom, dad, and five-year-old sister. Gramma tells me how she played alongside the wagon with her sister, picked wildflowers, and used broken pieces of glass as play dishes for their ragdolls.

The wagon trip took almost two weeks to complete. Her dad's wagon had been retrofitted with a bonnet: cotton canvas stretched over bows made of hardwood and attached to the inside of the wagon to provide shelter for everything they owned. Traveling inside the bouncing wagon was uncomfortable, but walking alongside was, too, because the girls were dressed in sun bonnets, ankle-length dresses, petticoats, stockings, and high-top button shoes.

Two mules pulled the wagon filled with their possessions while hooked over the sides were a butter churn, water barrel, farm equipment, chicken coop, and feed trough. They carried bacon packed in cornmeal, coffee, beans, spices, flour, and sugar. Sourdough starter had been mixed with enough flour to form soft balls that were stored with the rest of the flour. Balls of dough were mixed with enough water to thin them to the right consistency for batter to make sourdough pancakes cooked in an iron skillet on a campfire or sourdough bread baked in a Dutch oven hung over the campfire.

Early one morning after breakfast, the two little sisters sat in towering grass, playing with ragdolls and broken glass dishes. When shouts from their parents signaling time to leave never came, Gramma stood up for a quick look. "They're *gone!*" she screamed. After a hard run on a rutted track, they spotted a distant lumbering wagon shimmering in the early morning sun. They ran and ran to catch up to the wagon that never slowed down for them. When the girls finally reached the wagon, their dad stopped. As they climbed in, he said he thought they were asleep in the back. Gramma was sure her mother knew they weren't and meant to abandon them both on the trail. Gramma adored her dad, but she wouldn't have him much longer.

Gramma was still very young when her dad died in Galena. Her mother quickly remarried, and Gramma never saw or heard from her again. Gramma lost track of her sister and was shuffled around between relatives, spending the most time with an aunt.

Several years later when she was a teenager, Gramma walked downstairs early one morning and saw her dad standing in the kitchen, looking up at her. She screamed and ran the rest of the way down the stairs to where her aunt was carving the morning meat. The aunt still had a butcher knife in her hand when she turned to grab her hysterical niece. The bridge of Gramma's nose was accidentally cut, and it bled profusely, so her aunt grabbed coal dust from the coal bucket to stanch the bleeding. Gramma knew she had seen her dad, or his ghost or spirit, but her aunt hadn't seen anything. Gramma was convinced her dad came back to make sure she was all right and tell her that he loved her. Gramma had a long, thin black scar on her nose for the rest of her life. Whenever someone asked how she got the scar, Gramma always replied with a laugh, "From sticking my nose into other people's business."

After returning home across the river to Burley in January, Gramma has another heart attack and is taken to Cottage Hospital where I was born. During that time, all the aunts and uncles stay with us. Mom says the reason we built the New House was to have room for everyone while Gramma's sick. Ronnie's back home and cries when he returns from the hospital. I want to go, too, but no one lets me.

At school, I tell my third-grade teacher that Gramma had a heart attack. "Oh, that's a shame. I need my house painted in the spring," Mrs. Coal replies, meaning Gramma and Del had previously painted it, and she will want them again.

Mrs. Coal is old, short, and stout with frizzy black hair and a grim face. She regularly smacks my butt or hits my hand with her ruler without warning. The ruler whacks and butt smacks never caused the uproar Mrs. Cole's comment did. Mom, Aunt Ruth, and Aunt Mary head directly to the school. For the first time, I feel sorry for Mrs. Cole; I sure wouldn't want to be in her shoes with those three after me. I don't know what was said, but the next day, Mrs. Coal tells me she is sorry for my Gramma's illness. And she doesn't whack or smack me again during the short time I remain in her class.

In my dream, I see only clustered, crying faces: Mom, Dad, the boys, aunts, and uncles. They stop crying when Gramma's face appears, but she leaves and the faces cry again. When I walk outside to get away from all the sadness, Gramma's standing in front of our white fence, smiling at me.

"Gramma!" I yell, running to her.

She's still smiling at me as she rises just above the fence. Before I can touch her, she's out of reach and drifting away, silhouetted against white clouds high above in the dark sky. I'm jumping higher and higher, trying to grab her legs.

With tears streaming down her face, Mom shakes me awake to say Gramma died.

I know. I saw her leave, I think to myself.

I know Mom's too sad to listen if I try to tell her about my dream, then I never tell her because if I do, she'll cry.

Gramma's so still and white lying in a casket. Looking at her, I remember Mom telling Gramma about a dream she had. Gramma was dead in the dream, and Mom was scared.

"Oh, you wouldn't be scared of me, would you?" Gramma had asked Mom.

I'm not scared of her now, but no one lets me kiss her like they do. No one hears when I ask to be picked up so I can reach Gramma. I sit by an aunt during the service, and when I cough, she shakes my arm and glares at me. I bite the inside of my lip to keep from coughing again, listening to "Beautiful Isle of Somewhere" and wondering if it's all right to like it.

My family of seven ceases being one after Gramma died.

7

"Gotta Travel On"

BILLY GRAMMER

Everything changes fast. Ronnie marries Kathy and moves across the river to Burley, and we will leave Idaho for the last time, heading to Tucson, Arizona. Our neighbors from my Barracks Home, Paul and Blanche Coffey, have moved around since their boys left home, and they're currently in Arizona. I guess that's why we're heading there.

It doesn't matter where we are heading because we won't be there long. We had all hoped Mom would be satisfied and stay at the New House. But we're packing our things again. Even though moving has been my normal for more than half of my life, I'm dreading leaving this house and Idaho.

I won't see the New House in Heyburn again until my attempt at twenty-two to capture remnants of my family. Visiting what was supposed to be our "forever home," it looks just as I remember. "7Ls" still displays outside on the chimney, my bedroom has the original light-green paint, and the fireplace wall with the best of Mom's rock collection is still beautiful, although there's a crack in the wall caused by settling. The crack in my family was caused by moving. The former adds character; the latter destroyed a family.

Dad, Carson, and Craig stay until the New House is sold. Mom, Dean, and I leave in the pickup, packed solid with a tarp over the bed, for Las Vegas, Nevada, where Aunt Ruth lives now. Mom and her little sister always have a good relationship, unlike Mom and her older sisters, and because we'll go through Las Vegas on the way to Arizona anyway, it's a good place to wait for Dad and the boys.

When Mom gets turned around in Elko, Nevada, on a gas stop, she points, asking a cowboy if that's the direction to Las Vegas.

"Yep," he replies.

Mom thanks him and turns to leave.

"It'll take ya a long time tho. Be better ta go thata way," he says, smiling and pointing in the opposite direction.

Mom thanks him again then shoos Dean and me to the pickup. She keeps her mind off Gramma and crying by telling stories about her first driving experiences around Burley before and during WWII.

Mom's first car was an old Buick named Susie since dependable automobiles are always referred to as females. Mom was one of the few people around with a car, so she drove CCC guys to one of the CCC Camps around Burley. After work, Mom and Aunt Ruth went dancing and drove soldiers back to Camp Rupert, a prisoner-of-war camp close to Paul across the Snake from Burley, where a few thousand Germans and Italians were held to work in fields, harvesting potatoes. Mom also drove servicemen to Minidoka, where they were stationed at a detention camp for Americans of Japanese descent being held while the United States was at war with Japan. The detention camp was a misleading name for a prisoner-of-war camp for Americans who had committed no crimes.

Mom couldn't find, or afford, tires for Susie during the war and quickly wore out ones scavenged at the dump. Many times, the short trips took longer because driving on a rim after the tire blew was tricky. Aunt Mary went along for the ride sometimes, too, and when she didn't think Mom could navigate a curve in the road on just the rim and flat rubber, she'd merrily shout, "Bend'er, girl! You can do it!"

For the rest of the trip, Dean and I shout "Bend'er, girl! You can do it!" at every curve in the road. I know now her stories and our antics helped Mom keep her sadness under control, her loneliness for Gramma at bay, and the emptiness we were never able to fill for her at arm's length.

We stay with Aunt Ruth in Las Vegas on Boulder Highway in a little cabin motel unit for over a month, waiting for Dad and the boys. Dean and I are in heaven with no school, even though we should be in one somewhere. We play with Aunt Ruth's baby, but mostly we play in the desert behind the cabin, where several Model T cars have rusted out. We manage to open doors on two of them and spend days being Al Capone and the Untouchables. Our first experience with an ice cream truck is messy when we each buy a huge Popsicle that drips down our hands in the desert heat as we run to the gangster cars.

Mom and Aunt Ruth take care of the baby, talk about Gramma, play Solitaire, sing songs, and cry. The most often repeated is "The Prisoner's Song," and each time they hit the high part, neither can quite reach it, so they dissolve into giggles. They talk about Gramma again only to break out in song, giggles, and tears. When Dean and I hear "Do you remember when Mom ...?" we head to the cars because we're helpless in their grief.

Dad and the boys finally arrive in a large rental truck holding the rest of our things, Zip, and Trix. I wish Toy had come, too, but Dad says there wasn't room for her. I feel sad but know there isn't anything that can be done to change it.

Dad hires a man to drive the rental so he can drive the pickup, and we're on our way again. A hundred miles south of Las Vegas in Kingman, Arizona, Mom meets the Mother Road: Route 66. We follow Route 66 only a few miles—it continues east and we're heading south—but after only a few short months in Tucson, Mom will have us back on Route 66, heading east to the end of the road for my world.

My current world: a place I take for granted like every kid should be able to do. I have food to eat, clothes that fit, a bed to sleep in, and the knowing that I'm protected by adults around me. Home is where my family is, whether in a house somewhere or in a pickup packed solid moving to a house somewhere. Dad provides for me, Mom loves me, and I have Dean for fights, getting into trouble, and exploring. And I always will.

I've never gone to bed hungry once in my nine years, and it never occurs to me that I ever will. I'll learn the hard way at ten that we're responsible for our actions no matter the circumstances. And I'll learn how very long an eternity is when dealing with the ache of losing those who are most important to me. But that's all more than a year away. For now, in my blissful nine-year-old ignorance, I take everything for granted and join in another roaming adventure.

We stay at the Town and Country Motel in Tucson for several days until Dad finds a bidding job for a construction company. After that, we move into a house on Root Lane, which means we have to go back to school, even though there are only a few weeks left of the school year. Spanish is a required subject, even in third grade, and it's total Greek to me. The grading scale is 1 through 5 instead of A through F. Everything's different, and I miss Idaho. But I know we'll never go back because Gramma isn't there anymore.

We take Sunday drives, even in the Arizona summer heat. The boys pile in the back of the pickup, and Dad drives with Mom and me in the cab. We always take *the old road*. If there isn't an old road, we drive until we find one. An old road is necessary for good rock and wood hunting, and with kids, someone always has to go to the bathroom. I envy the boys' ability to stand and pee. It's complicated to stay hidden behind something, pull down your pants, and squat and pee without getting wet pants or shoes. But getting wet pants is better than using public restrooms because they're all filthy by Mom's standards. I'd rather have a flying whipping with a stick than go into a women's restroom with her. Unfortunately, sometimes we have to.

"Don't touch anything!" Mom orders as soon as the door shuts.

We occupy a stall barely big enough for one person let alone two. Disposable seat covers aren't widely available, so Mom covers the seat with toilet paper. She lifts me up and sits me down on the paper-covered seat. It usually takes a couple more tries because the paper slips off before I'm seated. And heaven help me if I grab the sides of the dirty seat to steady myself. Back outside, the boys come out of the men's restroom looking normal, happy, and not on the verge of tears from letting the paper slide off too many times. Oh, to be a boy and pee in peace.

Dad discovers Orange Grove Road during one Sunday drive. We follow it until we come to an orchard where oranges can be picked for a minimal fee. After picking a couple of bags, we head back and stop for ice cream cones at an A&W drive-in. I have to get in the back with the boys to eat my cone while Dad continues driving home. It's tricky eating cones in the open bed of a moving pickup and almost impossible not to have some ice cream fly into someone's face. Carson selects who he wants to torture for their ice cream hitting him, whether it did or not, and it's wrist-burn time until Mom yells out the side window to stop acting like morons.

We've lived on Root Lane a short time when Dad buys a large mobile home, and we live in Silent Wheels Trailer Park for a shorter time. The park has a swimming pool the boys and I live in until we're shriveled up, but I can't get used to the chlorinated water. I'd rather be in a canal back in Idaho where my hair didn't turn a sickly, pale-green color. Mom's never happy having close neighbors, so Dad has the mobile home moved to a lot by a dry riverbed away from neighbors and the swimming pool. Then she decides she wants to move to Missouri.

8

"There's a Long, Long Trail"

SONS OF THE PIONEERS

Mom wants to move to Missouri. Dad doesn't. He says it'll be like walking through a graveyard because he hasn't been back for over thirty years, has no reason to go, and those he knew are probably long gone. But Dad still wants Mom happy more than he doesn't want to move, so he hitchhikes from Tucson to El Dorado Springs to find our life there: a house and a job.

Knowing my dad, the first place he went when he arrived in the small, rural community was the tavern. Dad never asks for directions or information at a service station, only in a bar where the information's more accurate and the company easier. Dad's easygoing and friendly, and I imagine he made a stir when they found out his last name. Lots of Lancasters still live in and around town. Dad's Uncle Leo still lives with Aunt Minnie on Main Street, and his elderly father lives close by too. Dad learns that Mildred Edwards, the woman who cared for him as a baby, is very ill, and he goes to see her. She's now ninety years old, frail, and tiny in bed.

"Hello, Mildred," Dad says.

"Oh! Hello!" Mildred recognizes him instantly. She says she's so very happy to see him one last time. She dies only a few days later.

Dad calls Mom to say he found a job and a house. He tells her the farmhouse has an outhouse and a pump. Mom assumes the pump is an electric water pump, and an outhouse can be tolerated again, so she agrees. While Dad hitchhikes 1,253 miles back to Tucson, we start packing for the next move with Mom happily singing "Gotta Travel On."

Carson doesn't want to go this time because he has a job and wants to stay in Tucson with Trix. Mom and Dad find a little house on Romero Road for rent with a small corral in back for Trix. I didn't think Mom would allow it because Carson's her favorite, but he's seventeen years old when we leave him behind. I hate that Ronnie and Carson are both gone. I've lost the peacemaker, the tease, and the only cushion Dean and I have from Craig.

We arrive in El Dorado Springs, Missouri, on a cold, damp, gray October day. We spend the night at Uncle Leo's and the next morning, drive less than two miles on a gravel road to a small, black-and-gray tarpapered farmhouse with a small freestanding garage. The house has five rooms: front room, bedroom, kitchen, dining room, and storage room. The dining room is used for my bedroom, and the bunkbed fits in the storage room with little leftover space for Craig and Dean. It's tiny and ugly compared to our New House, but the worst for Mom is just outside the back door.

The pump, or pumps, I should say, turn out to be the old iron kind that must be primed before the first use of the day and require only arm power to work. One large pump stands outside the back door, and a second smaller one is attached to the kitchen sink. Mom's furious but continues unpacking.

We've lived in many places with outhouses, and though not preferred, they aren't the worst to live with—they just smell bad, even with lime regularly shoveled down the hole. As a kid, the best scare in the world is carrying a flashlight for the long walk to the outhouse on a cold, moonless night. After pulling open the creaky wood door and stepping inside, I place one hand on the seat to steady myself while I stick my head and flashlight partially down the seat hole to make sure no critters are waiting to bite my butt. To endure this odorous task with both hands already in use, my nose must be plugged using the soft palate behind the roof of my mouth to block air to and from my nostrils. After I finish my business, I have to get back to the house in one piece. There's always that last small hop, skip, and urgent little jump to get inside just before something grabs me from behind. I've even seen Mom's small hop, skip, and urgent little jump coming back inside at night.

Dad tells us about the time he pushed over an outhouse for a Halloween prank and slipped into the hole. We won't topple any because we don't want to fall in one.

"It'd be easier to make another kid rather than clean you up if you did fall in," Mom laughs.

A big creek flows alongside the property and runs under a small, arched bridge on the gravel road in front of our house. A little creek runs a distance behind the house and flows into the big creek. The surrounding area is a kids' paradise to explore, which Dean and I do at every opportunity. It doesn't take us long to become Missourians complete with accent, acceptance of snakes, and brown-staining, smelly, awful-tasting sulfur water. Later comes chiggers with everything else that crawls, slithers, or buzzes.

Mom likes having a baby around, so Randy, Aunt Ruth's little boy, is living with us. Aunt Ruth brought him to Tucson a few months after we'd arrived. She'd recently divorced and was struggling with everything, so Mom will care for Randy until Aunt Ruth gets back on track.

Randy's a cute little guy just learning to walk, and he's the first to break out in painful abscesses. Mom says the lousy water's probably causing them. But the doctor who shaved Randy's head because it's covered with boils said sulfur doesn't cause boils but a bacteria that normally lives on our skin can. Randy's so miserable, we all take turns walking him while he cries. Mom, Craig, and Dean have at least one painful boil, but Dad and I are spared. We never discover what caused the outbreak and, thankfully, it never strikes again.

When we're not in school, we take over pumping water for Mom. We pump water to heat for our baths in a galvanized tub. Being the youngest and only girl does have advantages: I get to bathe first. After I'm finished, Mom adds another pot of boiling water for the boys to bathe together. When I pass one of them on his way to the tub, I whisper, "I peed in the tub," which causes an uproar. Mom assures them it isn't true, but they never really know for sure.

We pump and pump enough water to fill two tubs on Mom's Maytag Ringer washing machine. Because the sulfur water begins to stain everything a dull brown, we drive to town each week to use a laundromat instead. There, only an occasional splat stains a particular area of clothing instead of everything.

After several weeks, Mom and Randy fly to Las Vegas, where Aunt Ruth's ready to have her baby back. Mom's gone only a few days, but it seems like forever since I've never been away from her this long. On the day she's due back, the boys and I fly off the school bus and tear through the back door. When she's nowhere to be seen, we stand in the kitchen, arguing.

"I told you she wouldn't be home today," Dean says.

"She said she would be!" I wail.

"Well, you're wrong as usual," Craig sneers.

"Shut up, butt face," I sneer back.

"Well, I am home!" Mom says, leaning over the chair arm in the front room so we can see her. We freeze for only a second as I think about how lucky I am that I didn't call Craig something worse. Then we charge to Mom and hug her until she's nearly squished.

"Okay, okay," Mom laughs. "I don't suppose anyone's hungry, are they?" Mom's back where we always need her to be: with us.

Not long after we move in, a man drives out from town to give Dad an old trunk that belonged to the Edwards family because no one claimed it after Mildred died. Edward E. Edwards's discharge papers from the Civil War are in the trunk along with a small, ancient family Bible inscribed to Mrs. Rachel Edwards from her mother, Elizabeth Todd, in 1865. Recorded on the pages are births and deaths of the Todd and Edwards families from the early 1800s to the mid-1900s. My Dad's birth is documented in the Bible, and the fact that E. E. and Mildred Edwards took him to raise. This is the first written proof Dad's seen that he had been born.

I like the idea of going to the same grade school Dad attended when he was little, but it takes getting used to my fourth-grade teacher. On my first day when I flub the answer to a question, she says it's okay to be ignorant. Ignorant and stupid mean the same thing to me, so I sink in my chair. When the teacher makes ice cream cones later for an afternoon treat, she walks up and down the rows of desks, making sure no kid licks their ice cream; instead, we have to bite off small pieces to eat. I think that's pretty stupid; an ice cream cone's made to lick.

After the boys and I come home from school and finish homework and a snack, we watch cowboy shows on TV. I look for *Horton Hatches the Egg* or *Mighty Mouse* when the cartoons start. Finally, it's time for Mom to start cooking dinner. Once again, scrumptious aromas fill the house and make our stomachs think our throats have been cut. We beg for bites until we're run out of the kitchen with a threat of the stick, even though she never uses it anymore.

"If wishes were fishes, we'd have a big fry. If horse turds were dumplings, we'd eat till we die," Mom says. Then she gives us each a tantalizing bite of fried potatoes speared on toothpicks.

After dinner, it's time for evening TV. We watch *Red Skelton* and *Milton Berle*, but Westerns are our favorites, like *The Rifleman* and *Death Valley Days*. Who knew Ronald Reagan would go on to run the country? We love *Wagon Train*, *Gunsmoke*, Richard Boone's *Have Gun Will Travel*, and oooh, Clint Eastwood in *Rawhide*. I have the world in front of me on three black-and-white TV channels with foil wrapped around rabbit ears and my world—my family—watching it with me.

On weekends, we take trips around the countryside, visiting places Dad remembers. On the first excursion, we drive out to the old homestead where he was born. The house is still standing, although it was abandoned long ago. The grounds are an overgrown mess, yet wild roses are blooming everywhere. Dad says his mother planted roses when she first moved there. Mom cries and dabs her eyes with the ever-ready tissue, probably remembering Gramma.

We drive far out into the country to visit Dad's ancient Aunt Ida. She lives in a small farmhouse enclosed by a run-down fence that keeps chickens, pigs, and some goats from running away, but there's nothing to keep them off the little porch; their company doesn't bother Aunt Ida at all. She's feisty and chews tobacco but switches to a corncob pipe to be polite, I think. I'm fascinated. Mom's polite but quiet. Dad's happy and thoroughly enjoys the visit, although we never go back.

Dad drives us to town for the Fourth of July celebration, where we play in Spring Park, waiting for the parade to begin. It's one giant picnic at the huge park with people from near and far. Dean and I chase each other around the rock columns and arches of a big goldfish pond that Dad says, as a small boy, he had helped his stonemason Uncle Jack build.

After the parade down Main Street finishes, the band sets up in an old-fashioned bandstand in Spring Park to continue playing. Old men, including a couple of Civil War veterans dressed in ancient uniforms for the parade, gather around water escaping from two small, stained pipes that emerge from a stone-enforced face of a basin close by the bandstand. The old men briefly scare me when Dean chases me down cement steps to a little pool of water under the stained pipes. When I screech to a halt, rheumy eyes, sunken cheeks, and snaggle-tooth grins surround me as the old men cackle and offer us a drink. They're drinking the free-running, smelly sulfur water in small, dented tin cups and tell us it's the water that helps them live for so long.

Spring Park is why El Dorado Springs began, when early travelers stopped at the spring to camp and water their animals. El Dorado grew into the small town it is while Spring Park grew into a huge, lush park where Dad first played.

Dad played baseball in Spring Park when he was little. During that time, August Busch Sr.'s wife—of Anheuser-Busch Brewing Company in St. Louis, Missouri—spent summer holiday in El Dorado Springs with her two young sons. She took them to the town kids' swimming hole to swim and play. While she watched them, her chauffeur unpacked a huge picnic lunch for all the kids, rich and poor alike, to eat. Then the chauffeur drove Mrs. Busch and sons, along with as many poor kids who could squish into or on the vehicle, to Spring Park to play baseball. Dad injured his little finger during one game but paid no attention so he wouldn't miss any fun or food. The tip of his little finger at the joint was bent down for the rest of his life. After the game, Mrs. Busch treated them all to something else delicious to eat. The only brand of beer Dad drank his whole life was Budweiser because of those times.

At home, Dean and I catch fireflies when the weather's calm on summer evenings. During the day, we fish the big creek's bluegills to feed the farm cats. I'd rather be trying to keep up with Dad fishing at Caplinger Mills because I like fishing with him, and I didn't see any snakes there. Standing on the bridge over the big creek, lots of snakes are around. I throw a rock and nail a sunning water moccasin curled up on a large boulder in the creek—apparently hitting it just right because he shot straight up and crumpled slowly back down on the boulder. Must'a killed him good. I won't fish until I clear out all the snakes

I see. Sometimes Dean and I jump from boulder to boulder exploring the big creek, but we carry a supply of rocks to make the snakes slither out of our way.

A huge tree toppled across the little creek sometime during a storm, and the fallen tree and debris had created a fairly large pond below. After Craig cleared brush and junk away from the sides, we have a kid-size swimming hole. Mom gives us a bar of soap when we go swimming to save pumping water for baths.

The fallen tree is perfect to jump from into the pond five or six feet below. I have to be careful walking on the tree because jagged limbs and rough bark are murder on bare feet. It's a slow-go but worth the trouble when I cannonball into the pond, making the boys yell their heads off.

Gingerly taking the first step on the fallen tree, to work my way to the middle of the pond, my toes feel something smooth and pliable. Uh-oh! Looking down, I see a water moccasin's tail under my toes. I realize how huge he is when his head lifts and slowly dips, swinging around to look at me from the other side of the pond. We're both pretty startled. I freeze and don't move anything—even my toes. After a very long time, the snake slithers off the tree into our pond, with its tail still under my toes as its head hits the water.

"Oh, shit! Snake! Huge!" I scream at the boys.

The snake barely makes a ripple as it disappears below the surface of our pond. The boys catch only a glimpse of it, but that's enough to send them flying out. We never convince Mom to come to our pond after that. Even I have a hard time going back because that snake was huge around—and as long as Dad is tall. Now we make lots of noise at the pond, throwing lots of rocks into the water before we swim.

While Dad's still at work on Saturdays, Mom gives us each money to go to a movie in town where the show will either be a love movie or a good movie, which is anything other than a love movie. When we get to town, Craig disappears to do whatever he does before the show, while Dean and I stop at Luther Thatch's grocery store to steal a jar of maraschino cherries to eat during the movie.

Craig's good at sneaking into the movie without paying. If he can't sneak in, he crouches down in front of the old-fashioned ticket cage, reaching up to the counter with money in hand. The ticket man thinks he's a kid under ten and sells him a cheaper ticket.

Sometimes Dean and I sneak in with a crowd so we'll have more money after the movie to spend on comic books and penny candy. Mom would be outraged, putting the stick to good use again if she knew. But what we do isn't for malicious reasons; it's just what we do at the time. We know it's wrong, but because of our vagabond mentality, we don't care. We won't be living here very long anyway, so why does it matter what we do?

On the walk back home, Dean and I stuff as many pieces of Bazooka bubble gum into our mouths as can fit. We stop stuffing when we can't read the comic out loud that's packaged with the gum because there's no room for our tongues to move. We're nearly home before the gum's chewed up enough to blow gigantic bubbles.

Mom pours out each sack of candy, dividing it all up four ways so there's no fighting over it. Then Mom and each kid pick out a comic book to read while eating our own pile of candy. On these Saturday afternoons, Mom has the opportunity to be a kid with us.

My curiosity about geodes started with Uncle Leo's porch supports and the old bandstand in Spring Park, all of which are covered with geodes that had been set in wet cement. The smaller rocks look like balls of cookie dough with cinnamon sprinkled on them. A hard crack with a hammer breaks the geode in two, and many have beautiful crystal formations inside. Some in town show the crystal formations while others are left intact, looking like cookie dough.

I started searching for geodes on the gravel road in front of our house after it was graded and around the farm after Dad said I'd probably find a bucketful without much trouble. I'll soon find more because there's a road grader coming up behind us as we walk home from town one Saturday afternoon. I know the grader blade will uncover many more geodes.

The *man* on the road grader stops to ask if we want a ride, but we say "no thanks" because we don't know *him*. *He* convinces us it's okay, which doesn't take much because we really want to ride in a real road grader. When *he* stops in front of our house, Mom runs out the door but stops short and doesn't say anything. I have a feeling she's seen *him* before. Afterward, she says the usual about not riding with strangers. But in time, I'll learn *he's* not a stranger.

On Saturday nights, Mom and Dad go out to dance at a bar. The boys and I have something easy for dinner, and Mom makes something delicious for dessert with three pieces on plates ready for us. As soon as they're out the door, we dive for the dessert. Craig never lets Dean or me eat ours and harasses us until we give him half. He's bigger, stronger, and a bully. We hate him more every day.

It turns out that the *man* on the road grader is at the bar, too, because once, *he* comes home with Mom and Dad. They drink beer and play spoons in time to music on my little box record player that Ronnie gave me during our last Christmas in Idaho.

As the summer progresses, Mom isn't talking about moving, but she's crying more than usual and takes long walks in the evenings, telling me to come too. Mom doesn't see the parallels between her childhood and what she's doing to ours. I can't point out the obvious similarities, obvious even to a ten-year-old, because she wants me to listen and not talk when she tells stories of her sad life before Dad, the boys, and me. So, I listen.

Mom had already moved times beyond counting when she was fourteen and met Herman Mangum. When she told Gramma she was going to marry him, Gramma said she could if she took eight-year-old Ruth with her when she left. One day, Ruth asked Mom if she could play with some kids across the road. When Mom hesitated, Ruth told her to come and play, too, but Mom couldn't because she was pregnant and supposed to be a grownup. She was fifteen when Herman left before Ronnie was born.

About two years later, Mom married Florian Robison and had a second son, Carson. When he was about two years old, his dad and a woman died in a car from carbon monoxide poisoning after they made love then fell asleep with the engine running. After that tragedy, Mom moved her two little sons to Heyburn, Idaho, to live with Gramma, who had kicked Del out. Gramma was living in an old farmhouse with Ruth and Del's daughter Louise, who was about the same age as Ruth.

Living in Heyburn with Gramma, Mom found her first paying job, where she and Aunt Ruth worked swing shift at a potato dehydrating plant while Gramma babysat Mom's two little boys. The potatoes were boiled and skinned before they came down a long conveyor belt, where Mom and Aunt Ruth stood shoulder-to-shoulder with other women, all using knives to cut out bad spots.

Canned potatoes that looked, smelled, and tasted like pineapple were made at the plant and shipped overseas to servicemen during WWII. The plant stank like rotten potatoes, and the women wore ugly uniforms and hairnets. That wasn't Mom and Aunt Ruth's idea of glamorous, and they hated the job.

Gramma eventually let Del come back, but Mom still hated him and certainly didn't want to live with him again. It was during this time that Mom stopped in at Boyd's Lounge after work. She had seen a handsome new bartender there the week before and wanted to see if he was as handsome as she remembered.

After Mom tells the stories on her mind, I ask her to tell some I want to hear: funny ones or scary ones. But as the hot, humid, snake- and insect-infested Missouri summer wears on, Mom only tells sad stories. I never see her breaking the boys' hearts with her stories—only mine. They're never around during the telling, and I wonder why.

After a long walk, Mom tires of stories and crying. So we sing songs like "Tie Me to Your Apron Strings Again," which makes her cry again, and "Driftwood on the River" as we walk back home. *Maybe now she'll stay happy for a little while,* I think. I wish with all my heart Gramma was still in Burley.

I think a lot about Mom's story when she was three years old in Burke, Idaho, and Gramma had smallpox. A doctor put Gramma in a sanitarium to either die or get well; he didn't know which one. Mom was put in the same locked room because she had been exposed to smallpox with no one to care for her. She remembered wiping Gramma's face over and over with a cold, wet rag to cool her fever. She combed Gramma's hair and held a cup for her parched lips to sip water because Gramma's fingers were swollen and curved like claws with pus-engorged sores filling both hands. Mom was terrified Gramma would die and leave her. Gramma recovered, and Mom never developed smallpox, so they went home only to leave again in the middle of the night the following year when Gramma left her tyrant husband.

Gramma loved Mom, but unintentionally or not, Gramma left her emotionally empty most of her childhood. Mom adored Gramma and, judging by her stories and actions, craved Gramma's acceptance. She wanted Gramma to love her and want her there but was never sure that Gramma felt the same. I can't put it into words at ten years old, but I know Mom's doing the same thing to me, and I'm terrified. She still cries about her childhood, yet she's causing mine to be just as painful. I don't understand why Mom can't see what she's doing.

Everything feels so different this time—something's really wrong. I wonder what she's going to do because she's crying constantly without talking about moving. I can't ask because if I do, the question may make *something worse* real. I just try to make her happy.

And Dean stutters. I wet the bed. And Craig picks on us.

It's almost the end of summer vacation. Mom stays in bed late every morning now—something she's never done. Dad's at work, and Craig's gone somewhere by the time Dean and I get up. We quietly dress and go outside, keeping ourselves busy until we know she's up.

Dean makes gladiator armor and helmets out of cardboard for us to wear, fighting with wooden swords. He found some tasseled cord and decorated our armor more elegantly than any Roman ever had. He has a scar below the corner of his mouth from the one battle I definitely won.

When Dean decides we need to be blood brothers, we crouch behind the garage as he cuts two slits and clutches our bleeding thumbs in his fist. "We'll always be together now, Sherrie. Always," he solemnly tells me. I think he knew we were soon to be torn to pieces.

The new school year starts after Labor Day.

In October, a year after we'd arrived, *that day* happens. Mom is gone, and she has no intention of ever seeing us again.

Life Without Mom

9

"Hello Walls"

FARON YOUNG

It's a long, lousy, straight-through drive from El Dorado Springs back to Tucson, Arizona, where we lived prior to moving to Missouri. Craig, Dean, and I are fourteen, twelve, and ten, respectively, and we fight like cats and dogs. When we pile back in, arguing after a gas stop, Dad doesn't start the car, waiting until we stop.

"I can't have you kids fighting all the time. You have to stop it."

And we do, mostly, for the rest of the trip.

I don't know how Dad survives. He looks so sad and has to deal with us too. I'm experiencing independence on this trip for the first time out of Mom's reach and have moments of crazy-happy freedom. They can't last, though. Misery replaces crazy-happy even before I return to the car after another gas stop, leaving me lost again, and I have no idea how to handle it. By the time we hit Tucson, I'm a quiet, lost, miserable kid.

Dad doesn't unpack the little car in Tucson except for our clothes because we have no place to unpack it yet. I take out the Bible and the gray basket and chocolate box Gramma gave me and keep them in a couple of grocery sacks. I'm glad I did because it isn't long before Craig takes Dad's car and leaves town heading east.

Craig has the same peculiar relationship with Mom that she has with her three older sisters. He wants to be with Mom but can't stand it when he is. It would've been a disaster if he made it back to Missouri, but he didn't make it. When he ran out of gas money, Craig came back without the car. Dad didn't get the car or our stuff back because he didn't have money to pay the impound charges. Everything I own is now in a couple of paper sacks.

I don't know or care where Dad, Dean, and Craig sleep during these first weeks. I'm numb and silent. When someone talks to me, I look but don't listen. *If I can just live through today*, I think, *maybe I'll wake up and things will be right again.* They're probably on someone's couch somewhere, like me, maybe in the same house; I don't know.

Carson still lives in the little house on Romero Road, and Dad or the boys might be sleeping there like I sometimes do. They might be sleeping at Ronnie and Kathy's, who had moved here from Burley shortly after their first child was born and live in a big house on Romero Road close to Carson's little house. They're just starting their family, and I'm certain they don't need or want a readymade family, minus the mom, hanging around.

Dad knows a couple with two daughters, and I stay with them for a while. It's all so confusing. I walk around in a fog, dying inside every day. How can I not belong anywhere? How can Mom not want me? Dad and Dean mirror what I feel when I see them, and I'm afraid when they look at me, they'll see Mom's face, then I'll lose them, too, and I'm ashamed. I keep my stuff packed in two paper sacks and wonder where I'll go next. I don't ask; I just show up on a couch.

After several weeks of confusion, Dean and I gravitate to each other again. We decide religion is the answer after he starts attending a Baptist church.

We know God will bring Mom back if I'm with Dean. We go to the little church practically every day. We sign up for every activity they offer, and we spend entirely too much time there on Sundays. We're both in the Christmas play—I'm the heralding angel, and Dean's one of the wise men. We're faithful, model children and even get baptized to guarantee Mom's home by Christmas.

When Christmas comes without her, Dean and I are at Ronnie and Kathy's. Dad gave me money when I asked to buy a little black Bible at the church for Dean's Christmas present. I asked Dad to inscribe it to Dean from me because I didn't trust myself to write it correctly. Dad wrote to "Gary Dean Lancaster" from "Sherrie Lyn Lancaster" dated "Xmas 1961." I still give it to Dean, but the hope, along with the happiness of the gift, is gone.

During this short Christmas morning, Dean and I need to keep apart and ignore each other to endure the day without Mom. But when Dean leaves without me, I don't think I can live anymore. For the first time, I hit the streets of Tucson and walk most of the day until well after dark, singing every song I know, looking for any kind of relief from this misery that is suffocating me.

Eventually, songs become my only comfort when I walk because Mom started singing them with me and when she sings, she's happy, so maybe I'll be happy too. But for now, I walk until I'm so tired I can go to sleep on whatever couch I'm staying on—it's Ronnie and Kathy's for tonight.

I don't wet the bed anymore and haven't since Mom left. I suppose it's because I cry myself to sleep every night. Mom always said the more you bawl, the less you'll pee. Around the same time, Dean stopped stuttering, too, but Craig never stops picking on us.

After New Year's Day, I tag along with Dad to a little bar downtown. He lets me walk next door to a music store, where I order two 45-rpm records: "Wagon Wheels" because they will take me home, and "If I Could See the World Through the Eyes of a Child" where there isn't any pain for kids. I won't have money to pay for them, and I don't have a record player anyway because Mom took my little box player when she moved out. But I still order the records and pretend I'll be able to get them. With no radio or record player, the only music I have is in my mind or when I listen to a jukebox in a bar with Dad, where I can pick out a piece of my life in almost every country-western song I hear.

I move four times during these first months without Mom and have already gone to three different schools. When Dean is around, he helps me register at a new school, but I go by myself most of the time. No matter where we are, Dad checks to make sure we're both in school.

The fifth move finally brings Dad, Dean, and me back together when Dad rents a house for us. It's a run-down, one-bedroom house on a dirt road: Buckeye Lane. The delicious smell of light bread baking won't happen, but I love it here because I'm not living out of a paper sack anymore and sleeping on a couch in someone's home where they would just as soon not have me there.

Craig stays at Buckeye Lane for only a few weeks and goes to school even less. He checks out *The Little Shepherd of Kingdom Come* by John Fox Jr. from the school library, and after he reads it, Dean and I do too. We fall in love with the book because it's easy to identify with the orphaned boy and his dog. I think it reminds us of Mom's leaving, and it has a sort of happy ending—poignant with hope—and that's what we're waiting for. When Craig tells Dean to take the book back to the library, I steal it, starting what becomes a fun way to stay connected. For the next thirty years, Dean and I steal the book from one another, devising elaborate schemes to get our hands on it and gloating until it's stolen away again.

I finally manage to turn eleven years old. On my birthday, TVs are placed around the basketball court at Iola Franz Elementary, then school lets out early so kids can watch John Glenn and the launch of the first US orbital space flight. It's exciting and the only fun there is today. No one remembers birthdays anymore. Nine days earlier, I'd forgotten it was Dean's birthday.

February is rodeo time in Tucson, and Dad's riding Trix in the parade downtown. I find my way close to where Dad's sitting on a leather saddle astride Trix, waiting for his turn to start down the parade route. Trix paws the ground and prances sideways, making musical clicking noises on the pavement. He strains at the bit and snorts warm air that turns to white clouds on this cold morning. When it's finally time to begin his walk, Trix rears up, pawing the air, and lunges forward as though he's going to gallop at breakneck speed. But when his front hooves hit the pavement, Trix immediately settles into a rhythmic, prancing walk with his head proudly raising and lowering in time with his stride. Dad's relaxed and handsome in Western clothes, boots, and a cowboy hat as he lightly holds the reins in one hand with the other resting on his leg. I'm so proud of Dad I think I'll bust. That's my dad in a parade! And for the first time in months, Dad doesn't look quite so sad.

Dean and I each have a little wooden treasure box. When Dean makes an acrylic red heart in school, he gives it to me as a present. I know he wants to give it to Mom, but I'll have to do. I keep it in my treasure box along with other things he's given me: an amethyst rock and a little locket with Mom's picture. It's the only picture I have of her. It's the only picture I have, period.

I'm looking through my treasure box when Dean comes home, so he gets his out, too, to compare stuff. After a while, Dean puts his away and heads for the door.

"Can I come with ya?" I ask.

"No."

"Oh, c'mon!"

"No."

I head for the door a few days later when Dean's there again.

"Wait up. I'll go with ya," Dean says.

"No ya won't," I reply to get even with him. I wait outside, hoping he'll come out anyway, but he doesn't.

We don't ask each other to come along anymore now.

A desert field of scrub brush separates Buckeye Lane from Hooligan's, the neighborhood bar. About the same time every day, I climb a mulberry tree and jump on top of our little garage to look for Dad's company pickup in the Hooligan's parking lot. There are usually several pickups, but I always know Dad's is the one with a crawler crane painted on each door. Dad gets to keep it because he bids jobs for a construction company. I snag a pomegranate from the neighbor's bush to eat while I wait. I know Dad should be off work and sipping his beer about now. Dad must have sipped at least one beer every day of his life, yet I never saw him drunk or heard him raise his voice to anyone.

When I finally spot his pickup, I run down a twisted path through desert scrub to the back door of the bar. Hooligan's is rectangular shaped with a long bar along one side, tables and booths that fill the length on the other, and a dance floor that takes up all the space in between. A jukebox sits against the back wall next to a narrow hallway with two tiny restrooms, a storage room, and the back door leading to my desert path.

I find my hug from Dad, climb up on an empty stool next to him, and order a Pepsi and a pickled egg from the bartender. I live on Pepsi and pickled eggs. The hardboiled eggs are swimming in a huge glass jar of brine that turns the eggs a light greenish-brown color. Jim the bartender uses a big spoon, doing his best to capture the egg I point out. The egg's skin feels like rubber and fills my mouth with salt and sour, making it necessary to eat something sweet afterward. So for dessert, I have a package of sugared beer nuts.

Dad dances with me sometimes now, and I love it. He goes slow so I can learn the steps that are increasingly more intricate. When I was little, he used to stand me on top of his feet, hold my hands, and dance around my Barracks Home.

"Don't worry. You'll get this in no time, so stop looking at your feet. You have your dad's rhythm, after all," Dad assures me.

We practice nearly every day because when Dad's in Hooligan's, I'm usually not far behind. But he always sends me home at 9 p.m. Sometimes Dean's home, but most of the time, it's just me. Craig's in and out but never stays. I don't know if he lives anywhere—I think he just bums around from place to place.

Sometimes the tavern owner's wife sends a pot of something home-cooked for us to eat, but the pot's empty in no time. That's a problem when you're a kid. It seems I'm always hungry, so I walk to the Food Giant grocery store to steal something: usually a Hostess fruit pie or a jar of maraschino cherries for dinner and another one of the two for dessert. If I do have something to heat in our little gas oven, I do what Dean does when he uses it. I turn the gas on with the oven door shut, and when I remember, I throw a lit match inside and slam the door shut again. The little oven rocks, rolls, and twists, but it's lit. I never knew there was a possibility of blowing up the house.

I tramp all over Tucson during the day when I'm supposed to be in school and during the night when I can't stand the house anymore because it's so quiet it drives me crazy. That's when Faron Young sings "Hello Walls" in my mind, driving me outside. My walls are lonely too.

Only a lonely kid like me understands it's the most exhilarating feeling in the world, and the loneliest, to do anything you want because no one's there to say you can't. I walk, think about Mom, and wish I were listening to her stories again—the stories I want to hear: funny ones or scary ones. I never want to hear the sad ones again because I'm living them every day. I think about when I was a *kid* and things were how they were supposed to be. I think about Burley.

When I can't stand thinking anymore, I grab the trouble in my head with both hands and put it all in my pants pocket. When it starts bothering me again, I switch pockets. It keeps me sane. I walk and sing every song I know—with Mom singing along with me now. Time passes.

I want to steal a Ouija board. If I can just get my hands on one, it'll tell me when I'll see Mom again. I know it will because it told Mom and Aunt Ruth things when they were young and alone.

After Mom's first baby, they lived in an old cabin not far from Gramma. Ruth and Louise, Del's daughter, were both in the eighth grade but skipped school most days to spend it with baby Ronnie and Mom to play with a Ouija board. They sat around the table with their fingers barely touching the planchette, asking the board a question. The planchette moved around the board, pointing to letters of the alphabet, spelling out its answer.

They usually asked girl-like questions: "Will I meet someone wonderful and fall in love?" "Will I be happy?"

"Spirit, who are you?" the girls asked once.

"Fuck you," the planchette spelled out. They promptly put the board away because they knew a bad spirit had gotten hold of it.

Sometimes the planchette tried to spell out answers so fast it would fly out from under their fingertips. Many times, Mom shuddered as though a cold hand touched her neck while playing.

"I have to quit now. It won't leave me alone," Mom said, shivering and rubbing the back of her neck.

The most frequently told Ouija board story was when someone side-swiped Del's car in a tavern parking lot. The incident left dark-blue paint along the side of Del's white car. When Ruth and Louise told Mom about it on their next visit, they immediately set up the Ouija board to ask the spirits for the blue car owner's name. After the planchette spelled out a name, Ruth wrote it down to take home to Gramma. That same day, Del went back to the tavern and noticed a dark-blue car in the parking lot with some white paint on the fender. He got the owner's name from the bartender then went home to plan how he could get some money out of the guy, although there was little chance of that because Del was all bluster and no action. The name Del had was the same name on the scrap of paper Ruth had given Gramma earlier, but just as predicted, he never confronted the guy.

I stop at Ed's Grocery to steal an ice cream bar for breakfast on days I decide to go to school. Dad has a tab there, but the tab's always at its limit with no ability to charge anything until it's paid down. I wonder if Ed adds the ice cream to Dad's tab anyway. It's a tiny store, and he must see me take the bar. The only thing he says to me is "good morning." Ed's a nice man.

A coatimundi lives in the desert across the street from Ed's Grocery. He's a small, raccoon-like, furry animal with a long snout. I guess he must have escaped from the Sonora Desert Museum not far from Tucson. He's an outcast like me, so I share the ice cream bar with him. He trots alongside while I drop pieces into his mouth.

My teacher Mrs. Titus gives me a quarter to buy school lunch. She started giving it to me after she saw me throw away an unopened lunch sack in the schoolyard trash can as soon as I left her classroom. When she asked why I threw it away, I hemmed and hawed because I couldn't say I was embarrassed about not bringing a lunch sack or buying lunch like other kids. Mrs. Titus opened the discarded sack to find a pair of my socks that used to be white but now are black and board-stiff. I wondered if she could smell the stink as I sidled away then broke into a full run.

Now she always has a quarter in her desk drawer for me. When the lunch bell rings and kids rush for the door, she quietly puts the coin in my hand. I tell her I'll pay her back, but I never do. The quarter isn't the only reason I'll never forget her; it's how she gave it to me and didn't shame me.

Mrs. Titus seemed mad at me only one time. When she hands papers back one day, she stops at my desk. "You've never written with a back-slant before. Why are you now!?"

How can I say that I have to change me, to be different, so *she'll* come back? I don't know how, so I don't say anything.

Dad occasionally carries in groceries and puts everything away. He doesn't cook regular meals, probably because no one's home at regular mealtimes, including him. I guess he thinks if I'm hungry, I'll fix something to eat. Dad had to scrounge for food when he was a kid, and he turned out okay.

I do try to fry bacon and eggs. I crucify the bacon: it's burnt to a crisp, so I throw it away. I make a fried egg sandwich but don't cook the egg long enough—yellow yolk drips down the front of my clothes as I walk and eat. The yolk's there for who-knows-how-long before it finally wears off. Bread balls are a staple. I peel off and eat the crust from a couple slices of bread and squish the remaining bread into a tight ball. The resulting dough ball is tasty enough even when the bread's stale—and I can actually bite it like I'm eating something good. Anything that doesn't have to be cooked quickly disappears. When easy things are gone, I continue to snag sweet stuff at the stores to eat.

I've just finished a Hostess apple pie when I open the door to see Dad, Craig, and Dean sitting at the kitchen table. This is unusual with all three of them here, and I can tell right away it's not a happy table. When I turn to head back out, Dad tells me to sit down too. He's grilling the boys about where all the food's gone because he recently bought a bunch of groceries. Of course, they don't know. I doubt Craig's telling the truth, but maybe Dean is. We never lock the door; we don't have a key. Anyone can come or go—Craig does all the time—taking food and anything else if they want.

The next day, Carson shows up with three cleaned rabbits. Dad cuts them up and fries the meat. We eat like pigs, and not one piece is left. Hopefully, the rabbit farm never missed the rabbits. Another time, Dad fried liver and onions, and I have a conniption fit when I smell it cooking. Yuck! Dad says, "eat it or don't," and I eat like I'm starved—which I am.

Sometimes the girl next door brings over a pot of homemade tamales. She's around eleven and miserable, too, because she doesn't like her Mexican stepmom who can't speak English. I'm jealous she has a stepmom. And we're both really sick of tamales.

We're friends even after she got mad at me for stealing her blouse as she ripped it off me. She never knew I also stole her 45-rpm record "Ace in the Hole" by Roberta Sherwood. I still don't have a record player, but I want it just the same. I love the song because Dad and I dance to it at Hooligan's.

10

"Walkin' After Midnight"

PATSY CLINE

I'm walking down a sidewalk when something huge drops over my shoulder, eating my ice cream cone in one noisy, wet bite. Carson laughs as Trix gets his treat for the day. I like it when Carson shows up. He's happy, smiling, and not at all like Craig, who's always ready to explode into anger, or like Dean, who's as lost as I am.

When Carson says he's leaving for Wyoming to work on a ranch, I really want to go with him. I can't, of course, and pleading doesn't help. A smile with a quiet no has to do. The whispers say he's leaving fast to avoid trouble for a petty crime. Dad gives Carson a good talking to before handing over all the cash he has in his wallet.

Carson packs a Boy Scout mess kit, clothes, a few personal things, and a box of Quaker Oats in saddlebags. He ties a bedroll to the saddle, hooks a gun and canteen over the saddle horn, and rides Trix north to Wamsutter, Wyoming, somewhere between 675 miles as the crow files and 1,000 miles by road. He shoots rabbits along the way for dinner while Trix grazes. He stops in small towns to replace Trix's oats and occasionally buys himself a hamburger. Carson stays in Wyoming for a long time, working on ranches and oil rigs, and it'll be over three years before I hear about his adventures.

Soon after Carson leaves, Dad renovates a building that a man rented for a tavern and builds a long, nice bar. I'm the eleven-year-old bartender for a closed party the night before it officially opens. Standing on a tall crate so I can reach the draft beer handles, I fill mugs and send them sliding down the long bar to an open hand. After a few tries, I can load a mug with just the right amount of foam on top. It's even fun washing mugs in hot, soapy water in a sink with bristle brushes attached. The jukebox switch is on free, so I keep the music going between serving beer and washing mugs. The night's almost as much fun as Hooligan's but not quite. I'm so busy bartending I can't dance with Dad.

My dad's a handsome man with lots of women chasing him in Hooligan's. Early on, Dean and I liked Ms. Green, who was nice to us, but she was very stout, very tall, and nothing came of it. Now I like the Okie from Oklahoma. She's beautiful with long, wavy black hair, and I think Dad chases and catches her. Trouble is, she has a boyfriend or something.

One morning, I wake up to a horrible noise—a bubbling, wet, strangled breathing sound. When I realize Dad's making the awful noise in his sleep, I get close enough to see his nose is smashed sideways. Blood bubbles blow up then collapse with his breathing. I must have yelled because Dad wakes up with a jerk. He moans and tries to hold his face and calm me down at the same time. He says he's okay and not to worry. I try to clean him up, but he can't bear having a wet rag close to his face. In answer to my questions, Dad only says he took the Okie dancing and ran into the wrong end of a beer mug. Dad's nose heals just fine after he manages to pull it out straight, and I never saw the Okie in Hooligan's again.

Then there's Claribel. She chases everyone in Hooligan's, including Dad. I don't like her because I know she doesn't like me. She isn't very pretty but can be pleasant enough when she wants to be. She just never wants to be pleasant to me. I guess Dad doesn't notice because she's the one who eventually catches and keeps him.

About eight months after moving back to Tucson, Dean somehow finds Uncle Leo's telephone number in El Dorado Springs and uses someone's phone to call him. When Uncle Leo's wife answers the phone, Dean asks Aunt Minnie if Mom's still there. Dean cries when he tells me Aunt Minnie said our mom usually has a black eye or two when she sees her, and that *he* must beat her up pretty often. She said it's such a scandal, and Dean shouldn't call her anymore. Dean says Aunt Minnie wasn't friendly, like when we lived there. Maybe it's because Mom's still there with *him*, and it's such a scandal because *his* wife and kids are still there too.

I know Mom's crying a lot if *he* beats her up like Aunt Minnie said, and I hate the thought of it. The memories of Craig knocking her to the ground and the fight with Anna torture me. But a black eye or two can't be the result of a bad fight like the one with Anna. When *he* hits her, it has to be like what Craig did: one punch and it's over. If I can just find her. But how?

The only fun since my bartending job is the desert monsoon season when school lets out early because there's a heavy downpour. Looks like all the kids have someone to pick them up except for me and the girl next door. We're soaked to the skin by the time we hit the sidewalk, so we decide: Why not attempt body surfing down the deep, overflowing gutter?

After the rains, a *bazillion* toads will magically appear in a few days, just when we'll want them after our next football game. When the mud begins to dry up, kids gather to play football again—the only outside fun on the lane. I don't know any of the kids except the girl next door, but I still like to play. Every time we start, a potbellied man wearing a ten-gallon cowboy hat walks up the lane to cuss us out. He's not much taller than us even with his hat on and never says why we can't play; he just cusses. He calls the cops even though we're nowhere near his last house on the lane. Later, if we see a police car, we scatter. Before long, the girl next door and I get even with him.

The scrub brush desert between Buckeye Lane and Hooligan's had turned into a huge, shallow pond after the heavy rain, and it's alive with toads. We catch a bagful, throw them against a wall, and load the smashed toads back into the bag for delivery. We sneak down to the short man's house at midnight to scoop the smashed toads into his mailbox then sneak back home. The smell on our hands is terrible, but the smell in his mailbox will be even worse tomorrow in the desert heat.

I wonder why he always cusses us out. I figure he's just another one who's completely forgot what it's like to be a kid, so he's always mad. My long-ago adventuring with the boys helps me not forget.

During the school year on Buckeye Lane, I learn that keeping myself in school supplies is easier than food or clothes. When I'm hungry after a late-night walk, I have to wait until morning for stores to open to steal food. I have no idea how to get some new clothes. School supplies are different.

Flowing Wells High School has open-air hallways lined with lockers. I cut through the school on my way home one night when I absentmindedly tug on a locker handle. It opens. The lock must have been left on the last combination number for easy access. When I want school supplies now, I go shopping at the lockers at night where I open several and choose what I want.

I like how paper feels and sounds when I flip through notebook pages, and I love the smell of yellow wood pencils. Picking out more than I need, I carry it all home where I stack everything neatly hidden under my cot. School supplies are my one luxury. Very little of the stash gets used—I skip school a lot—but it feels good having a bunch of something that's mine.

～

Living in the same place for so long, we begin to know others around us. Johanna lives across the dirt lane from us. I think she must be the meanest person alive because around the clock, I hear her screaming at her little kids. One day, she walks over to ask Dad if he wants some apricots from her loaded tree. When Dad sends Dean and me to pick them for her, Johanna's friendly, saying she'll keep some to make jam for us. Afterward, sometimes Dean or I walk over to see her. She seems to like my company. I guess she must be lonely too.

Another woman down the lane asks me to babysit. I think that's pretty neat because I'll make some money, so I don't tell her I've never babysat in my life because I figure I can handle it. Her boyfriend works for Shamrock Dairy, so she shows me her supply of pint ice cream cartons in all different flavors. Forget the money! I charge her two pints to babysit. Her kids are asleep, so I just watch TV and eat two pints of ice cream. It's heaven. I would have paid her if I had any money just to watch her TV. Then I take two pints home.

Dean babysat for her once, too, but his charge was for her to wash our dirty dishes. The kitchen sink is always full of dirty dishes that stink and hide a breeding ground for mosquitoes and who-knows-what-else that crawls or flies. I don't think she liked washing them because she never asked us to babysit after that.

Dirty dishes are piled high in the sink again, so Dean and I decide it's time to clean up the place to surprise Dad. Picking dishes out of the sink with one hand and holding our noses with the other, we head outside to hose them off. Then we fight off a horde of mosquitoes when we come back inside. While Dean washes dishes, I mop the floor. We don't have a bucket, so I dunk the mop into the never-cleaned toilet to wet it. I won't wring it out like I saw Mom do because I don't want to touch toilet water. The place looks a lot better when we finish.

I think that was the first and last time the little house was cleaned—if that's what you'd call it.

Hooligan's is still where I want to be when Dad's there. Lately, Betty and Dallas are regulars at Hooligan's too. They have four kids with the two oldest, George and Tammy, a little younger than me at eleven. Sometimes we meet our respective adults at the bar and hang around together and play. I don't like Dallas very much because of comments he makes about me when I'm standing right there.

"Why doesn't she ever talk? Why doesn't she ever smile like a normal kid?"

Comments like that really piss me off because he doesn't talk or smile until he drinks his first beers of the day. I think it's obvious I'm the furthest thing there is from a normal kid. It's not my fault, so why does he have to bring it up?

Sometimes Dad pays Betty to do our laundry, but she doesn't like doing it because she has enough of her own to do. I occasionally hang around their house when the two oldest have to babysit the two youngest. Other times, the three of us take off to play and usually end up eating ice cream cones on the roof of Iola Franz Elementary School.

Betty and her family are planning a vacation to Missouri. When she asks if I want to go with them, I can't believe it! I daydream I'll find Mom. I have no idea where in Missouri we're going, but at least I'll be in the same state as her. I plan to run away and find her as soon as we arrive.

The next evening, George, Tammy, and I pick a bunch of mostly green apricots from Johanna's tree to eat. The next morning before daylight, we're leaving on vacation. We haven't gone far when I start feeling sick. I usually don't get carsick this fast, so maybe it's just the green apricots I ate. Luckily, I'm sitting in the back seat by a window because I throw up all the way to Missouri. We travel straight through with Betty and Dallas taking turns driving. When we get to Dallas's mother's house, Betty puts me to bed where I'm so sick I throw up in my sleep. Betty stays close by to clean up the bed and me. I'm so ashamed. I don't want to be sick, and I don't want to spoil their vacation or my chance to find Mom. Betty's very kind taking care of me. When I finally stop throwing up, I'm so weak I think I'll still die.

When we head back to Tucson days later, they have to regularly stop for me to find some cover to hide behind and go to the bathroom. On one stop, I have to walk a long way for a small desert bush. I'm so weak I don't think I'll make it back to the car. If I die or not doesn't much matter because I've screwed up the only chance I've had to find Mom. I'm not better until a few days after I'm home, but then it's too late to run away and find her. I'm stuck in Tucson again with nothing to do and no reason to do anything.

Within days, I decide to be perfect. If I'm perfect and do everything I should, maybe Mom will come back. I start by going to school every day. I sleep when I should and get up when I should. I had stopped bathing without really realizing it, probably because I didn't care about anything anymore and no one made me. But now I wash my face and brush my teeth every day—almost. It hurts when I wash my hair, but I do it anyway. At the time, I can't figure out that filth from not washing it causes the sores I always have on my scalp: crusty things that ooze and bleed when I pick off the scabs.

I even try to curl my hair for the first time using bobby pins I swiped to anchor pin curls the way I saw Mom do. She tried to show me how to take care of myself before she left. Because she always did everything for me, I never cut my nails or did anything with my hair. When I cried, she started crying, too, and said when I had to do those things I would. I'm sure if I'm perfect she'll come back, but I still can't seem to take care of myself. I can't get the hang of cutting my nails, so I usually chew them off. My hair is beyond help. I can't do anything right, I tell myself.

She must love me again by now, I think over and over. It's been so long. Sometimes I steal a letter out of someone's mailbox to read and pretend it's to me from Mom. One letter is so long and boring it helps me break the habit.

In a short time, I decide to kill myself. I break an empty jar and choose a jagged piece of glass to cut my wrists. Something has to be on the outside to show how I hurt on the inside. But I can't do this right either and only manage a few deep scratches on each wrist that ooze enough blood for long thick scabs. I guess I'm chicken too. I'm lost and don't have the slightest idea what to do about it.

Dean hasn't been around for a while, and Dad isn't home. We can't stand to spend too much time together at home because when we do, it's more apparent Mom's still gone. I have to know Dad and Dean are around some-where, even though it's easier to get through a day without them. But I really need to talk to someone.

I walk to Johanna's and pour out how I want to find Mom. I tell her I wrote to Aunt Mary only once—because she knows Mom's address—right after we moved back, when I was living with Ronnie and Kathy. Later, Kathy handed me the reply from Mom via Aunt Mary and told Dad on me as soon as she saw him. Dad told me to never write Aunt Mary or Mom again. Johanna offers to help me. She tells me that I can use her address for my return address and gives me a postage stamp and an envelope. I go home to write to Aunt Mary and ask her to send my letter to Mom.

What seems like an eternity later, Johanna screams for me to come over one day. She hands me a letter, but my hands shake so hard I can't open it. Johanna opens it for me then leaves the room. I don't remember what Mom said because I tore it up as soon as I read it, like she told me to do in the letter. But I'm so happy! *She must still love me!*

Days later after the happy wears off, I wonder again for the millionth time how she could leave me. She is my mother. I don't write again for a long time, and Johanna moves, so I can't use her address again. It always takes Mom so long to reply anyway. She never writes first, and that hurts too.

A small, black-and-white TV with rabbit ears is waiting for me one day when I get home from school. We haven't had one since Missouri. I run to Hooligan's to hug Dad, who knew I would love it, and run back home to watch TV. There's nice noise in the house now! I watch *Ozzie and Harriet, Leave It to Beaver,* and

My Three Sons and pretend I have a real family. I love watching the 11:30 p.m. late movie. One of the first was *The Jazz Singer* with Al Jolson. I didn't like the show—the dad was way too mean for me—but I fell in love with Al Jolson's singing. Oh, those "Mammy" songs! I want my mother too! The TV keeps me home at night and not walking the streets where I never once made sense of anything anyway. With no one to care what was happening except me, on those walks I would spit out my baby molars when permanent teeth pushed through.

After a month of nice noise watching TV, I wake up in a panic. A horrible uproar is happening, and the house sounds like it's exploding. I can see the empty bunkbed, so Dad and Dean aren't home. What can this awful noise be? I peek out the bedroom door to see someone throwing everything he puts his hands on. Through a fog of sleep and fear, I realize it's Craig.

My fishbowl crashes through a window, and I slip in water on the floor and fall with a thud when I try to scoop up my guppies that are flopping around me. I crush more than I save, and the rest die anyway. I scream when my TV crashes through another window. Kitchen chairs, dishes, pans, and more are flying over my head, bouncing off walls, or crashing through windows, landing in the front yard. I scream at him over and over to stop. *Why doesn't he trash wherever he's living and leave me alone?*

Craig finally stops his devastating rampage. He's drunk, cussing, and crying. He tells me he's sorry and leaves. I don't say anything and just stay out of his way because I'm scared of him, scared he'll pick me up and throw me through a window just because he can. He already chased me into the desert once, caught me, lifted me over his head, and threw me down as hard as he could over and over again. I was sore for a long time.

Now I'm shaking, crying, and scared to death he'll come back, but I still go outside to find my TV. It's totally busted up.

"You son-of-a-bitch Craig!" I scream, kicking the TV with my bare foot.

Hobbling back inside with my toe hurting, I look around at the awful mess. Then I start cleaning up.

I haven't been at it long when two policemen burst through the back door, crouching low, yelling, and each holding a gun with both hands pointed at me. They scare me absolutely to death. My feet fly out from under me, and I hit the floor again with a thud.

"What do YOU want?" I scream, crying.

I make it to my hands and knees then stand up, shaking so hard I think my knees are knocking together.

"Are you here alone?" one asks.

"Yeah."

"Who did this?"

"My brother. He left a while ago."

They say they have to take me to the juvenile detention facility, Mother Higgens.

"Why?"

I will myself to stop shaking. *I haven't done anything wrong. They can't know about the food I steal. I have to eat, don't I?*

They say I'm by myself, so they have to take me. I think for two policemen, they're pretty dumb. Of course I'm by myself. The only difference now is everything's busted up.

And I know with a sickening feeling if they take me away, I'll never get back home again and I'll lose Dad and Dean too.

"Who's gonna clean up this mess then? Besides, my dad will be home in a little while."

The policemen keep talking while I ignore them. I try to clean up, pretending they aren't staring at me. I try to will them away from me. I pretend I'm not ashamed of this mess and act like I always clean up stuff in the middle of the night by myself.

The policemen talk and walk slowly toward me.

"My dad will be home anytime, and he'll be mad if I'm not here where I'm supposed to be."

I back away slowly to keep from falling and turn my soaking wet butt toward them, dying of shame from wet pajamas with a rip on one cheek. I keep working, holding my breath. After I assure them again my dad will be home anytime, they finally give up and leave. I've never been so glad to see anyone leave in all my life and sob with relief.

Dad does come home soon after, visibly shaken. He quickly surveys the damage, and with care in his eyes, he reaches out for me.

"Are you all right?" he asks.

"Yeah."

"Ronnie's in the hospital. Craig beat him up pretty bad, but he'll be okay I think. I guess Craig's been here too," Dad says.

He picks up a kitchen chair that still has three legs attached, turns the kitchen table upright, and sits down. He sighs and shakes his head at the mess and broken windows.

"I have to go to the hospital to see Ronnie. Will you be okay?" Dad asks.

"Yeah. Some policemen just left a few minutes ago."

"I guess the neighbors called them. I won't be gone long. Don't worry, Craig won't be back tonight."

Ronnie spends several hours in the hospital before he's released, and I get most of the mess cleaned up. When the old landlady shows up in the morning, she raises holy hell about all the broken windows. Dad calms her down and promises to replace them all. I don't see Craig for a nice long time, and I hope it stays that way.

I never knew or asked why Craig beat up Ronnie that night or why he trashed Buckeye Lane. I didn't want to know—I already have more than enough to carry around. I just hope I'm not around the next time he explodes.

11

"Lonesome 7-7203"

HAWKSHAW HAWKINS

I'm still eleven years old. It seems I'll be eleven years old for a very, very long time.

I'm worried I don't know how to grow up right. Several kids on the lane are sitting around one night when I start giggling because a boy just tried to kiss me. He says, "Fuck you!" and doesn't try again. Now he completely ignores me. I don't know girl stuff, and I don't even want to be a girl, especially after the fuck you. I want to be like Carson and Craig: quit school, do what I want, and go find Mom. She'll tell me things I should know. I don't know when I'm supposed to start wearing a bra. What if I should be and I'm not? Dean tells me not to worry.

"I'll tell you when it's time to wear one," he says.

I feel better about the bra thing after that.

A few days later, I'm waiting for George and Tammy to finish their work so we can play. Out of nowhere, Betty starts telling me about menstruation.

I know Dad put her up to it. How can he do this to me? I have a mother, and she'll tell me this stuff someday when I find her. I remember Mom's stories when she started menstruating and had to save old rags to use and wash out for reuse. I didn't understand why that was so bad.

"Just wait," Mom had said in her knowing voice that made me crazy because I didn't know, and I knew she wasn't going to tell me.

Not long after Betty told me that stuff, I discover pubic hair. I didn't have any the last time I bothered to look. I know I should know things, but I don't know what the things are I should know. I suppose whatever's going to happen will either kill me or not—and I just don't care.

Dad is always patient with me, no matter my mood. He has to be both Mom and Dad, but he doesn't have a clue how to be a mom. And he's miserable just like me. Dad doesn't have the slightest idea what to do with me, and I don't know what to do with myself. He tries. He tries to help me with my hair when I bawl because it looks horrible. The haircut I gave myself doesn't help much, so he takes me to a beauty shop for a permanent. But the woman won't give me one because my lips are swollen with cold sores. She says the permanent won't hold because of the virus that causes them and suggests I come back after they're healed. I don't go back because I always have cold sores. Dad takes me shopping for a purse when I want one. We go to a bunch of stores and finally back to the first store where I want the first purse I saw. With a gentle smile and without a word, he buys it for me.

I wonder why all I really want is Mom. Dad doesn't leave me; he always comes home at night. Sometimes he comes home in the wee hours of the morning, but he always comes home. I check Dad's dresser every night after I get back from walking, and I've never once found his things gone. Still, all I want is Mom. I know she doesn't want me, but I never lose hope that someday I'll find her.

Dad takes care of me the best he knows how, but I'm not around much. I'm usually roaming the streets, wondering when I'll wake up with things right again. If I was ever in danger roaming Tucson's streets, I never knew it—except one time. The episode scared me and further alienated me from people. I'd noticed a high-school-size guy hanging around the grade school sometimes during recess. He retrieved a basketball and tossed it back to me. I saw him in the grocery store when I stopped to steal food. I saw him again when I was roaming the streets instead of being in school. Now, here he is again, walking in the same direction I am on the sidewalk, only he's on the other side of the oleander bushes.

"Hey! Come'er," he calls to me.

"Whaddya want?"

"I wanna talk to ya. Come'er."

"I hear ya just fine. Whaddya want?"

Suddenly, I'm yanked through the oleanders. He's grabbing, pulling, and touching me. The guy doesn't have an easy time. He doesn't know I've spent years battling four older brothers. I punch and kick and wildly slug and kick some more. I start running so fast I don't think my feet touch the ground until I'm home, where I climb the mulberry tree and jump on the garage in case he followed me.

That night, I tell Dad what happened. The next day, he finds Craig and they go to the high school. Dad tells the principal about the incident and asks to visit the classrooms. I don't think Dad expected to spot the guy based on my description, but I think he intended to scare him. Dad knew word would get around that two big guys are looking for him.

Apparently, Dad's strategy worked because I don't see him again for a long time. Weeks later, someone yells as I chase a ball during recess. When I turn around, a basketball flies into my stomach with such force it knocks the wind out of me, and I bend over double, gasping for air. When I straighten up, the same guy's standing directly in front of me, glaring without a word. Dozens of kids are yelling and playing all around me, but all I see is him. Then he turns and walks away. I never saw him again.

⌒

When someone drives to Nogales, Mexico, Dean and I go every chance we can—it's a break from another lousy day. Ronnie often makes the trip to take his kids on an outing. Other times, it's just to buy bottles of booze because they're cheap and you're allowed to bring three back across the border without declaring them at customs. Ronnie has hiding places in his '57 Chevy and usually brings back more than three. As soon as he crosses the border and finds a place to park, half-naked, dirty, little kids swarm the car.

"Chicle! Chicle!" the kids yell.

With huge smiles on their faces, they continue shouting as they elbow each other, jockeying for the prime spot closest to the driver's door. Ronnie always buys some of their gum and hires one or two to watch his car. Nothing bad ever happens to the car when a little kid's hired to watch it.

Dean and I scour the junk shops in Nogales. Decent switchblade knives are for sale cheap, and we buy one apiece every time we go with money Dad gave us. As soon as we get home and before the bottles are distributed, Dad frisks us and confiscates the switchblades. He tells us that he knows we're two smart kids, but we're still not acting like it.

"Smarten up and stop throwing money away. Use it for something you can keep," Dad says like he used to when he wasn't so sad.

Soon Dad's driving to my favorite place again because he knows it's my favorite place: Old Tucson. It's located in the foothills about twelve miles from Tucson. Old Tucson was built in the late 1930s as a movie studio with hundreds of Western movies filmed there; it opened to the public in 1960 as a theme park. Dad sips a beer in a saloon and lets me have fun. I wander around and pretend I'm a cowboy, free to jump on my horse and ride away. One time, Chuck Connors from *The Rifleman* is surrounded by dozens of kids while showing us how he handles his rifle. If I can just live long enough to grow up and be a cowboy, I'll be happy.

I love the drive home from Old Tucson after dark. When we come out of the foothills, the twinkling lights of Tucson are spread out before us. In my mind, I'm on the outskirts of Burley again, and Mom's sitting close to Dad. She always sat close to him, even when no kids were sitting in front with them.

⌒

Hooligan's is how home should be: people are there, life's happening, it's noisy, and there's music. I don't climb the mulberry tree on Friday afternoons anymore to look for Dad's pickup because I'm his dancing date now on Fridays. I lay dress clothes on his bunkbed ready for when he gets home.

Then I pick out my cleanest dirty outfit since Betty hasn't done our laundry for a long time. I can still fit into some of my old clothes because, since Mom left us, I've gotten skinny. They look pretty ratty, but that doesn't bother me as much as the huge tear in my slip does. The girls at school laugh when they see my slip in PE, and they always see it. It never occurs to me to sew it up; I just try to hide it. Besides, I don't know how to sew anyway.

Dad had given me a new dress recently. I don't know who helped pick it out, but it's a pretty summer dress with a scoop neck and buttons down the front, except I think the buttons are supposed to be in the back. It's really hard to button after I put it on.

A girl with clean hair and pretty clothes sits next to me in school and starts laughing when I proudly wear the new, clean dress. I don't know why she's laughing, and our teacher, Mrs. Titus, doesn't either, so she asks the girl what's so funny. The girl tells her—and the whole class—that I have my dress on backward. I silently die and get madder than hell when tears start slipping down my face.

Mrs. Titus takes the girl and me to the bathroom, where she sits on a closed toilet seat lid, holds my arms, and explains how dresses work. She explains to the girl with clean hair and pretty clothes that it isn't nice to laugh at someone less fortunate. Now I'm really pissed. I don't consider myself less fortunate; I just have trouble staying clean and having new clothes is all. Mrs. Titus makes the girl apologize and sends her back to class.

"Everyone has to learn things," Mrs. Titus says, putting her hands on my shoulders to make me look at her. Then she helps turn the dress around with the buttons in front. "You'll be okay now that you know how to pay attention to things. And this is a very pretty dress." She pats my arms and holds my hand as we walk back to class and my desk. The kids don't dare laugh with Mrs. Titus glaring at them.

Although I'm embarrassed beyond belief, I'm madder now than ever about that *someone less fortunate* crap. Nothing in my eleven years has let me be a normal kid, and for not being normal, I think I'm doing pretty damn good. If someone doesn't like how I am, they can just leave me the hell alone, and that's okay with me.

"If you don't like my apples, don't shake my tree," Gramma would have said.

I never wore the dress again.

Dad's finally home to wash up for our Friday night dance date. He's so handsome in a white, long-sleeve shirt, khaki jeans, Western belt buckle with a longhorn steer head inset, and cowboy boots. When I tell him he's handsome, he smiles a devilish little grin.

"Yes, and I'm pretty too," Dad says, making fun of girls.

On his upper arm, he has a tattoo of a woman's head and neck that he named Lucy. She's pretty but old-fashioned looking to me.

"You need a new tattoo, Dad."

"I like Lucy just fine. She's the only woman I know who doesn't talk back to me."

He finishes washing up and dresses, then we're off to Hooligan's. I still have to take the desert path back home at 9 p.m., but what fun first—I'm Dad's date! He dances with me and oh! can Dad dance. My job is to salt the floor before the Friday night crowd arrives. After the bartender, Irish Bob or Jim, hands me a carton of salt and a quarter, I sprinkle some salt all over the dance floor and drop the quarter in the jukebox slot to select a country song with the tempo Dad likes best. Now it's time to ask him for the first dance.

I love the sound of our feet slip-sliding on the salted floor. We have a special tune only we dance to because we're all over the dance floor during Johnny Horton's "Honky Tonk Man." We must make a sight flying around with the top of my head at Dad's stomach.

Dad occasionally sits out a song, but soon his feet are tap dancing around his barstool. When they break into dance steps, he flows off his stool and holds out his hand, asking me to dance. I grab his hand to slide off my bar stool, and he guides me into his arms and onto the dance floor. After many nights at Hooligan's, I've learned to keep up and glide—or fly, depending on the tempo—around the floor with him. He tries to mix me up then smiles down at me, squeezing my hand when my feet stay in sync with his and my rhythm matches his.

When I dance with Dad in my mind, I think about his smooth, rhythmic steps and see his gentle smile. He told me once with a smile that he liked dancing with me better than "your mother" because I never try to lead. Now, his smile tells me he wasn't trying to trick me—he was just completely enjoying what we could do together better than anyone else.

A lifetime ago, Mom danced with Dad. Wearing a dress Mom made me, a miniature of her dress, I went with them to Kelly's Bar a few miles from El Dorado Springs. I loved watching them dance. Dad asked me to dance for the first time that night to "It Wasn't God Who Made Honky Tonk Angels," sung by Kitty Wells.

I know Dad misses her as much as I do. We just never talk about it because I've learned from him how to grieve her without words.

12

"If I Could See the World Through the Eyes of a Child"

PATSY CLINE

A wonderful thing happened in Hooligan's one Friday evening while I was Dad's dancing date. I didn't realize then that my life would never be the same or how fortunate I was. I had long since decided to keep my troubles in my pockets, put one foot in front of the other, and keep walking until something made sense. I was about to learn there are truly wonderful people in this world, even in a neighborhood tavern on Prince Road.

As Dad and I whizz by the long bar, a man and woman smile at us from the back corner of the bar. After our dance, the man and woman move. She takes a seat next to me, and the man stands by Dad.

The man has dark hair cut in a short crew cut, and kind, crinkly eyes shine from a handsome, craggy face. He laughs and gestures with muscular arms as he talks to Dad. The woman has beautiful, warm-brown eyes, shoulder-length auburn hair, and a warm, friendly motherly manner. And she's talking—to me. She's a nice lady and keeps talking even though I don't reply. She asks several times if I need anything, and I finally say I'd really like a new slip. She says she'll pick me up the following day and take me to find a new slip.

The next morning, Dean's awake on the top bunk and Dad's sleeping on the bottom one. I tell Dean about the nice lady and that I don't want to go with her. I don't want to talk to anyone, especially an adult. I know Dean understands because when he's around, he does the talking for me. He knows what needs to be said.

"You're going," Dad quietly says then turns back to sleep.

The lady takes me shopping, and after she helps pick out a slip, she steers me to other clothes and buys me everything else, too, from the skin out: underwear, pajamas, dresses, tops, shorts, Levi's, socks, and shoes. I'm in absolute heaven. She offers assistance when necessary and lets me pick out things I like.

She takes me to lunch and says I can order anything I want from the menu. I eat a steak sandwich for the first time. It's delicious. After pie à la mode, we go to a house where the lady and her husband are staying with their daughter and her family. I think I'm going to freeze to death before she tells me what makes it so cold. It's the first time I've been in a home with central air conditioning.

"Now you know where I live. You can come over anytime," the lady tells me.

"You haven't come over yet to visit! Why not!?" the lady asks after giving me a big hug the next time I see her in Hooligan's.

All I can do is smile since I still don't know her name, and I won't ask. It takes a while to find the courage to walk to her house, and that's only after I hear someone call her by name in Hooligan's. I finally know what the lady's name is—it's Dorothy! And her husband's name is Harold.

Dorothy. Dorothy and Harold.

I walk to Dorothy's house the next day. I'm scared to ring the doorbell, so I don't. What if she changed her mind? What if she really doesn't want me here? What if she's not home? What if? What if? What if?

"Mom, Sherrie's here!" Dorothy's daughter Mary calls over her shoulder after answering the door.

Dorothy's laughing and running with outstretched arms.

"Are you hungry?" she asks, hugging me.

I can't remember the last time someone asked if I was hungry. I must have died and gone to heaven. Dorothy hugs me all the way to the kitchen, where she takes a pan out of the oven to make a hot meatloaf sandwich. It's delicious. I walk to Dorothy's house many times in the coming months.

As time passes, Dorothy becomes and stays the dearest person in my life. And without Harold's help, she never would have found me. They will always be Dorothy, Dorothy and Harold to me.

Years later, Harold laughs about the night I met them in Hooligan's. He'd seen me in there a few times with Dad before that night. He'd also told Dorothy about a great-looking female hanging out at the bar. Dorothy decided it was time to go with Harold and check out the woman who caught her husband's eye. Dorothy was dressed for bear, ready, willing, and able to put this menace in her place. When Harold pointed me out while Dad and I were dancing, Dorothy almost hurt him instead. Then Dorothy did exactly what Harold knew she would do. She took me into her heart and loved me.

13

"Bummin' Around"

HANK THOMPSON

I finally live to be twelve years old.

I learned to be inconspicuous between ten and twelve, and I don't hang around adults or ask anything of them. If I'm not in the way, they won't get tired of me. Mom doesn't want me—why should anyone else? Besides, I don't like most adults anyway. They usually make me die inside by what they say and don't say or do and don't do.

Before Dorothy, the exceptions to my rule were Dad and Hooligan's. Dad's quiet and lost without Mom, just like me, which makes it easy to hang out at the bar with him. And I love the music and dancing. Of course, the bar's filled to overflowing with adults, but adults in a bar are more like kids anyway. Dad sends me home at 9 p.m. because if the Saturday-night-fight happens, it's usually later in the evening. And he's probably ready to dance with someone taller.

Dorothy throws a bomb into my scheme of things. Her expressive, kind, warm-brown eyes see inside me. I'm certain she knows everything I've ever done wrong, everything I've stolen, and every lie I've told. And yet, she still loves me and wants me around. So, at twelve years old, I gradually try to be what I know I should be.

Years later, I asked Dorothy if she knew I was a pretty good thief when we met.

"Why do you think I always slipped you some money when I saw you? Any kid will steal if they don't have anything!" Dorothy replied with her characteristic hand-smack on the table for emphasis.

Not long after my first visit to Dorothy's, I'm really excited because Dorothy's coming to see me in an assembly at school. She bought the black skirt and white blouse I have to wear. My school shoes are scuffed, so I walk to a drug store for polish. Realizing I don't have enough money, I steal it. A man grabs my arm, jerking me around in the parking lot, and grabs the polish. He yells that I'm never to come inside the store again. My shoes are still scuffed, but Dorothy doesn't say anything after the assembly. She never says anything to embarrass me.

Soon after, I have pinkeye again with sore, crusty eyes. When Dad drives me to the same drug store for medicine, the man who caught me shoplifting waits on us. I'm scared he's going to say something to Dad, but he doesn't. Maybe hiding behind Dad's leg and my red, goopy eyes save me. That episode and Dorothy's eyes help me stop stealing things, even food, for a while.

During the next visit to Dorothy's, after I eat what she puts in front of me, she hands me the neatest thing I've ever had: a small, rectangular, pink-and-white transistor radio with a plastic wrist strap. Now I can take the music I love with me when I'm walking, and I don't have to wait to hear it in Hooligan's.

Several months after he replaced all the front windows from Craig's rampage, Dad's mad—which means he's quieter than usual. I threw a screwdriver at Dean after he made me mad for some reason or another. I missed him but not the replacement glass panel in the front door.

After I broke the glass, when Dean's around, we try not to fight, but we have to have someone to hate and blame for Mom's leaving. It's not Dad's fault, and we can't hate Mom. How can we hate someone we love so much it hurts? We see the effect of her desertion in each other's eyes and can't stand the sight of it. We hate each other because we're miserable, and though we don't understand it, we have to keep an emotional distance to cope with it all. So we argue and fight. We never stop trying to deal with it, but it's years before we begin to learn how.

We try again on the morning of Friday the thirteenth when we make a pact to stop fighting and shake hands just like in the old days. When we start goofing around, I throw a punch he blocks, and my fist explodes in pain, hitting his elbow. I jump around cussing while Dean laughs, not knowing my cussing's for real. Our experiment back into friendship has lasted long enough. When Dean asks if I'm okay, I say "yeah" because the pain's tapering off. Then he leaves.

The throbbing's back with a vengeance, so I run hot water over my hand. I use the bathroom faucet because the kitchen sink's full of dirty dishes and mosquitoes again. The water makes my hand feel better, but it swells up and turns red. Even so, it feels better with hot water running over it. The water heater runs out of hot water many times during a really long day.

It's not time for Dad to pick me up for our Friday night date, and I can't climb the mulberry tree to look for his pickup with my bum hand. So I walk next door to the Mexican stepmother who about kills me examining my hand. I can't pull it away; she won't let go. She sends the girl to Hooligan's to find Dad, who comes home in a hurry and takes me to a hospital. After a long wait, a doctor puts my hand in a soft cast because a bone is fractured.

I haven't eaten since the day before, and I'm dizzy from missing my pickled egg and Pepsi dinner. My hand hurts, and I'm woozy and about to throw up. I sit on the closest thing I can find: a wheelchair. When it's finally time to leave, a nurse gruffly tells me to get up because I'm perfectly able to walk. It's my hand that's hurt, not my feet, she says like I don't know that. When I won't get up because I know I'll throw up, she wheels me out, complaining the entire time. Damn, I hate adults. If she felt like I did, she'd probably be dead.

It's late when Dad drives to Hooligan's. I guess he's mad at me because he's really quiet again. After a while, Dad pats my leg and smiles between shifting gears.

"Use a club next time you need to hit someone. It's easier on the hands," he tells me, patting my leg again.

Dorothy and Harold are waiting for us in Hooligan's and soon take me to the 21 Club for a late dinner. I quickly learn how to eat left-handed after Dorothy cuts up the meat on my plate. Afterward, they take me home with them. Dorothy has me stay for several days and takes me to a doctor for a checkup. She keeps me until she knows I'm okay. I think she would've always kept me, but she knows I need to be with my dad. I need to be where I belong, even if I don't know for sure where that is.

Shortly after the soft cast comes off, I break out with three-day measles. Pinkeye and measles: I'm so disgusted. How can a big kid like me keep getting little kid's crap? I'm feverish and itchy, and I can't go to Hooligan's. That's the last straw; now I am miserable. Dorothy gives Dad a get-well card with a couple of dollars in it to give me. She writes that she's waiting for me to get well, and if I need anything, have my dad tell her.

Soon after the measles clear up, a brand-new, sparkling-clean bicycle is parked by the back door when I come home. It has multicolored streamers hanging from the handlebars with a basket attached to the front. I know Dorothy and Harold were here. I fly down my path on the new bike to Hooligan's, where they're waiting for me. After I hug and kiss them both,

Harold smiles while Dorothy quickly lays down the law about bicycle safety then hugs and kisses me back. She slips a dollar into my hand, and I'm off exploring Tucson on my beautiful bike.

Just days after the bicycle appeared, Dad tells me to invite Dorothy and Harold for dinner the following weekend. He says he'll cook something special. When I ask them if bologna sandwiches and Kool-Aid sound okay, they say it sounds wonderful and they'd love to come.

I straighten up the place and chase out mosquitoes while Dad washes dishes, fries chicken, and makes mashed potatoes and gravy. Dad's gravy is delicious, but it's so thick I can stand the spoon upright in the middle of the bowl without it falling over. Dorothy smacks my leg under the table with her foot and hides a smile behind her hand as she helps herself to more gravy.

Looking at Dorothy, Dad smiles his gentle smile and says, "Smack her once for me too."

It's a very special dinner that's thoroughly enjoyed by everyone. I'm so proud of the dinner Dad cooked for Dorothy and Harold, and I think he is too.

Things become boring as usual after our special dinner until the old landlady shows up asking for the rent. *Why not come when Dad's home?* I think. I don't have it, but she acts like she still wants me to give it to her. She's always mad, even when there are no broken windows. She comes back when Dad's home, and she's nice to me after Dad gives her the money. She says she has some kittens and asks if I want one. *Oh yeah! Something that's mine to love.* I can't wait!

I still have the old basket that Gramma gave me. She said it was a gift filled with newborn baby things when my mom was born. It survived the trip from Missouri, and I treasure it. I tie a rag bow around the handle and make a bed of rags inside for a kitten. I wait and wait. I rearrange the basket and wait some more. Days then weeks go by without the old landlady and a kitten showing up.

When I tell Dorothy and Harold about the kitten I never got, they take me to a home with several Chihuahua-terrier mix puppies. Harold tells me to pick one out and helps me choose a name for her: Ponchita. She's beautiful. And she sleeps with me—not in the basket.

During Ponchita's first days with me, I skip school and hide in the desert weeds if Dad hasn't left for work yet. Once he's gone, I slip back home so she won't be alone. During one long night, I train Ponchita to sit, stay, and come when I whistle. Ponchita learns the commands, and she's so content to be with me. We go to bed in the wee hours and sleep most of the next day. Then I ask the girl next door to ask her stepmother if she'll check on Ponchita during the day because I have to go back to school before Dad catches me ditching.

Craig shows up to tell me the latest things he's tattled to Dad. He's told him about my ditching school, the school supplies hidden under my cot, and hiding in the weeds until Dad leaves for work. He must sneak around here a lot when I don't know it. Dad doesn't mention any of it to me, and we both just avoid Craig's mean streak. I'm sure he's the one taking so much food, too, and responsible for most of the dirty dishes.

Ponchita sits in the basket and goes everywhere I go on my bicycle. We travel all over Tucson except when I have to go to school. I hate leaving her because she's so little, and I don't want her to be lonely. On the way home from school, I start whistling through my fingers once I reach the desert weeds. If someone's home to open the door, she tears across the desert and jumps into my arms, and if not, she tears up the house, trying to get out. She's my friend and constant companion.

During the next few weeks, secrets are happening in Hooligan's. I'm let in on it when I'm handed an invitation for Dad and me to attend a surprise thirtieth wedding anniversary party for Dorothy and Harold. Hooligan's is rented for the night, and what a party—with decorations, a live band, food, gifts, and an open bar. Pitchers of beer and Pepsi flow like water. Dancing the night away with Dad, I still have to go home at 9 p.m.

Twenty years later, I danced with Dad at Dorothy and Harold's fiftieth wedding anniversary, and I didn't go home at 9 p.m. It was snippy, but Claribel agreed I could take Dad to the party, and we had an absolutely wonderful time dancing. It was held at a lodge—a fitting location for the occasion—but if Hooligan's, my desert path, and Buckeye Lane hadn't become cement and apartment buildings, I would've been happy dancing there too. It was a lovely and very special party. And the last time I danced with Dad.

Ponchita's been mine for about three months, and I usually skip school at least once a week to stay home with her. One day after I return to school, my teacher stops our regular activity about thirty minutes early. She picks up a book from her desk and starts reading to the class. I'm mortified at first because I'm much too old and mature to be read to like a little kid, but it only takes a minute before I'm hooked. I think how lucky I didn't skip school today, and I don't skip again until she finishes the book. By then, I've already swiped a paperback copy for myself. I can't wait for those thirty minutes each day.

In the book, *To Kill a Mockingbird* by Harper Lee, the kids, Jem and Scout, are how Dean and I used to be, and Atticus is how Dad sometimes still is when he's not so sad. I'm captivated while the teacher reads and walks around the room. One afternoon when she takes a little hop to sit on her desk, her garter snaps loose and shoots across the room like a bullet. Luckily, the flying garter doesn't hit anyone because it could've killed a kid. The teacher doesn't miss a syllable, and there are a few snickers. Those who do are quickly stared down by the rest of us.

Listening to the book is a welcome change from hearing about the Cuban Missile Crisis. It scares me to death, considering how adults are acting. Even Hooligan's is subdued with everyone talking about it, and dread hangs in the air. I'm determined to keep Ponchita and me together when the Soviet Union and America start blowing up each other, so I braid long lengths of cord to make a collar and leash for her. I figure if I can't see her in the dust and smoke, I'll be able to hold on to her with the leash. I make a rag bag to tie to a belt loop and fill it with stuff for us to eat. Luckily, I don't have to use the leash Ponchita hates or eat the moldy stuff in the bag.

When I ask Dad if he'll have to go back to the army if something bad happens, he says no since he's too old and already did his part in WWII. He smiles, pats my leg, and tells me not to worry because everything will be okay. Of all the things Dad rarely talks about, WWII is the least mentioned. But he does tell me a couple of stories.

In 1943 after completing boot camp, Dad followed Patton's Third Army across Europe for two years and nine days as a construction foreman with the rank of First Sergeant. He was in the Army Corp of Engineers in awful places: Normandy, Ardennes, Northern France, and the Rhineland. He supervised crews building bridges, docks, airports, and roads, among other things. Dad was awarded a Bronze Star for bravery under fire while building a dock in Cherbourg, France, for Liberty ships to land Allied troops and equipment.

Dad was in Paris on VE Day—Victory in Europe Day—on May 8, 1945, where he partied in the streets and bars for three days with huge crowds of people. When he sobered up, he was sitting on a seat in a line of communal toilets with his pants around his ankles. His elbows were resting on bare knees with hands holding his aching head when a French accent asked him to pass the toilet paper. He glanced at the person who asked, sitting on the seat next to him. The accent belonged to the most beautiful French woman he'd ever seen. Dad handed the paper over as embarrassment silenced him even before he could formulate any words. He wasn't in a position to ask her out with his pants around his ankles, so he didn't. And that made him even more miserable than the hangover did.

I'm close in age at twelve to one of Dorothy's granddaughters, Carol, so she picks me up to spend weekends with her. One Friday after school when she arrives, I'm hiding out in the bedroom because I don't have any clean clothes to wear. Dad and Dorothy convince me to go, which doesn't take much because I always want to go with her. On the way, she says she has an errand. She says Carol needs a new outfit, and she might as well buy one for me while she's at it. Dorothy buys matching Western blouses and pants that we wear home. My other clothes are washed and folded when I get up the next morning.

I never take a pair of pajamas to Dorothy's when I spend the weekend. After she encourages me to wash up, Dorothy gives us each a soft, clean tee shirt of Harold's to sleep in. The tee shirts are like dresses on us with pockets where we stash candy cigarettes. We have blankets, pillows, popcorn, candy, and pop in the front room, where we watch the scariest movie on TV. Dorothy watches, too, until we start to fall asleep, then she quietly walks partway up the stairs to yell and throw pillows, scaring us to death only to say she's going to bed. She giggles the rest of the way to her room.

I love listening to Dorothy and Harold's banter, good-natured disagreements, and stories they tell about when they were first married. I love the way Dorothy talks and the words she uses, like case knife for butter knife, wheel for bicycle, pocketbook for purse, and square for a city block, even though it takes a while to catch on to some of their meanings. The first time she tells me to put my jacket in the press, I lay it on the couch because I don't know what she means.

"Not on the davenport. In the press." She picks up my jacket and opens the hall closet door. It's safe and easy to make mistakes with Dorothy because she always helps me find my way out of them.

Dorothy's the consummate mother. She raised all her children, several of her grandchildren, and me. She's a grand lady with a band of steel running the length of her spine, full of love, caring, and life. And Harold's the only man she's ever loved. I know because she told me so.

One summer weekend, Dorothy and Harold put Carol and me in their station wagon that's soon heading to Disneyland in California. I know it's a real place, but I thought the closest I'd ever get to it was watching *The Wonderful World of Disney* on Sunday nights when I'm lucky enough to be close to a TV set since Dad has never replaced the set Craig destroyed.

Disneyland's so utterly fantastic I never want to leave. Ticket books are handed out—ooh those E tickets!—and orders are given to meet up again at a certain time. After that, we are free to explore.

There's no Space Mountain, Bear Country, or Mission to Mars yet. There's no Electrical Parade, Haunted Mansion, Pirates of the Caribbean, or Small World. But, oh man, what's here to discover is amazing! There's a castle with a drawbridge and moat! Matterhorn bobsleds and Skyway buckets pass through the Matterhorn for me to ride. I can fly with Dumbo, ride the Casey Jr. Circus Train, and take Peter Pan's Flight—just like Dean's and my old picture book! I'm afloat on Mark Twain's Riverboat before exploring Tom Sawyer's Island and the Indian Village. I'm riding the Monorail and driving the Autopia then taking a submarine voyage and gliding on a Flying Saucer. I take a Jungle Cruise and practice my Chuck Connor rifle skills at the Safari Shooting Gallery. I eat a tuna sandwich from Peter Pan's pirate ship, Chicken of the Sea, and run around Skull Rock. I watch the marching Disneyland band, listen to the Dapper Dans Barbershop Quartet, and eat a caramel apple on Main Street. I quickly decide I could live in Swiss Family Robinson's treehouse and be completely happy for the rest of my life.

That's Dorothy and Harold—doing something fantastic to let kids be kids. They do that for me at every opportunity, and I think it makes them just as happy as it makes me. I've had a wonderful experience I'll never forget as long as I live.

After the Disneyland trip, when Dorothy asks why I'm not riding my wheel anymore, I have to tell her it doesn't have tires. Dean swiped some money from Ronnie then tried to ride his bicycle to Oregon to find Aunt Mary because she knows Mom's address. He thought that if he could find Aunt Mary, maybe he could find Mom. He didn't get very far when his tires blew out, so he came back to put my tires on his bike and tried again. When my tires blew out, Dean left his bike alongside the road and bought a bus ticket with the stolen money. He found Aunt Mary, but he didn't find Mom.

Aunt Mary wrote Dad a letter—which I read before Dad got home—asking for Dean's bus fare back to Tucson. She made a couple of comments in the letter about Dad being an unfit father. That really burned me up because Dad didn't abandon us: her sister did. Even though there're two things about Aunt Mary that really matter to me—I know her address, and she knows Mom's address—I still wrote a letter telling her off for telling off Dad. Both letters are ready for Dad when he gets home. He read them, wrote a check, put it along with my letter in an envelope, and sealed it without a word. Dean came home, but we still can't spend much time together even though we both want the same thing.

Years later, I learned from Mom that she and Aunt Mary thought Dad dictated the letter to me because it made a sound point about who abandoned who. At the time Mom asked me about it, I said Dad only read it after I'd written it.

"You and Dean always were deep," was her only comment.

Craig went to Aunt Mary's in search of Mom too. Craig, Dean, and I would have done anything to see her again. Craig escaped from Mother Higgens, the juvenile detention facility, with a butcher knife from the kitchen and made it all the way without getting caught. He stayed with Aunt Mary until an arrest warrant caught up with him and the authorities took him back to Tucson to complete his sentence. I never find out why he ended up in Mother Higgens. Whatever the reason, I don't think the time spent there helps him much.

After living on Buckeye Lane for about a year, Dad and I move to a small duplex across town on Monte Vista Street. I'm not sure why we move or where Dean stays because we don't keep track of each other anymore. After our move, I feel more isolated than ever. There are no Friday night dates, no Hooligan's, no pickled eggs and beer nuts, no jukebox, and no dancing. As time passes, I miss dancing with Dad almost as much as I miss Mom. But I still have Ponchita, my bike, and the transistor radio. I don't see Dad much because he's always with Claribel, and she still doesn't like me. I could've liked her if she liked me, but she never does. I only see Dorothy on weekends when she picks me up because we now live on opposite sides of Tucson.

I volunteer at school to be a crossing guard before school, during lunch, and after school. I'm proud, wearing the orange strap over my shoulder with a wide belt. I'm especially proud of the whistle on a chain around my neck. When I blow it, holding up a red-and-white stop sign, kids and cars alike must follow my directions. Me, a nobody, can do something important. I take the job seriously and don't skip school or come late.

A girl in my class walks home for lunch every day. If I don't make her wait long at the curb, she gives me a piece of hard candy I suck on to make my stomach stop growling. One day when I hold out my hand for the candy, she says she doesn't have any and hurries past me. After a while, I pass out on the street.

The next thing I know, someone puts a salad with small chunks of cheese in front of me in the cafeteria. It looks so good, but I have to go throw up. I'm so hungry my stomach's cramping, and I can't eat the salad with small chunks of cheese. After that, a woman takes my crossing guard stuff away from me, and I lose the job that made me feel I was worth something.

I spend a lot of time walking, trying to make sense of my life. I hate not being able to go to Hooligan's anymore, and Buckeye Lane was a lot better than being stuck in a small duplex in the middle of a patch of desert with nothing around. I stay with Dorothy and Harold lots of times on weekends, I move in and out of Ronnie and Kathy's house a couple of times, and I stay with Mary, Dorothy's daughter—although I don't stay anywhere very long. They all have what I've lost: family. Ponchita goes with me everywhere I go—we're inseparable.

I keep wandering because I'm miserable and I'm looking for where I belong. I want an adult to be an adult and not let me have the choice to leave. I want them to want me there. At least that's what I thought at the time. I think now if anyone had ordered me to stay anywhere, I would've bolted like a wild animal.

I never go to a school long enough to have any friends because when I leave one place for another, there's a different grade school to attend. I'm always the new kid on the block and a very quiet one. When a girl starts to talk to me as we walk home from school one day, she asks about my family. I say my parents are divorced and hurry away. The next day, the same girl tells me not to be so sad because lots of kids' parents are divorced. I can't even begin to explain to her the difference between being divorced and being abandoned by your mother. The one person who's supposed to care about you and want you there doesn't. How do I live with that? Where do I keep it so it doesn't hurt? How do I forget about it? I'm so ashamed that I start to walk home from school a different way to avoid her.

During this latest wandering time, after I'm back with Ronnie and Kathy, Dorothy and Harold stop in at Hooligan's one Friday afternoon and see Claribel and Kathy sitting at the bar. Dorothy's leery of them both because they will talk about someone behind their back then turn and look them straight in the face. The only reason Kathy ever wants me around is for babysitting and ironing Ronnie's shirts. Claribel's telling Kathy that she isn't getting the work out of me that she should, and Kathy agrees. Dorothy overhears the comment, and she's livid.

Harold stays at Hooligan's while Dorothy drives to Ronnie's house. I'm not home, so she drives around to find me walking and asks me to get in the car. Dorothy says she wants me to stay with her and Harold and not just on weekends. She asks if I would like that. After Dorothy and Harold talk to Dad, I move in with them permanently. I hope I can stay until I somehow find Mom.

Dorothy cleans me up and helps me stay that way while I'm with her. She encourages me to brush my teeth and take care of myself. Dorothy keeps my clothes clean and expects the same of me. One morning, she grabs her pocketbook and heads for the door.

"Come on," she tells me. "We have some shopping to do!"

Dorothy drives to Sears Department Store and heads for the juniors' department and the underwear aisle. There she picks out my first bras.

"It'll feel just like a straitjacket for a while until you get used to it," Dorothy tells me. "Then it'll still feel like a straitjacket. But don't worry; it gets easier as time goes on," she says, adjusting her straps and smiling.

After we get home, I stuff them in the back of my drawer. I don't want them or these *things* growing on my chest. They embarrass me and make me feel weird. I wish they'd just go away. But they don't. After several days, Dorothy corners me in my room as I'm dressing for school.

"It's time, Sherrie," she gently says, handing me a bra before heading back to the kitchen. I put the damn thing on, and then immediately, I'm not me anymore. It's forcing me to be something I don't know how to be: a girl. After Dorothy tells me how nice I look, I feel a little better. But I still don't like it much.

Dorothy holds me to her with a silver thread. She shows me every day that she wants me here. And she makes it easy to stay by not taking away my freedom.

She had new tires put on my wheel, so on weekends, I head for the door and my bike with Ponchita in my arms.

"Be home before dark and be careful," Dorothy tells me.

Sometimes Dorothy phones Dad to tell him it's time to come over and see me. When Dad arrives, Dorothy stands close in front of him and quietly reads him the riot act for not coming over more often. Harold sips his beer while Dad stands silently at attention until Dorothy finishes, then he leans down to kiss her forehead. Still muttering, Dorothy serves Dad a beer and food, and we all sit at the table and talk. I love these times because they like each other, and I love them.

Everyone usually comes to Dorothy and Harold's on the weekends: kids, grandkids, in-laws, and friends. Dorothy has tons of food cooked and ready whenever someone's hungry because the adults are playing euchre—a card game played by two sets of partners using nines through aces. Wild games are usually in progress at two or three tables, but Dorothy never plays with Harold as her partner. She says they could never have stayed married as long as they have if she played partners with him because he's too ferocious when he plays the game.

I use Dorothy's return address when I write Mom via Aunt Mary. I don't write often because it still takes her a long time to answer. When Dorothy hands me a letter one day, it's not from Aunt Mary. The return address on the envelope is Mom's in Illinois. Now I know where she is! Mom tells me they have a baby boy, Stevie. I mope around, certain she still doesn't love me because she has a new baby. Harold says I'm down in the dumps and tries to cheer me up.

Dorothy's two older sisters are visiting, and Harold plans a vacation to take them back home to Indianapolis, Indiana. I'm going too.

"How far is Illinois from Indiana?" I ask Harold.

"It isn't very far. Why?"

"Mom's in Illinois. Can we go by there on the trip?"

"Yes," Harold replies without a moment's hesitation.

He immediately looks at Dorothy, who's already looking at him. She's at the kitchen counter chopping something for dinner. The chopping's louder now, and words are flying silently between them. I pray Harold wins the wordless disagreement. After an eternity, Dorothy tells me to write Mom back and ask if it's okay to stop and see her. Mom replies and says yes. I am paralyzed with excitement.

14

"Tie Me to Your Apron Strings Again"

EDDY ARNOLD

The car trip from Tucson to Roseville, Illinois, takes two and a half days. Harold has us up at daybreak and in the car shortly thereafter. When Harold gets behind a steering wheel, he drives with purpose.

"God help us if we have to go to the bathroom!" Dorothy says with a wink.

Dorothy, her two sisters, and I fly in the car with him to Illinois. For the first time, I don't embarrass myself by getting carsick. In fact, I never do again.

We arrive in Roseville just after noon. Mom included her phone number in the letter to call when we arrive and said she'll drive into town to show us the way. Harold spots a telephone booth and parks in front of a fire station next to an old, austere-looking grade school across the street from an old, even more austere-looking high school. While Harold calls, I'm sitting in the front seat, unable to breathe, listening to my heart pound in my ears. Dorothy straightens my blouse, smooths my hair, pats my arms, and tells me to tie my tennis shoes. I think I'll explode soon. I hear a couple of cars, but I know without looking they're not her. I know the third one is. I'm flying around the front of both cars where I finally find Mom. We hug, kiss, laugh, and cry over and over.

Mom pulls away to wipe her eyes and says I need to introduce her to my friends. I wonder why Dorothy and Harold don't get out of the car. It's only after I finish introductions that I see tears streaming down Dorothy and Harold's faces and the sisters' faces too. Tears are still streaming down mine when I ask if I can ride with Mom while they follow on the country roads to the farm where *he* works.

Mom's home is a small, square, one-story white farmhouse that sits down a long lane from the main gravel road. It reminds me of my Barracks Home. A narrow sidewalk cuts through green grass that borders a chicken-wire pen for hens, a rooster, and the coop then continues to the back door. Just beyond is Mom's rock garden with her flower beds in brilliant bloom.

We follow her down the sidewalk and through a screen door into the house. A turn to the left leads up three steps to the kitchen, and straight ahead are basement stairs. *He* sits with Stevie, snuggled in an infant seat on the kitchen table. While Mom introduces *him*, I meet my little brother and immediately fall in love with him. He has Mom's nose, just like me.

They have a beer while everyone gets to know each other as I stay quietly out of the way, filling my eyes with Mom, who regularly finds me for a hug. I'm so happy because she's so happy to see me. It's heaven, but I'm already dreading the end of it. Dinner's cooked and eaten with everyone talking and happy.

I could've been led blindfolded by strangers into this house, and I'd still know it's Mom's. It feels like her, although an old-fashioned upright piano in the front room is new to me. After dinner, *he* plays, and everyone sings the songs I remember so well from Mom singing them.

By this time, Mom and I have convinced Dorothy to let me stay for a few more days. I'll catch a bus to Indianapolis on Saturday, and Dorothy will pick me up at the bus station. She gives me money for a ticket and makes me promise I'll catch the bus. At least I can be in Mom's world for a little longer. I wish it wouldn't end, but I know it will—Mom hasn't asked me to stay. I'll have a few extra days, so it's okay that the evening's over. Mom has room for everyone: Dorothy and Harold on a feather bed in the basement and the sisters on a pull-out couch.

I wake up slowly—safe, warm, in heaven. I don't open my eyes because I don't want to spoil the feeling. I can hear the long-ago familiar sounds from her kitchen. The radio is on low, and she's humming while making sounds of cooking. The wonderful odor of her biscuits in the oven fills my room.

Stevie starts fretting in his crib next to where I'm snuggling in bed. He's three months old and so little and cute. Mom changes his diaper and gives him a bottle propped up by a cute stuffed bunny then turns to pull up the warm bedding around me. I drift back to sleep, listening to Stevie softly suck on his bottle. I've never been so completely happy in my whole life of twelve and a half years.

Mom cooks and we eat a big breakfast before it's time for Dorothy, Harold, and the sisters to leave. They still have to drive to Indianapolis, and Harold wants to make it before dark. As they're leaving, Dorothy hugs me and whispers, reminding me that I promised to be on the bus. I hug her back and promise again I'll be on the bus.

"It's probably been five years since I saw you, Mom."

"It's only two years."

She's looking at me with that look: the one that pierces through me; the one I never figure out.

"It's sure been a really long time," I reply.

"Do you ever cry yourself to sleep?" is the only question Mom asks me.

She says she did when she was little and missed her mother. I shake my head no. I'll never admit anything that'll hurt her or make her cry, so I'm relieved when she doesn't ask anything more about my life since she left us.

We're walking arm and arm down the lane where one side is the house, yard, chicken coop, flowerbeds, and rock garden. On the other is a garage with farm equipment, barn, corn crib, and a huge pen filled with a dozen hogs, each weighing over six hundred pounds. They're filthy, noisy, terrifying, and fascinating. The farm is framed on three sides by cornfields stretching farther than I can see. A herd of Black Angus cattle grazes somewhere beyond the fields. The corn is grown to fatten them up before their trip to Chicago for slaughter. The hogs are turned loose to root through cow piles, taking advantage of all the corn that passes undigested through the cattle. Ugh.

He works the farm during the few days I visit, so I have Mom and Stevie all to myself. She cooks a delicious dinner each evening while they have a few beers before we eat. After Stevie's in bed, we watch television. It's a wonderful visit, but emptiness never leaves me: Mom has a family that doesn't include me.

After the few days fly by, Mom drives me to the bus station in Monmouth. She hugs me, cries, and says she'll see me again.

"Take care of her. That's my little girl," she tells the bus driver.

The driver says he will. *But if I am her little girl, then why won't she keep me?* I wonder. Fighting tears, I begin the first of several long bus rides to—and away—from her.

Dorothy's waiting for me. She's happy as always to see me but also relieved, and it wouldn't be until much later that I understand why. I would've put her in an awkward position if I'd been able to stay with Mom. How could Dorothy explain to Dad that she left me with Mom after Mom deserted us all? Dorothy loves me and cares for my dad, and she would never betray his trust. She also could never understand how a mother would willingly abandon her children for any reason.

I meet many of Dorothy and Harold's relatives in Indianapolis. She drives around the city, showing me where they lived while raising their family. She takes me to the Indianapolis Speedway Museum. Then, on my very first taxicab ride, we're delivered downtown to the center of the business district at Monument Circle. Before shopping, we visit the Soldiers and Sailors Monument, where Dorothy waits while I climb many, many stairs to the top of the monument. Afterward, she explains how Harold and his crew strung the exterior of the monument with Christmas lights every holiday season when he became an electrician after they were married. She also tells me the story of how they met.

Dorothy's dad dropped her off on his way to work each morning at her aunt's house, where she waited for a city bus to take her to high school. Dorothy first saw Harold from Aunt Sarah's kitchen window. He was stripped to the waist, glistening with sweat and sparkling black dust, shoveling coal from the bed of a Model T pickup down a chute to Aunt Sarah's coal bin in the basement. Harold saw Dorothy watching when he paused to wipe sweat from his face. When their eyes met, they smiled before looking away. Dorothy later said he looked like a Greek god. She then noted that after thirty years of marriage and six kids, he now looked like a goddamn Greek, which provoked the expected response from Harold, and good-natured arguing at its finest was underway.

Dorothy's cousin Sammy and Harold were friends, giving Harold the perfect excuse to drop by and find out the pretty girl's name who smiled at him from the kitchen window. Sammy told Dorothy that Harold was interested in meeting her and arranged to have him and several friends at the house when she returned from school. That afternoon they were able to talk and get to know each other.

Dorothy wasn't old enough to date, so after she finished her homework a few days later, Sammy walked her to the movies. At a prearranged spot a few squares away, Harold was waiting on the street corner to escort Dorothy the rest of the way. Sammy kept a respectable distance while they talked and held hands.

Dorothy was fifteen years old and too young to marry, so she eloped with Harold, who was five years her senior. Because it was during the Depression and times were hard, Dorothy's parents gave them the space they needed in her family home to begin their life together.

Thirteen family members lived there during those Depression years, and only Dorothy's dad had a steady job. The other men looked daily for any kind of work they could find. Ninety-eight cents bought a good pair of shoes, and one dollar and twenty-five cents bought a fancy pair. Bus fare was five cents with an additional two cents for a transfer. A movie cost ten cents before 7 p.m. and fifteen cents after. A bag of flour cost sixteen cents with four pounds of lard at twenty-five cents, and those cents were hard to come by. A basket of food was available from a CCC office when work couldn't be found. A set number of hours had to be spent doing community work, like patrolling neighborhood parks at night, to claim the basket.

When the coal-shoveling job ended, Harold found work sacking manure for a fertilizer factory, earning eleven dollars a week. Dorothy's dad was an electrician and boss at the Indianapolis Power and Light Company, and he eventually got Harold hired. Everyone in the house was relieved, especially Dorothy, because Harold reeked of manure when he came home at night.

Harold's first job at the power company was digging post holes with a pickax and shovel. Soon, with his father-in-law's help, Harold learned the electrical trade and was an electrician and a union man for the rest of his life. In those early years, Harold attached spikes to his work boots and took a running leap to sink the spikes into an electrical pole in need of repair. He scaled the pole hand over hand to complete necessary repairs after summer thunderstorms or winter ice storms. Harold's daily work lunch consisted of six White Castle hamburgers and two glasses of beer: all for twenty-five cents.

Dorothy's first baby was born on her sixteenth birthday. The doctor charged twenty-five dollars to deliver at home, but Harold didn't have the full amount when the baby decided to be born. Dorothy's little sister Juanita came to the rescue by contributing money from her piggy bank to pay the bill in full. Minutes after the birth of their son, Harold told Dorothy she would never have to go through such pain again. Once was enough, he assured her.

The baby was premature and sickly, and some thought he wouldn't live through the night. Still, Dorothy's grandfather wrapped the baby in a small blanket and laid him in a shoebox by a radiator heater to keep him warm. He fed the baby warm drops of milk along with a tiny amount of whiskey throughout the night while Dorothy's mom took care of her. The baby boy lived and soon had three brothers and two sisters.

Dorothy and Harold eventually got their own place. When they moved, Dorothy's dad told Harold, "If you get tired of her, don't hit her, beat her, and don't mistreat her. Just bring her back to me."

They saved for a down payment on a refrigerator: their first appliance. It had a locked metal box attached that required two quarters to be dropped through a slot each day or the power would automatically shut off. A bill collector came for the quarters monthly, so payments were made on the refrigerator. Dorothy had two children before she had her first stove: a coal oil stove with a removable oven on top and an oil tank attached to the side with two lines to feed two burners.

Harold was old enough to go to a tavern on Saturday nights, but Dorothy was still underage. So with kids to look after, she stayed home. She cleaned and mopped the floors after her kids were asleep then checked on them. She patted their heads, stroked their cheeks, and thought each night that she wouldn't spank them for anything they did the following day because they looked like little sleeping angels. Each morning found her smacking someone's butt just hard enough to get their attention or chasing another one for some childhood mischief. Dorothy told me she grew up with her kids.

The first vehicle Dorothy and Harold owned was an old Model T Ford pickup. It had to be parked on a slope facing downward to give it a running start. The floorboard had two removable pieces of wood on the driver's side so Harold could put his shoes on the pavement to help with the running start when necessary.

Dorothy and Harold had a circle of family and friends who met once a week at someone's home to play cards, and to play cards meant euchre and homebrew brewed in a large crock. Dorothy's job was siphoning the brew into bottles, and Harold's sister-in-law capped each bottle. Usually, they were both happily tipsy by the time their chores were finished after Dorothy had to swallow some from the siphoning tube rather than spill it, and her sister-in-law had to take a sip from a too-full bottle before capping it.

When the United States entered WWII, Harold was temporarily exempt because of his large family. Dorothy managed rationing during the war in the same way she did everything: with fortitude and imagination. She had an excess of sugar rations with six kids, so she made them sugar pies with sugar, flour, canned milk, butter, and cinnamon—a most delicious pie. Then she traded sugar stamps for coffee stamps. She traded any ration stamps she had, whether she needed them or not, for shoe stamps to keep her kids in shoes. Harold was adamant about that because of the times when he didn't have shoes while growing up.

Dorothy couldn't buy nylons because nylon was used to make parachutes for the war effort. The hose she could buy did more to hide women's legs than enhance them and had a dark, vertical seam on the back from top to bottom.

"The seam had to be straight, or Harold would tell you!" she said with a table smack.

Ladies' wartime hose were made from thick silk, and the result was anything but sheer. Dorothy bought them when she could get them and guarded them with her life. When her last pair had a run, she smoothed leg makeup over her legs to give the appearance of wearing nylons.

If there was a line of people in a dime store or drug store, it was almost certain the store had hose or cigarettes for sale. If the store had cigarettes, you could buy one pack of whatever brand they had, mostly off-brands, because the others were sent to soldiers overseas. Movie theaters had a barrel in the lobby with a sign that read, "Drop a dime in here, put a pack over there." Dorothy had a rolling machine she used when a pack of cigarettes was impossible to buy, and a daily chore was rolling cigarettes for Harold's next-day use.

The war ended before Harold's exemption expired. A few years after the war, Juanita moved to Tucson, Arizona, with her husband. Shortly after, Dorothy and Harold moved their family to Tucson, too, where I would meet them over a decade later.

Dorothy and Harold provide a great time for me in Indianapolis. Adults and kids visit the state fair, where I ride every ride and visit every booth. Later, we spend hours at an amusement park, where I ride the roller coaster a dozen times. When I think I'm finished, Dorothy coaxes me to go again while she patiently waits.

After a terrific time, we're on our way home. When we pick up Ponchita from friends, Dorothy realizes something's wrong and takes her to a vet, who diagnoses distemper and keeps her for nearly a month. At first, Dorothy takes me to the vet's office to see her but soon says she's too busy. I know why—Ponchita's dying. I'm on my bike by myself, traveling the length and width of Tucson, singing every song I know then chanting a poem over and over again that hangs in the vet's office about losing your dog.

Harold's home from work early—sitting at the kitchen table with Dorothy—when I walk in from school one day. I immediately see a little thing slip-sliding on the floor, trying to make traction and come to me. My dropped books scatter as I kneel for Ponchita to scamper into my arms. She's so skinny and her short hair's falling out by the handfuls, but she's well and back with me. And that's all that matters. Dorothy will fatten her up again like she did me.

If Dorothy's sons or nephew drop by for dinner, we have contests to see who can eat the most bread with gravy over it. Sometimes, someone flips a teaspoon of gravy at someone else. Sandwiches are made with a tissue placed between slices of meat, and ice cream sundaes are topped with shaving cream instead of whipped cream. Dorothy laughs and eggs us on.

"One boy is a boy, two boys are half a boy, and three boys are no boy at all," she says.

On days when there's no school, Dorothy and I watch the original *Jeopardy!* with Art Fleming. We watch the John F. Kennedy murder tragedy. We're watching when Jack Ruby steps out of a crowd and shoots Lee Harvey Oswald, and we both jump off the davenport. We see the little boy John F. Kennedy Jr. salute his father during the funeral procession, and we both cry.

These times add to my sadness because there's still a hole in my heart for what used to be my family. I hardly ever see Dad because he's always with Claribel, and I never see any of the boys. I don't travel the same streets they do now that I live with Dorothy and Harold, so I don't run into them anymore. I really miss Dean and ache to see Mom again.

Dorothy and Harold provide everything for Ponchita and me; we want for nothing. I love them both, but I still wake up every morning lonely and ashamed. *This isn't where I belong*, I think. *I should be with Mom*. Somehow, I need to be with her, but I don't understand that need. When I finally find the courage to write and ask if I can live with her, I can't believe it when she says yes! Showing Dorothy and Harold the letter, I ask if they'll take care of Ponchita for me.

"I miss you already, and you're not even gone," Dorothy tells me.

She gives me a suitcase for my clothes, and Harold helps me pack other possessions into a couple of cardboard boxes. They buy a bus ticket for me, and I leave Tucson for Roseville, Illinois, six months after my visit with Mom and the day after my thirteenth birthday.

Wandering

15

"Wagon Wheels"

SONS OF THE PIONEERS

It takes three days and two nights, stopping in every big or little town. I'm scared to get off the bus, but I have to. I'm scared to go to the bathroom, but I need to. I'm trying to be an adult when I couldn't finish being a kid. I'm pretending I'm not intimidated by women of every size, shape, and color in the filthy bathroom, with some sleeping on small benches or making incredible noises in the stalls. Some are stripped to the waist, washing in sinks, as others comb hair or adjust makeup. I see young mothers exhausted by children in their care and obvious prostitutes working the terminal. They all look like they could eat me for a midnight snack. I'm in and out as fast as possible and back to the mainstream of the big or little bus terminal that's filled to overflowing with men, women, and kids. And others who could be male or female, but I can never tell for sure. I stay away from people talking to themselves or stumbling and nearly falling with every step.

After I buy a Pepsi and candy bar, the driver calls us to get back on board—back to the safety of my window seat. I shiver with cold, curl up facing the window, and will myself to sleep so I won't have to talk with anyone sitting by me. Then the miles slowly start to melt away again.

The smell of diesel fuel and exhaust, the sound of a whining transmission, whirring engine, and hissing air brakes, along with a floating sensation from the sway of the bus, lull me to sleep. A million headlights all heading in the wrong direction finally end in Monmouth, Illinois, where Mom's waiting to take me back to the little farmhouse. At long last, I'm where I need to be. I'm home … I'm home.

I'm through the door and up the steps to the kitchen before I see Dean smiling at me. I'm so crazy-happy to see him that I nearly knock him over for a hug. I didn't know he beat me to Illinois and has been living with Mom for a couple of months. I'm so incredibly happy. I have Mom, and Dean and I will be best friends again because we both have what we need. And we have this beautiful little baby to play with too. I'll have to be around *him*, but what a small price to pay for all these wonderful things. How wrong can a thirteen-year-old be?

One of the first things I do is call Dorothy so she'll know I've arrived safe and sound. A person-to-person collect call to myself does the trick and doesn't cost anyone a dime. *He* comes in from working the farm shortly after and orders the first beer of the day. It's Thursday afternoon. Several beers later, Mom tells us to make sandwiches for our dinner and cuts thick slices of her wonderful, homemade light bread to use. Dean and I fall back into our teasing-fighting-fun routine, and Mom seems to enjoy it as much as we do. When I'm not bantering with Dean, I sit and watch Mom. I can't get enough of her in my eyes. She smiles and hugs me on her way to a couple more beers.

Dean goes to bed in the basement on the old iron-framed, feather-mattress bed piled high with Mom's quilts. I'm in Stevie's room in the bed next to his crib, where I fall asleep in the very same house with my Mom and Dean.

Dean stays home from school the next day, Friday, and *he* doesn't work the farm. Looks like I'm the reason for a party. I quickly learn they don't need an excuse to drink day and night. Mom makes her big breakfast: fried pota-toes, homemade biscuits, ham, gravy, eggs, and sliced tomatoes, pickles, and sweet onion. It's delicious. *He* and Mom have beers while she cooks, then after breakfast, they have beers all day and into the night. By early evening, Dean and I are doing our best to stay out of their way in the little house. We take Stevie to the basement to play on the soft feather bed, but *he* immediately yells to come back upstairs. *He* seems to want us watching them drink, or *he* doesn't trust us out of *his* sight—it's one or the other or both.

After Stevie's in bed, we're finally allowed to watch TV. It's not long before talking in the kitchen is louder, beers are set down harder, and the atmosphere becomes strained, with Mom's voice small and crying and *his* voice gruff, gravelly, and mean. Suddenly, Mom yells as *he* storms out of the house. The door opens and slams and opens and slams again. I look at Dean, who is calmly watching TV.

"Better get used to it. They do this all the time," he says matter-of-factly.

I can't sit still. How can Dean watch TV when there's yelling outside? The car door slams shut several times, then I see headlights follow the lane to the gravel road and turn toward town. I hear Mom crying when she opens the back door. I see her holding her head as she stumbles to the bathroom. I look at Dean. He shrugs his shoulders and says again, "Get used to it."

A long time later, Mom comes out of the bathroom with her hair dripping wet and a towel draped over her shoulders. She's not wearing her blouse. I've never seen her bra before, but all I see now is bright-red blood on the towel. I jump up to help her, but she pushes past me to sit at the kitchen table. The back of her head is laid open top to bottom, and the long gash steadily drips bright-red blood. When I ask, she says *he* hit her with *his* gun when she tried to get in the car with *him*. She won't let me do anything for her and takes her drink to sit on the steps by the back door. She's still there, crying and drinking, when Dean and I go to bed.

I wonder why she left my gentle Dad and us to go with *him*: a mean—many times brutal—coarse hillbilly. *His* growling voice and her bloody head keep me awake. It's my second night in Mom's world.

I learn the drill well during this first long weekend. *He* came home sometime in the early morning hours. Breakfast is cold cereal. They have beers. Now *he's* ignoring Mom completely but very talkative to Dean and me. It breaks my heart to see her treated like this. I hate *his* guts and want to ignore *him* like *he* ignores Mom, but I'm afraid to. What if *he* takes it out on Mom if I ignore *him*? What if *he* hits her again because I ignore *him*? I answer when *he* speaks to me.

By afternoon, we're driving to town because they're out of Fox Deluxe beer. A case costs a little over $3.00 and will last a long day when supplemented with shots of peppermint schnapps. I see my first drive-through business: a liquor store with a drive-through window where two cases of beer are handed to the back seat and coupons silently passed to Mom. We drive home in strained silence with a lump in the pit of my stomach that nearly makes me sick.

We're back home to watch them drink more and more beer. I learn from watching Dean to act happy while treading on eggshells. I learn to go to bed soon after dinner to get away from the miserable feelings. Going to bed early now, I'm thankful a fight hasn't erupted.

I've been asleep only a few seconds, it seems, when noises wake me up: cussing, crying, loud thuds. I fly into Mom's bedroom as she's picking herself up off the floor to sit on the bed. *He* sits up to viciously slap her, knocking her back on the bed, then uses both feet to kick her out of bed again, and she hits the floor with another thud. When I scream at *him* to leave her alone, *he* drunkenly mumbles and turns away from Mom. She tells me to go back to bed. She says she'll be okay now.

It's my third night in Mom's house, and I'd spent years trying to get here. My thoughts explode. The two of them were nothing like this when I'd spent a few days with them last summer. How am I going to get out of this insanity? But I can't leave her like she left me. She's my mother.

Mom doesn't drink on this first Sunday; instead, she cooks and cries all day. Dean and I take care of Stevie. He's such a sweet little baby. What kind of life is he going to have? What chance will he have in this mess? Maybe I can take Stevie with me if I do leave. Maybe.

While Mom cooks, *he's* drunk at the kitchen table, telling Dean and me over and over how awful they were treated in El Dorado Springs after they got together. It was so bad they had to move to Illinois, and *he* can't understand the injustice of it all. It's quite a performance. *He* keeps drinking and wanting sympathy for his occasional tear until he finally goes to bed. *He* never once mentioned the four kids he left behind or the three Mom left. And *he* didn't mention the back of Mom's head or his brutality in bed the previous night.

After *he's* in bed, Mom watches TV with us. When I sit on the couch and snuggle up to her warm arm, she hugs me and pats my leg. Maybe I can stay with her a while longer. Maybe they won't drink tomorrow.

I learn that Monday through Wednesday are usually nights they don't drink. I guess they have to rest up for the following four.

The fights and beatings keep the wide gulf between Dean and me. We can't be best friends again because we'd have to talk about it all—her leaving us then and the fighting now—and that's something we just can't do. We won't talk about it for years until we're both in our thirties and best friends again. But even when we do, the only thing Dean tells me is that when he hears a fist hitting flesh on TV, it still makes him sick.

When he told me to "get used to it" on my second night at Mom's, he didn't know what else to do. Neither did I. We had to live with it or without our Mom, and we had just barely found her.

Dean and I catch a school bus to Roseville. I'm in seventh grade in the old grade school, and Dean's in ninth grade in the old high school across the street. I have a large school binder, and Dean has a thin, plain binder. We like each other's, so we trade.

The next weekend, Dean and I stay home with Stevie when they go to town. After they're back, I can tell *he's* mad. Mom loves oranges and comes home with a bagful. She leaves the groceries on the table, grabs her drink, and sits down on the padded arm of the chair I'm sitting on in the front room. *He* walks in, holding up an orange stuck on the blade of *his* pocketknife. *He* bends down to Mom's face and cusses her as *he* cuts the orange in half and presses the tip of the blade down her cheek and chin, leaving angry red marks. Mom doesn't move and makes whimpering sounds.

"See what I could do if I want?" *he* growls.

He smashes the orange on Mom's face, violently rubbing pulp and juice all over. Then *he* drops both halves on her lap and walks back to the kitchen, cussing and wiping the knife's blade back and forth on *his* pant leg. Mom cries and whispers for us to switch the school binders back because *he* bought Dean that binder. We do immediately. *He's* made it abundantly clear any infraction on our part will be taken out on our mom. I start being *very* perfect: careful what I say, how I say it, and how I act so maybe he won't hurt her again.

I soon learn if I try to stop a fight in the beginning by yelling at *him* to leave her alone, they both yell back at me. But if I wait to yell at *him* until *he* hits her, *he'll* usually stop. But it won't stop the arguing or crying or heavy, black feelings. And I can do nothing to help when they go out and she's been beaten when they come home. Mom cries and never lets me console her. Dean pretends nothing's happened. We both live for the few hours when we're alone with Mom and Stevie and she's not crying. Freud would have had a field day with us.

⌒

There are many tornadoes while I'm here. When the wild air outside turns still, thick, and pea-green, we run to the basement. The bus ride to school on mornings after a tornado is awful. The countryside looks like a devastated war zone, with huge trees uprooted, a barn roof perched on top of a house, a house flattened, a tractor upside down in a pond, and piles of unidentifiable things in twisted heaps. It seems the worst tornadoes happen on weekends, with Monday morning's outside air noticeably quiet and still. Tornado season matches the devastation of a drunk weekend with black eyes, swollen face, cut lips, bruises, and piles of aching emotions everywhere in twisted heaps, with Monday morning in the house always deadly quiet and still.

One Sunday evening after they'd drunk themselves sober, we all watch TV after Stevie's in bed. It's a balmy evening, so Mom opens all the windows, and a nice breeze gently blows the curtains. *The Twilight Zone* has a storyline about all the meanness in the world, then during Rod Serling's recap, he says something like, "There's too much meanness in the world, and it might end because of it." The second he finishes speaking, the electricity goes out as something roars through the house. The noise is deafening. I feel like I'm being squeezed to death, then it lets go, and I fall back on the couch. Mom stands up but can't walk. Dean tries to talk but can't.

The whole incident lasts less than a *very long* minute, I think. *He* grabs a flashlight and runs outside as Mom and I rush to the baby's room, where Stevie's still fast asleep. From the damage outside, *he* figures the open windows let a tornado pass through instead of breaking through the house. We quietly sit for a long time before going to bed. I'm thinking about all the meanness in this house, and I think Dean and Mom are too.

Dean and I never want to go when they go to town. We ask to stay home with Stevie so we can do more things with him. Most times, we're told we have to go anyway. *He* drives to some store and into the parking lot of some bar, where we sit in the back seat with Stevie between us the rest of the afternoon and well into the evening. Dean and I play with Stevie, give him a bottle, and change his diaper—all in the back seat. When *he* comes out carrying two cokes for us, which we don't want because we already have to go to the bathroom, I can briefly hear music from inside the bar. *He* says they won't be much longer.

"Take your time. We're fine," we always reply.

We moan in agony because we're not supposed to unlock the doors, let alone get out and stretch or pee. Damn, I miss Tucson. At least there I'd be inside the bar listening to the music.

One weekend, *he's* ten cents short for a case of beer. *He* tells Mom *he* remembers dropping a dime down the dashboard of *his* car then spends the weekend tearing out the dashboard and putting it back together. But *he* doesn't find the dime.

"Mom, I have a dime," I tell her.

"Keep it," she says.

He earns fifty dollars a month and free rent working as a hired man on the farm. In addition, *he's* given half a hog every month and a side of beef every six months. Mom broke out in giant hives from eating too much pork and had to see a doctor, but *he* still buys beer and schnapps with *his* money rather than something other than pork for her to eat. Vegetables are grown in the garden to can, and we scour the countryside, looking for wild strawberries and mushrooms to pick.

Mom makes most of Stevie's baby clothes. She replaces broken laces in her shoes with dime store string and wears the same clothes she had worn when we left Arizona for Missouri a lifetime ago. Her name's not on *his* checking account, car, or anything else. *He*, on the other hand, buys a sixty-dollar Stetson hat. And after *he* comments to Mom in front of me how nice my dad's cowboy boots and shirts always looked, *he* soon has *his* first pair of cowboy boots and two new shirts.

We're in Minnesota on a weeklong fishing trip for summer vacation. The little cabin we're staying in on the shore of a lake belongs to a Missouri drinking buddy of *his*. It's Stevie's second summer, and he's fussy.

"The second summer complaint," Mom says.

Dean and I play him into a good mood most of the time.

The first two days are a lot of fun. After a swim, Dean and I hurry through a glob of moss floating on the water close to shore then race up many, many stairs to the little cabin's porch. We're laughing and panting at the door when we start jumping around, yelling for Mom. She flies out to see what's wrong and yells and jumps around with us, pulling leeches off our legs that leave behind little bloody marks.

He even invites me to get up before dawn and go out in a little boat to fish. I love fishing but would rather fish alone. Dean prefers to sleep in, so I accept because one of us should try to keep the peace. My pole bends nearly double, and the line screams out, chasing a hook that's firmly attached to something bucking and swimming. I work and work to reel in a northern pike that's the biggest catch of the day. Luckily, nothing sets *him* off, even me catching the biggest fish, so it's a good day.

The third day, Dean and I are watching Mom feed Stevie lunch when *he* explodes at the baby's fussing. Mom screams as *he* yanks Stevie out of the highchair by one baby arm, knocking the highchair over. *He* grabs a baby leg to flip Stevie upside down. Cussing, *he* slaps him several times. Mom's trying to grab Stevie, so *he* flips *his* back to her, drops Stevie with a sickening thud, and steps over him to grab a beer and leave for the lake. Mom screams at *him* before picking up the pitifully sobbing baby. It had all taken only seconds.

That evening when we try to eat dinner, *he* picks a fight with Mom, who usually responds when *he* starts. Now *he* has *his* excuse to tell her to pack. We drive all night back to Roseville with Dean and me desperately trying to keep Stevie quiet in the back seat while *he* drinks, drives, and regularly pops Mom with the back of *his* hand. Mom cries the whole trip. I sing Bobby Vinton's

"Tell Me Why" in my head all night. Then *his* personality completely changes for a short time.

After such a really terrible time, you couldn't be around a nicer person. *He* even suggests fun things for us to do. Dean drives the tractor around the farm, and I drive the car on the way to town. Mom's not beaten; Stevie's not slapped. But *he* picks on Dean for how he drives the tractor and tells me to pull over because I'm not driving right. Now the same cruel *thing* is back, and so are Mom's black eyes.

Dorothy calls and writes regularly, telling me how Ponchita's doing. One day, she calls to say it's almost time for some new school clothes and do I need some? Yes please, I tell her, and Dean needs shoes too. She tells me to cut a piece of string the length of Dean's foot so she can send him a pair when she sends the clothes. The shoes fit Dean perfectly.

Before school starts, I decide to write Dorothy and Harold and ask if I can come back to Tucson. They send a bus ticket—no questions asked. Dean says he's going to stay with Mom after I tell him I'm leaving. Mom doesn't say anything when I tell her, but Dean says she really doesn't want me to leave.

I walk down to the basement where Mom's doing laundry. *Will I ever see her again?* I wonder. I can change my mind and stay. *No, I have to leave*, I tell myself. I can't stand watching what *he* does anymore. Mom continues working when she sees me. She says she understands why I want to leave, but it isn't that bad here. She says I can stay if I want.

If only I could. My mind's screaming. I want to tell her to leave with me because Stevie and Dean will come too. I want to scream at her to leave the *bastard* before *he* kills her, but I know she won't. I only say I'm going back to Tucson and walk back upstairs. I've been with her almost six months.

16

"Everybody's Somebody's Fool"

CONNIE FRANCIS

Why do adults screw stuff up so bad? I miss her and know I always will, but I have to get away from *him* and *his* horrible fights, beatings, and humiliations. I need to be somewhere normal, but I don't seem to belong in normal places. I'm the outsider trying to get in—the poor kid with nowhere else to go. I can't fit in because I don't belong, so I don't want to be anywhere. I decide the trick is to be sane after everything you're forced to put up with as a kid.

I knew Dorothy and Harold were on their way back to Indiana to live, so I'd arranged to stay with Ronnie and Kathy. My things are barely through the front door when I'm put in charge of babysitting, and they walk around my things to leave. It's dark inside and outside, the kids are asleep, and I suffocate from the all-too-familiar loneliness.

Mary, Dorothy's daughter, says I can live with her and start eighth grade, so I do. Dorothy had left Ponchita with Mary for me, which is wonderful because I love that little dog. I like it here because Mary shows me it's okay I'm here. Mary's like her mother: thoughtful and caring. She does weekly baking on Thursday mornings, and many times I skip second period to walk home with a girlfriend. Mary greets us with a smile and gives us a glass of milk and something delicious to eat as she comments how amazing it is that second period is canceled so many times on Thursdays.

Mary and I watch the Beatles on TV. She encourages me to go out with my friends and have fun. It's easier to make friends when I realize if I just talk, some of the girls will usually talk back. As I grow into my teenage years, it's more important to have friends—it takes the edge off the isolation. Mary encourages me to bring my friends home and plays games with us.

Mary plans my first slumber party for my fourteenth birthday. When she told me, I was ecstatic! I've overheard lots of girls at school talking about their slumber parties and thought I'd never go to one, let alone have one.

We spend a couple hours at a roller-skating rink, and Mary has food, cake, and ice cream ready when we return. She tells us to stay up all night because it's a slumber party, then she goes to bed. We don't make it all night, but we have tons of fun until the wee hours of the morning.

But I still wake up each morning with the same shame and emptiness. The shame from being abandoned still hangs around my neck like a neon sign. If I'd been the daughter she wanted, maybe she wouldn't have left. I'm completely empty; I can't even remember anymore what order the boys stood in our family picture.

My first crush happens at school. Don Bowersox lives with his dad and misses his mother, too, so we have a lot in common. It's *neat* to have someone who wants to hold my hand. We kiss walking home one evening from a school function—a quick kiss but a kiss, nonetheless. It's a sweet one: a lingering peck on the lips with feeling that makes me walk on air.

Dorothy's nephew Norman asks me out to a movie, and I say yes. Don asks me to a school dance, and I say yes. When I realize they're both on the same Saturday night, I quietly panic and don't know what to do. Dad calls Saturday morning, asking if I want to go to Tombstone, Arizona, with him and Claribel. Dean's going, too, and that clinches it. I didn't know he was back, and Dad and Dean planned this excursion to surprise me. Now I have the perfect out from two dates on the same night. My huge mistake is not telling either guy I won't be home.

We have a great time in Tombstone. Dean and I wander around town to take it all in. We walk the old graveyard to read names on all the tombstones. We explore the shops and walk the street where the famous gunfight took place in 1881 between the Earp Brothers, Doc Holliday, and the Clantons. The only thing we don't do is talk about *him* and Mom.

Dean and I order sarsaparillas at a bar with only a foot rail and spittoons—no bar stools. Dad even asks me to dance when someone fires up a jukebox. I'm in heaven; it's been so long. We can only dance once, though, because Claribel becomes testy. I won't dance with Dad again for about sixteen years.

After Dad delivers me back to Mary's, she tells me Norman had been here to take me to a movie. Then she says Don had been here, too, and hands me the flowers he left. The flowers are wilted, and for some reason, I don't understand why that makes me want to cry. Mary quietly tells me that I should have handled it better to avoid being rude to two very nice guys. Norman never asks me out again. Don understands I wanted to see Dad and Dean, so thankfully, we still go to dances at school together.

It's springtime, and Mary and her family are going on vacation to see Dorothy and Harold in Indiana, and I'm going too. Before we leave, I write Mom, asking if I can stay with her again, and she says I can. Mary asks if I'm sure that's what I want. I've decided I'll stay where I belong, no matter how bad it gets, because I still just want to be with Mom. Dean isn't there anymore, and I can't leave Mom alone with *him*. Besides, it'll be different this time—I just know it. I'll make it different. I know I'll be a babysitter again, but I don't mind because babysitting Stevie's a sweet chore. Don says he'll write to me. He says we'll still be best friends, and he'll really miss me.

Ponchita makes the trip, although I already know I won't be able to keep her with me in Illinois; Mom won't have inside dogs. So Mary takes her on to Indianapolis, where Dorothy and Harold will care for her again. The very first thing I do when I have a minute to myself is write Don. For days then weeks, I look for a letter, but he never replies, even after I send a second one.

"Short or tall, fat or small, they're all alike," Dorothy says with a table smack, referring to males.

I settle back in with Mom and finish the last few weeks of eighth grade in the same school where I finished seventh grade the year before. Mom's glad I'm back. I'm company for her, and I help a lot with Stevie. She has no friends, so I'm the only one she talks to other than *him*. We develop a good friendship and enjoy each other's company. But when *he* comes home, I'm an expendable kid again and expected to stay out of the way. They still drink and argue, but the beatings have mercifully slowed down. Sometimes weeks go by without one, but when it happens, it's more savage.

Before I start ninth grade, Dorothy and Harold drive over from Indianapolis for a visit, and it's a good one. *He* mostly behaves *himself* when other people are around and always does with Dorothy and Harold. They take me back with them to stay for a couple of weeks before school starts. Dorothy takes me shopping for school clothes and buys me a warm winter coat in July. We both laugh because heat and humidity make trying on coats hard to do.

I start ninth grade in the old high school in Roseville. A few weeks later, we move to Biggsville, Illinois, because *he* has a new job working a farm for

Bob Burkett. We'll temporarily live in O'Leary's old farmhouse until Burkett's is available. I continue school at Union High in Biggsville, which isn't big at all with a population around three hundred. A couple of girls quickly latch on to me, so I fit in this school quicker than anywhere I've ever been. It's great. But an even greater thing is about to happen.

Mom and I cry and jump for joy when Carson unexpectedly shows up. He drove from Wamsutter, Wyoming, with a huge dog in a '57 Ford Thunderbird with a T-top. Mom laughs and wonders how they fit in that tiny car. I haven't seen Carson since he left Tucson riding Trix to Wyoming, and Mom hasn't seen him since we left Tucson for El Dorado Springs. We're both ecstatic to see him.

Carson discovers his dog's an egg snatcher after he breaks into the coop the first day, sending chickens flying as he eats eggs and demolishes their nests. Carson smiles but could have killed the dog and keeps him tied up the rest of the visit. I hold my breath, hoping Mom won't be beaten because of the eggs. Then Carson will leave and the visit will be ruined. I'm still too green to understand bullies never show their true colors when someone's around who's strong enough to take them on, so the visit isn't ruined.

We freeze to death in O'Leary's house when winter hits. The old place is a small, two-story farmhouse with a wood heating stove in the front room. We live on the first floor and keep the door to the upstairs closed in an attempt to keep the heat downstairs, but it's still really cold downstairs. I keep my clothes over the back of the couch I sleep on, and before I get up in the mornings, I dress under the covers and snuggle into the winter coat Dorothy bought me. I thank her again every morning for that coat.

I'm about to bust with excitement on our way to the biggest town around on the last weekend before Christmas. Monmouth Square—downtown Monmouth, Illinois—at Christmastime looks like a scene from a Currier and Ives picture, with bustling shoppers and excitement. It's mid-afternoon with snow falling and streetlights twinkling. While *he* and Mom do some Christmas shopping, I hold Stevie's hand to weave in and out of groups of people and stores. When women comment on my handsome son, Stevie giggles as I thank them and pull him along with me. It's so peaceful and happy that I wish Stevie and I could be here on Christmas morning since I know it won't be peaceful and happy at home.

In January, we move into Burkett's farmhouse on the new farm *he* works. What an awesome old house. Built in the 1890s, it's a large, two-story house with a small living room, huge dining room, and beautiful hardwood floors. A carved wood banister leads to four upstairs bedrooms with one converted into a bathroom.

A long lane leads to a gravel road that leads to the blacktop that leads to town. Not only are there snow days in the winter when the school bus can't come, but there are also mud days in the spring when the bus can't come either. On one of those days, Mom lets me go through a box of pictures she has of my family. She lets me pick out ones I want and later buys me a photo album for them. I'm so happy I finally have pictures of my brothers, Mom, Dad, and me. Now I have proof that we really were a family once, and I know what order the boys were standing in for our family picture.

A large pond not far from the house is loaded with frogs and all kinds of critters. There are chickens and hogs on this farm, too, but now Mom also cooks venison, squirrel, and many other unidentifiable things *he* hunts. A skinned squirrel looks like a human baby, so it's not very appetizing. I'm nearly ready to try Rocky Mountain oysters when I see a bucketful swinging through the kitchen, still whole, round, and bloody after the hogs were castrated—that ends that. And I never get close to trying frogs' legs after *he* goes gigging in the evenings and brings home a bagful.

He raises rabbits and skins them alive, saying it makes the meat taste better. I think *he's* a cruel son-of-a-bitch. Mom cries and turns up the radio volume so she can't hear the screams. I can't stand the pitiful screams either and wonder what *he'd* think if I could do that to *him*.

I think I'm trapped here, much like Mom, although she'll never admit it. I'm fifteen now and cringe at the many times I asked Ronnie and Kathy to move in with them but left because I hated it. If I hadn't been miserable missing Mom, maybe I could have made it work. But I was too miserable to try. Ronnie was a brother, not a mother, and probably didn't know how to help me. I cringe thinking about when I asked anyone, even Mary, although I felt welcome with her. Dorothy and Harold bought several bus tickets in the past, but I won't ask for more. Besides, they still buy all my school clothes, and Dorothy always includes a few dollars when she writes.

I have to make this work because I just want to be where Mom is, and I won't ask again to move in with anyone. I tell myself I can make it until I graduate and find a job. If *he* had just a little decency, Mom and I wouldn't be stuck and could be happy.

At three and a half years old, Stevie's an adorable little guy and so much fun to play with in the yard, where I hide behind huge trees and he tries to find me. One tree has a branch just the right height to boost Stevie up to sit.

"I kime a tee!" Stevie happily says.

I tickle him and hold him tight. After he stops giggling, I tell him not to tell Mom he climbed a tree.

"Otay," he tells me.

"Mama! I kime a tee," Stevie proudly tells Mom as soon as we're back inside.

"Sherrie!"

"Oh Mom, he just sat on a branch." She knows I won't let Stevie hurt himself.

There are lots of fun school activities now that I'm in high school, but most of the time, I can't attend because I have to babysit Stevie so they can go out to drink and fight. I try to convince them to let me take Stevie, too, because he would love to see a game. *He* never lets me. Occasionally, I'm allowed to attend an event after school. Transportation isn't a problem because one of my girlfriends' parents always offers to drive me home.

Mom tells me why she doesn't drive anymore when I ask. *He* wrecked *his* car coming home dead drunk one night, and *he* made Mom change places with *him. He* said *he* couldn't lose *his* license, or *he'd* lose *his* job. Because Mom was sitting in the driver's seat when the police came, they charged her with drunk driving, took her license, and she never drove again. She says making *him* do all the driving is one way to get even. *It also keeps you trapped*, I thought.

I'm allowed to escape the "always possible" fight and go to a sleepover on Halloween. After a party at school, dozens of kids form a human chain to weave through the entire little town, in and out of buildings and by houses. With lots of adults egging us on, we happily grab candy and snacks. When we pass someone's house, that kid drops out of the chain. Cheryl's the only one of our school group who lives in town, so several of us drop out with her. Her dad wears a scary mask and stalks us most of the evening, suddenly appearing and merrily scaring us to death. How fun to be normal.

On babysitting nights, Stevie stays up past bedtime to sneak snacks, play hide-and-seek, and watch TV with me. I like *The Andy Williams Show* when the Osmond Brothers are guests, and *The King Family Singers*. Stevie doesn't like either, so he turns off the TV. I turn it on then tackle and tickle him, but he wiggles out to turn it off again. When I turn it back on, the TV makes a poof sound and dies. Stevie turns pale; I feel sick. We hook pinkie fingers and swear not to tell them. At only four years old, Stevie understands the significance of why we have to do this. We don't tell so no one's beat or slapped. Mom and I faithfully watch *Dark Shadows*, about a compassionate vampire, on TV each afternoon, and I know we'll miss many episodes in the future.

⌒

After the school year is over, I help Mom pack the car the day before we are leaving on vacation to visit her sisters Anna and Mary in Oregon. We are all going, including *him*. On the way, we plan to stop in Wamsutter, Wyoming, for a surprise visit with Carson.

A pickup with my girlfriend Cheryl and most of the softball team in the back comes down the lane while we're working. They're here to ask if I can play because they're one player short and don't want to forfeit the game. I really want to go with them, but it turns out that I can't. I tell *him* and Mom the kids will wait until I finish my work, but *he* growls no. I tell *him* I'll be back as soon as the game's over, and *he* still growls no. *He* doesn't bother looking at me or the kids. *He* just growls. Mom goes into the house. The kids say it's okay and not to worry before they pile back in the pickup and leave.

What would it hurt for me to play a softball game? I wonder after they take off. For the rest of the afternoon, I stand around with nothing to do. It only takes so long to pack a car. *He's* such an asshole!

When we arrive in Wamsutter, Carson isn't there. We soon find out that he's in a hospital in Rawlings, Wyoming. A piece of oil rig machinery fell on his left foot, and his big toe was amputated. He's one surprised, happy guy when we walk into his hospital room. Soon after Carson's discharged, we head for Oregon.

We stay one night with Aunt Mary and Uncle Don in Zig Zag, which is the same as being home: I babysit Stevie so they can go out. It only takes until the second night before a fight breaks out and Mom shakes me awake, but this time, it's *him* against Aunt Mary. *He* says she started it, but I don't believe that. They've only just met.

He and Mom have graduated to whiskey and drink almost every weekday night now, along with weekends. Many times, I've watched *him* "slug" Mom's drink when *he* mixes it. *He* caught me watching once as *he* poured enough liquor into her glass for three drinks. *He* smirked at me because *he* knew I couldn't do anything about it—either way, Mom will lose. If I tell her, there'll be a fight. If I don't tell her, she'll be easier to beat up. I'm sure something like that happened with Aunt Mary, but we still leave in the middle of the night to stay with Anna and Ade in Portland. I expected a fight at Anna's house—not Aunt Mary's.

He stages *his* mean look, drinking at Anna's kitchen table. *He* tucks *his* head down, furrows *his* brow, and looks up through *his* eyebrows while *he* trashes Aunt Mary. When that doesn't get the desired response, *he* switches tactics and goes for sympathy. *He* can squeeze out a tear when *he* wants others to believe *he's* been wronged. When *he* does that with Anna, it works like a charm.

"It takes a real man to cry," Anna says.

I think it only takes a phony bastard.

On the way back to Illinois, we visit Gramma's grave in Burley, Idaho. It seems like I've lived two lifetimes since I saw her standing by our white fence, smiling at me.

I have the same circle of friends when I start tenth grade in Biggsville, and I'm looking forward to a fun year. If only there were no holidays. I hate them now because that's when it happens. Without fail, Mom's beaten just before, during, or directly after a holiday. When she fights back, she's beaten the worst. After getting in the middle of *his* many slugfests to make *him* stop hitting her, I go outside even if it's freezing cold and dark. Turning up the volume on the transistor radio Dorothy gave me, I walk the fields.

Mom's crying on the back steps when I return with my radio blaring late one evening. I've been gone much longer than usual. I turn down the volume and sit beside her.

"You were going to run away and changed your mind, didn't you," Mom says.

I'm ashamed she can read my mind so easily and knows I can even consider leaving her alone with *him*.

"There's no place to go," I shrug.

"I know," Mom says. She wipes her eyes, pats my knee, and goes back inside.

Everything would be okay if *he* just wouldn't hit her. I'd even try to like *him*. Dean and I could be best friends again, and I'd tell him to move back because it's okay now. Mom wouldn't get mad at *him* anymore because *he* doesn't hurt her anymore. I'd invite a girlfriend over to spend the night. Stevie would grow up in a normal home. If *he* just wouldn't hit her. When Mom calls *him* pitiful during a fight, I can count on not recognizing her face the next morning, and the sight makes me sick.

Mom hasn't had black eyes for a couple of months, and we're sitting at the kitchen table while Stevie plays on the floor. We each have a wet sponge to dampen glue on S&H green stamps and press them onto empty pages in the green stamp books. The stamps are a gimmick to encourage shoppers to patronize certain stores. The filled books are redeemed for all sorts of products like toys, kitchen gadgets, dishes, and furniture. A *Sperry and Hutchinson Idea Book* of merchandise available at redemption stores is open on the table. Several pages are dog-eared and, to me, sad. I know Mom will never save enough green stamps to trade for the pretty things she wants—things like she had when Dad, the boys, and I were her family.

"Why do you stay with *him*, Mom?"

"I've made my bed, now I'll lie in it. Besides, *he* has *his* good points."

She didn't elaborate, and I know better than to press the subject. We never mention it again. I don't think being a brutal tyrant is a good point, and I detest *him*. It's hard to reply when *he* speaks to me. It's hard to keep my face neutral and not show the total disgust I feel for *him*. I made up my mind long ago that if *he* ever came after me, I'd kill *him* or die trying. I'm not sure why, but *he* never turns on me even when I get in the middle of *him* beating

Mom. *He's* increasingly sarcastic and arrogant toward me but not so much *he* can't laugh it off.

I turn my little transistor radio on low every night after I go to bed. If it's late enough, I can tune into Chicago station WHB, the "World's Happiest Broadcasters." I fall asleep every night listening to Dottie West's "If You Go Away," Ronnie Dove's "Cry," and Jerry Vale's "Where Were You When I Needed You." I tell myself I can make it to graduation, get a job, and Mom and Stevie can live with me.

Then I think again how lucky *his* kids are because *he* left them. They're not watching *him* beat their mother regularly or her leaving them time after time to slip into an increasingly alcoholic world. But maybe their mother was like that, too, so she could endure *him*. Maybe they were slapped; maybe they saw those terrible things. I don't know. I hope she was happy after *he* left. I hope she stayed with her kids and raised them. And I hope they don't turn out like *him*.

17

"King of the Road"

ROGER MILLER

I can't believe *he's* allowing a slumber party for my sixteenth birthday! Because *he's* behaved *himself* during Dorothy and Harold's visits and with Carson, I convince myself *he* will this time too. I invite the best friends I've ever had: Debbie, Cheryl, Susie, and Betty Jo.

After *he* takes Mom out for the evening, I make hamburgers for our dinner. When Stevie's in bed, we start the party in earnest. Throwing sleeping bags, blankets, and pillows over the front room floor, we giggle, laugh, and talk about boys. We watch TV, eat snacks, play games, and talk about boys some more. The ones who've kissed a boy—really kissed a boy—talk about it while the rest groan with envy. After midnight, we drop off to sleep one by one. Soon after, the phone rings.

Susie's boyfriend's in the army and just returned for a surprise visit before shipping out to Vietnam, so her mom and boyfriend are coming to pick her up. Susie's so excited and dodges thrown pillows as we die with jealousy. A skiff of snow covers the yard by the time there's a knock, and Susie flies out the door and into the arms of her boyfriend. After they're gone, we fall asleep again, scattered over the floor.

Out of nowhere, Mom shakes me awake, telling me to get in the kitchen. Damn! I hate being shaken awake. It's happened a million times, and it's never good. I stumble to the kitchen with my heart in my mouth, trying to wake up to find *him* drinking and growling at the kitchen table. Mom sits down as *he* asks who'd been in the house after they left.

"No one."

"You're a goddamn liar! I'm not stupid!" I beg *him* to not wake up my friends.

"This is *my* house! Fuck your goddamn friends! Who's been here?"

"Just the girls *you* let me invite."

"There's a place for someone like you, ya know."

"What are *you* talking about?"

"You had fucking boys in here, that's what, tramp!"

"No, I didn't!"

"There's footprints in the snow. You had two boys in here!"

"Susie's mom came to pick her up at midnight."

"There's two sets of tracks!"

"It was only her mom and her boyfriend."

"See! I knew it!"

"Her mom was here! She went home with her mom because her boyfriend just came home on leave."

"Gimme her phone number! I'll prove you're a fucking liar!"

"It's two in the morning. Please wait."

"Get out of my sight, tramp!" *he* growls.

I grab my sleeping bag and tiptoe to a little storage room. I'm so ashamed. Debbie and Cheryl creep in to whisper they've gone upstairs and it's safe to go back to the front room.

He tells me to get up so *he* can take everyone home. Mom was going to make a big breakfast, but I bet that won't happen now. When I go upstairs to the bathroom, she's dressed and lying on her back across the bed with one arm over her eyes. Back downstairs, I sit next to my friends. They whisper they had fun. Breakfast isn't offered.

He drives with Mom and Stevie in front and the rest squished in back. It's very quiet until *he* cheerfully thanks each one for coming as *he* drops her off. I wish I could die. On the way home, I'm ignored when I ask if *he* still wants Susie's phone number. Like so many other things, this just never happened. I know I'll never invite a girlfriend over again, but I didn't realize it'll be for a completely different reason.

I'm babysitting as usual the following Saturday night. Stevie's in bed, and I'm watching TV when I light one of *his* cigarettes. *He* always leaves a partial pack laying around, and I usually have one on Saturday nights. Suddenly, the front door flies open, and in *he* walks. It scares me to death because we never use that door. I stamp the cigarette out, but I know *he* saw it. I wonder why Mom didn't come in. *He* doesn't say a word or look at me as *he* stalks by me and into the kitchen. *He* stays only a second then leaves using the front door again. I didn't see headlights coming down the lane, and I don't know why they came back. At least when *he* cusses me out this time, it won't be in front of anyone.

The next morning's ominously quiet when I go downstairs. I know I'm in for it. The subject is what's to be done with me, how I should be put in that place for girls like me, how disgusting I am, and how dare I take *his* cigarettes after all *he's* done for me.

He's done absolutely nothing for me except make life hell. Dorothy still buys all my school clothes and sends money for things I need—not *him*. I've always worked in the school cafeteria for a free lunch both times I've lived with them, and I think all the babysitting I do covers what I eat for dinner and a weekly cigarette.

But the only thing to do is put me on a bus to my dad. I don't know how it'd been arranged, but I'm being kicked out. And I can't go to Dorothy and Harold's because *he* won't let me use the phone to call them.

In bed listening to my radio, I finally understand. *He* drove down the lane with the headlights off or hadn't left at all. I wonder how long *he* waited, peeking in the window, before I lit a cigarette. By smoking it, I gave them what they want. It turns out that they really want rid of me, too, because for the first time, they buy the bus ticket. They won't let me call my friends to say goodbye. I wonder who'll watch Stevie so they can go out, drink, and fight. I wish I could take Stevie with me.

I wonder why Mom turned against me. I know she's ashamed for me to see what she puts up with to stay with *him*. She still cries over Gramma and loathes Del. How alike we are and how very different.

She cries and hugs me. She's kicking me out and crying because I'm leaving. I get on the bus and know I'll never again live with her. I wonder if I'll ever see her again. And I hate myself for caring.

Carson lives in Las Vegas now, so he picks me up three days and two nights later at the bus station to drive me across the California border to Mountain Pass, where Dad and Claribel live. Dean stays with them on weekends and holidays, which is the only good thing about coming here. During the week, he boards with a lady in Barstow, California, to attend school. The state pays for boarding because it's such a long bus ride to Las Vegas for school. I figure I'll be able to survive weekends and holidays in Claribel's house because the rest of the time, I'll board in Barstow—hopefully with Dean.

Claribel has different ideas. I have to stay at her house and take the long ride to school. When I ask Dad if I can go to Barstow with Dean, he says no. I know he won't cross Claribel. She still really dislikes me; I still don't know why. I'm completely stuck now. Once again, as much as I want to be considered, I'm not.

Dad wakes me each school morning at 4:30 a.m. Claribel's still asleep when we leave at 5 a.m. He drives sixteen miles to State Line and drops me off at the Tower Club Casino then drives back to work at the Mountain Pass mine. A woman and her daughter pick me up and drive twelve miles to Jean, Nevada, where kids wait in a café for a school bus. The bus takes us forty-one miles to an intersection outside Blue Diamond, Nevada, and drops us off—whether it's raining or blowing a million miles an hour—in the dark in the middle of nowhere next to a stop sign to wait for the next school bus. This one delivers us twenty-three miles later to Las Vegas High School around 8 a.m., just before the bell rings. I've traveled ninety-two miles to get to school Monday morning, and I'll travel 920 miles by the time I'm back at Mountain Pass after school on Friday. I hate it. It would only be 194 miles round-trip to Barstow once a week.

The best part of a school day is lunchtime, when a short walk puts me on the most glamorous street in the world: Fremont Street—where I'm putting one foot in front of the other, walking up one side and down the other, trying to make sense of what has happened in my life again. Why can't Dad stand up to Claribel? And what about Mom? Why did she up and leave us? Why did they use the first reason they could find to kick me out? I still love Mom and still don't know why I do, but I hate *him* with every part of me. I can't wait until I'm old enough to live on my own away from everyone.

But even in my most earnest moments of freedom fighting, I still see the boys and me walking the same street when we were little, visiting Aunt Ruth. We stand in a casino's air-conditioned entryway to get out of the desert heat only to be immediately ordered out by security guards because we're kids. Then we scour the shops to cool off. I'd gladly give anything to be with Mom, Dad, and the boys again.

I'm a numb, silent loner at school again. I don't have the will to try and be normal anymore. After school, I make my way back to the Tower Club by the same routes. If Dad isn't there soon after I arrive, I wait in the café, knowing

Claribel will be coming with him, which she usually does. I have to wait until she finishes drinking and gambling before we can leave. Dad's ready long before she is because we're the only two who get up so early, but we're rarely home before 10 or 11 p.m. The only redeeming factors are a pool table and a jukebox. After I finish my homework at a booth in the café, I play "Theme from a Summer Place" on the jukebox, and I play pool. I play every night, and I'm getting pretty good at it. After Dad buys me something for dinner, he gives me pointers on the game. I know he enjoys playing with me, which he does until Claribel complains.

I clean Claribel's house and do laundry every weekend because her back hurts. She can crawl on and off a bar stool multiple times all night, every night, but she can't clean or do laundry. I wonder who did it before I had to come here. It's spring, so there's lots of extras that need to be done: wash the walls, treat the wood paneling, wash the ceilings, and shampoo the carpet. Dad slips me a few dollars each weekend when I'm finished so I'll have money to play pool and the jukebox before he comes to get me.

Dean found a job in Barstow, rarely coming home now, and I'm so glad when he does. The next time he makes it, we drive to Las Vegas to see Aunt Ruth and Uncle Woody. They had met and married in Vegas after Mom left us, so I've never met him. It's wonderful to see my favorite Ant Root again and meet Uncle Woody. We spend the afternoon talking and laughing without ever mentioning the elephant in the room: Mom. Long before I'm ready, it's time to drive back to the Mountain.

On the way, I beg Dean to help talk Dad into letting me go to Barstow with him, but he won't. He says Dad isn't the problem, and Claribel will never let me. Apparently, she enjoys making my life hell. We don't decide our differences of opinions with slugs anymore, although we regularly strike sparks off each other. But I know Dean's usually right, and I trust him. He tells me to be patient; I last two months.

One morning, I pack a pair of jeans, shirt, and tennis shoes in a sack. When the bus drops me off at Las Vegas High School, I walk across the street to a service station bathroom and change out of my school clothes. Then I walk across town to Aunt Ruth's house. She's surprised and happy to see me, and we have another great time talking before she drives me to school in time for the rides back to Mountain Pass.

Soon after, Dean tells me that he asked Aunt Ruth if I can stay with her. He understands how miserable the drive to school is, and he knows how much Claribel dislikes me because he hears it all the time. He lived with Aunt Ruth for a while and figures it's the best place for me. Aunt Ruth tells Dean, "Of course she can stay here!"

The next school morning, another sack is loaded with a change of clothes, and I use the same service station bathroom. Then I make the long walk to Aunt Ruth's house to stay this time. The following weekend, a friend of Dean's drives me to Mountain Pass for my things. I'm relieved no one's home because I've developed a loathing for confrontations—even quiet ones. After throwing my things together, I put the house key on the kitchen table and leave.

Finishing the last few weeks of my sophomore year at Las Vegas High with Aunt Ruth and Uncle Woody, I'm so thankful to be living here.

18

"Those Lazy, Hazy, Crazy Days of Summer"

NAT KING COLE

Lake Mead is smooth as glass with the early morning sun peeking over the distant mountain range. The air's motionless, and the only sounds are the hum of an inboard-outboard motor, water lapping around me, and my heart pounding in my ears. I shiver with cold and fear as the ski rope pops between the handle I'm holding and the boat. I always experience a moment of fear just before the boat pulls me upright, but the feeling quickly turns to exhilaration as I fly on my slalom ski, crisscrossing in and out of the boat's wake in excess of 60 mph. I love it.

A bit of fear remains on a calm morning like this one. When the lake's smooth, I usually take the worst tumbles, flying head-over-heels before I can roll into a ball and sink in the water. The lake was rough and rolling with whitecaps during the two weekends Uncle Woody patiently spent teaching me to water ski. He insisted I learn on a slalom ski because he and Aunt Ruth had been through the agony of learning on two skis. Now, try as he might, Uncle Woody can't dunk me when the water's rough, no matter how many contortions he puts the boat and me through.

When the boat suddenly slows, I gather up ski rope hand over hand, keeping it taunt to avoid slowly sinking in the water then let the rope out as he speeds up. When he drives in a fast, continuous "S" pattern, I've learned to jump the wake higher and turn on a dime, ready for the next wake jump.

Sitting on the lookout seat facing the rear of the boat, Aunt Ruth cheers me on. Occasionally, I see her chewing out Uncle Woody for going too fast or turning so sharp. Uncle Woody looks my way, holding out his hand palm up, asking how I like the speed. I reply with a thumb up, then I'm flying again.

My undoing is my own fault. Uncle Woody deposits me close to shore, but I swing too far out on the rope before dropping the handle. The skeg digs into the rocks and mud just beneath the water's surface, causing me to fly out of my ski and land in a patch of scrub brush several feet from the water's edge. Aunt Ruth spends quite some time picking stickers out of my backside and lecturing on skiing safety. Then Aunt Ruth brings Uncle Woody in too close to shore.

"Oh shit!" Aunt Ruth says.

But it's too late to correct her mistake, and Uncle Woody rolls down the beach before he can stop himself. Aunt Ruth puts the boat in neutral and floats offshore.

"We've got to make sure he's okay," she says to no one in particular. "He's standing up; evidently, he's not hurt. I can't keep us out here forever."

Auth Ruth talks herself and the boat onto the beach, where Uncle Woody's standing with one hand on his hip and the other knocking dirt out of his ears as he waits for her. But it's not his nature to be mad, so we're still taking turns skiing and laughing about Aunt Ruth trying to do him in again.

We start skiing the first weekend of April and continue well into October, depending on the weather. Aunt Ruth makes fried chicken and potato salad and fills coolers with the food, pop, beer, coffee cakes, and snacks. Most of the time, we leave for the lake as soon as Uncle Woody's home from work on Friday and won't return until Sunday evening or later if there's a holiday.

On the last ski weekend of the season, Aunt Ruth and I decide not to swim because the water's way too cold. As for skiing, we've perfected a dry start by standing in a foot of water with the left knee bent and holding the tow handle with both hands. The right foot is secured in the ski with the top half of the ski hovering just up above water. That way, we start a tow without being immersed in freezing water up to our necks. The trick is not to fall: we want to ski—not swim.

"Chickens," Uncle Woody says.

"Oh, go jump in the lake," Aunt Ruth replies, and he does.

Uncle Woody dives from the boat and says the water feels perfect, convincing us to follow him. We dive into freezing water and straight up again to climb the ladder and wrap up in towels while he chuckles.

Uncle Woody's a sweetheart of a man. Tall, gentle, and handsome, he's very much in love with Aunt Ruth. They're good together, and they take care of each other, even though they drink too much. Everyone drinks too much. The absolutely astonishing fact to me about Uncle Woody is that he was born and raised in El Dorado Springs, Missouri, just like *him* and Dad. Two outta three ain't bad, I guess.

Just like Mom, Aunt Ruth keeps her home immaculately clean and cries when she talks about her childhood. She tells me how she'd been told her dad died in the mines when she was three years old, only to find out Gramma left him after he raped my mom when she was nine years old. That's one story I'd never heard.

I wonder if Mom's crying jags and acceptance of brutal beatings are remnants of that rape. It's horrible it happened, but it doesn't explain the similarities between Mom and Gramma's alternating acceptance then rejection of their children: they turn their love on and off on a dime so the kids never know where they stand with their mother. And it doesn't explain how a mother can willingly abandon her children or leave a husband who took such good care of her. It doesn't answer the question I need answered: How could she just up and leave us or, for that matter, kick me out?

Aunt Ruth and I talk about Mom sometimes. I know Mom doesn't want me telling things that happened while I lived with them, and I don't. I don't think anyone would believe me anyway. Aunt Ruth and I actually have a lot in common. She loves Mom, too, and had similar experiences of alternating acceptance and rejection with her and Gramma.

"But when I needed someone, your Mom was always there for me," Aunt Ruth says.

Mom has an uncanny knack for calling at just the time when Aunt Ruth's sick or depressed and needs to talk. Time after time when things weren't going right, Mom called. "Hi, Ruth. Are you okay? What's wrong?"

I ask Aunt Ruth why I still love Mom after all that's happened.

"Because no one can help but love her. It's who she is."

Aunt Ruth's my closest connection to Mom. And she has an emotional connection to Mom, too, because Mom basically raised her, even though Mom's only six years older. I've known since I was little that Aunt Ruth was Mom's favorite sister and vice versa. And she's always been my favorite aunt. They were close until Mom abandoned her family. Aunt Ruth says they rarely talk now, and she misses her too. It's a relief to finally talk to someone about Mom, although I don't very often. I only do when I'm certain I won't cry, which helps Aunt Ruth not cry too.

Aunt Ruth first came to Las Vegas in the mid-1950s between moves to Kansas City, Missouri, and Knoxville, Tennessee. She worked as a shill for a mob-owned casino then as a cocktail waitress, before deciding to move on again in another effort to outrun her unhappiness. When she came back in 1960, Aunt Ruth ended up staying for over a decade. She's a strikingly attractive woman and posed for several publicity photos for casinos. Aunt Ruth joined a union and started working cocktails at the Nevada Club on Fremont Street. She worked at most of the casinos downtown, including the Fremont, Mint, Golden Nugget, Four Queens, and the Pioneer Club.

Aunt Ruth saw firsthand what casinos would do to keep high rollers gambling. In the wee hours of the morning, rich women hit the slots, dressed only in robes, gowns, and slippers. They wet themselves rather than lose the machine they were playing then summoned a cocktail waitress to have someone mop up the floor. If a male high roller hit big and left, the boss sent several girls to entice him back to play, and hopefully lose, to the casino where he had just won.

It was easy to lose and find a job in those days. If Aunt Ruth was miffed for some reason, she walked across the street to a new job. She worked the showrooms, craps and 21 pits, slots, and poker rooms. She averaged only a few dollars a day in salary but usually made around five hundred dollars in tips during a shift.

She also worked for many Strip hotels like The Desert Inn, Tropicana, Frontier, Riviera, Flamingo, and Stardust. Many times, a pit boss asked her to look out for dealers she thought might be cheating. This was before eye-in-the-sky technology that used cameras aimed at the casino's action and watched twenty-four hours a day for signs of anyone cheating. Dealers honed many ways to steal chips, and the pit bosses knew it. One way to combat the problem was enlisting the help of cocktail waitresses. Aunt Ruth knew what happened to dealers when caught, so she always maintained she had been too busy to notice anything. In truth, she never looked.

"The less I knew, the safer I was," Aunt Ruth told me.

When caught in the act, a dealer was walked to a back room by the pit boss and security guards. He might be warned once, depending on the circumstances, but he usually never worked again and was lucky if he ended up in a hospital—as opposed to dead in the desert—with arms and legs broken, kneecaps smashed, nose broken, and a concussion thrown in for good measure.

Each hotel had their own call girls: high-class prostitutes. Aunt Ruth was approached to be a call girl, a showgirl, and an escort, which equated to a good-looking broad on the arm of a mobster sent to Vegas to cool off (hide out) because he was too hot (wanted by police) in another state, but she always declined the offers. Emotionally, Aunt Ruth couldn't have handled those jobs. She already had three sets of scars on her wrists from suicide attempts, and she figured she was earning enough money legally.

Call girls earned two to five grand a night, and escorts earned on average fifteen hundred. Trouble was that catering to mob clientele, they could end up dead in the desolate desert surrounding Las Vegas for hearing too much information after their date drank too much. Hotel employees knew about the latest body in the desert through the grapevine long before it hit the newspapers—if it ever did. The employees knew to keep their mouths shut.

Aunt Ruth was leery of all casino bosses because of their mob connections. She was scared to say yes or no when a boss approached her for a date or asked her to change professions. If she said yes, she could end up in the desert. And she was always afraid that when she said no, she might end up there anyway. Fortunately, each time she was asked and refused, the boss asking was gracious and the subject dropped.

However, one Italian pit boss told Aunt Ruth he was infatuated with her, and she got worried when he wouldn't stop hitting on her. She told her troubles to another waitress while on break one day.

"Oh, don't worry, honey. You don't have to go out with him if you don't want to," the waitress replied.

The casino grapevine was always on top of any new story. The next day, Aunt Ruth learned the waitress she had poured out her troubles to was the

Italian pit boss's mistress. Aunt Ruth walked across the street to a new job that day.

My aunt was a romantic at heart and knew someday her Prince Charming would come along. Eventually Uncle Woody did, but not before she married a few too many frogs, although she only gave me a mischievous smile when I asked how many.

One marriage ended abruptly after he became violent and boxed her ears, rupturing both eardrums. Aunt Ruth was hurt and angry, and figured she could play the mob game like everyone else. You could get anything you wanted in Vegas, including illegal drugs or phone numbers of hit men. Aunt Ruth called a number she'd been given.

"Yeah?" a voice answers.

"I understand for five hundred dollars you'll take care of someone?" Aunt Ruth asked, hiding her anxiety.

"How did ya get this number?"

Aunt Ruth replied with a code word she'd been instructed to use.

"Okay. What's his name, lady?"

Aunt Ruth replied with the name of her soon-to-be ex-husband.

"It'll be taken care of," the voice said.

"Well ... what'll you do?"

"You don't need to know."

"I just want him beat up."

"We don't do that, lady. He'll disappear."

"I'm not sure ... I don't want that."

"Look, lady, before you call again, make damn sure you know what you want. This ain't a game," the voice growled.

"Maybe I'd better think about it some more ..."

"Take the rest of your life, lady!" the cold voice said, slamming the receiver.

Aunt Ruth never called back.

⌒

Aunt Ruth and I watch the afternoon movie hosted by local Gus Giuffre. He makes us want to watch the movie even when it's really bad. I like catching the bus downtown to the El Portal theater on Fremont for a movie. If Aunt Ruth wants to see it, too, she drives while we listen to local Red McIlvaine on the car radio. We laugh when he says "Las Vegas" because he makes it sound like "Lost Wages."

You never know who you might see shopping in mob-controlled Vegas, but what you won't see is gang violence, prostitutes, and drug dealers hanging out on corners or gun violence because the mob controls those things. We usually shop at Wonder World, Vegas Village, or Maryland Square, where we've had conversations with entertainers Jim Nabors and Jerry Vale—two of my many favorite singers. But for my first Strip show, Aunt Ruth takes me shopping at Ronzone's for my first grownup dress and high heels.

I'm still sixteen when Aunt Ruth and Uncle Woody take me to the Sahara showroom to see the Smothers Brothers and Vikki Carr opening with her beautiful voice. I enjoy every minute and feel like a grownup, even though high heels are murder. Give me rubber flip-flops any day.

Must-sees on TV are *I Spy*, *Hee Haw*, *The Flip Wilson Show*, *Rowan and Martin's Laugh-In*, and *The Smothers Brothers Comedy Hour*. "Here come da judge," and "Mom always liked you best!" become staple retorts in Aunt Ruth's house. There is a lightness of living here with Aunt Ruth and Uncle Woody that I have rarely experienced. I love it.

Dean visits regularly, and Carson still lives in Vegas too. One evening, someone knocks at the door while we're watching TV. When Aunt Ruth opens the door, Carson walks in, smiling, as Aunt Ruth gasps and nearly faints. Carson laughs and says the other guy looks a lot worse. His nose is broken, and there's cuts, bumps, and bruises on his face and arms from a pool cue fight at some bar. The next time he visits, Carson's scabbed up over most of his body from road burns after crashing his motorcycle. But he never loses his smile.

Dean says I can take his car out for a while one Saturday evening when he's visiting. "The only thing you can't do is cruise Fremont Street because my car will overheat," he tells me. When Dean tells me not to do something, it's a dare to do it at seventeen, so I pick up a girlfriend to cruise Fremont Street.

The blinking, pulsating neon against a backdrop of dark, gray-blue sky is awesome for a teenager driving up and down Glitter Gulch. This is the place for teenagers to hang out at night because cruising Fremont is about the only activity we can do legally, besides a movie or bowling. We can't stick even a toe inside a casino.

We cross Main Street at the west end of Fremont and follow a loop through a little park in front of the Train Depot—owned by the Union Pacific Railroad—where the Plaza Hotel sits now. The loop puts us back on Fremont heading east, where we turn around again at The Blue Onion drive-in. The street is bumper to bumper with rowdy teenagers shouting. When I see steam escaping from the hood after several trips, I pull into the loop by a water faucet and wait while some kids finish filling their steaming radiator. I didn't tell Dean about it for years, but I did tell Aunt Ruth. She laughed and said she was going to blackmail me.

When Dean visits, we constantly tease Aunt Ruth, calling her our old teenager aunt. She's only twenty years older than me, and she does act like a happy teenager; however, over time, I recognize the consequences of her early years always churning just below the surface. But for now in the safety of her presence, Dean and I are learning how to be friends again.

As time goes on, wherever Dean is I usually end up, and wherever I am Dean isn't too far behind. In the meantime, though, he joins the army, and I know I won't see him for a long time. I can't keep anyone together; someone's always leaving. Dean's gone, and Carson comes by to tell us he's moving to California.

I start my junior year at Western High School and complete it at Western High School. It's the first time I've gone to one school for an entire school year without moving.

Just before my senior year starts, I decide to move.

19

"The Key's in the Mailbox"

FREDDIE HART

Dorothy and Harold sent an airplane ticket for me to visit them in Indianapolis during summer break. I'm so glad Ponchita still remembers me. Dorothy listens to my adventures about trying to find a job in Vegas and laughs when I had the audacity to apply at McDonald's because they hire only male workers. A man took my application, looked at me like I had three eyes, and threw it in the trash as I walked out. I had submitted applications to Wonder World (known as WOW), Skaggs Drug, and Dairy Queen without a single bite.

Dorothy says I'll be able to find a job here if I want to stay with them for my senior year. That and the thought of being a day's drive from Mom are tempting. I want to earn my own way, and I want Mom to come to my graduation after I convince myself that she would come. Only two older brothers out of four graduated: Ronnie and Dean, and she's only been to Ronnie's. Maybe she'll come to mine. I keep Dorothy's offer in mind and have great times on my vacation. One of those great times was illegal.

Two of Dorothy's nieces are twenty-one to my seventeen and a half. They loan me clothes, put makeup on my face, and assure me that I look at least twenty-two years old. Then we go out to a popular nightspot. Using one of their IDs that states I'm twenty-one with brown hair and brown eyes—I have blond hair and blue eyes—I successfully enter the nightclub, order my first illegal drink, and watch Little Richard sing and play the piano. It's amazing. I'm so ready to be grown up.

After a wonderful visit and shopping spree with Dorothy, it's time to head back to Vegas. Dorothy lets me trade the plane ticket in for a bus ticket so I can go through Illinois to see Mom. Being this close, I have to see her—it's my fix I can't live without.

Cheryl picks me up to stay with her in Biggsville, and several other Union High School friends come over for a great time hanging out and catching up. The next morning, Cheryl drops me off at Mom's. I didn't tell her I was coming because we haven't talked since they kicked me out seventeen months earlier. I arrive after *he's* gone to work, and Cheryl will pick me up in time to guarantee I'm gone before *he's* back.

I almost faint when Dean answers the door. He's on leave before attending Officers Candidate School in Baltimore, Maryland. We're flabbergasted we're both at Mom's at the same time, and so is Mom. The day's a wonderful visit for each of us.

It's curious, my relationship with Dean. We genuinely like and trust each other, and we always have, even when we were very little. But after Mom left, we couldn't handle being *us* anymore because she had been such an important part of that. Of all the things I still regret about those times, I regret most of all that Dean and I had to stay emotionally and physically apart to cope with each day. But now, as the years roll by, we're getting our *us* back again each time we're together. We never call and rarely write, and we never know when we'll see each other again—we're just confident that we will. And when we do, we strike sparks off each other as always and torment each other every chance we get.

After the visit with Mom, Stevie, and Dean, Cheryl picks me up before *he* gets home then takes me to visit Debbie, another friend from school, and her family. Her dad announces it's been too long since their last vacation and decides on the spot to drive me home rather than have me take the bus. He says it's a good opportunity to see a section of the country they've never seen. Debbie and I are beyond excited. I cash in my ticket and contribute to trip expenses when her dad will let me. We drive to Vegas with lots of sightseeing and fun along the way.

Aunt Ruth's sad when I decide to take Dorothy and Harold's offer and move to Indianapolis before school starts. But she understands the wanderlust because she's had it most of her life too. I'm in Indianapolis for my senior year two weeks before school starts, and I'm kicked out before the first day. The Indianapolis School District won't let me attend because I'm not living with my parents or a legal guardian—a problem I didn't realize existed because it never happened in Tucson or Las Vegas. Dorothy and Harold rescue me again, and I start school two weeks late after they become my legal guardians.

After my last early-afternoon class, I catch a city bus downtown to Block's Department Store and work until 9 p.m. My first job is transferring sales data to computer cards as a keypunch operator. The keypunch machine cuts small holes in the cards as I type. Later, the cards are fed into a mainframe computer that transfers the data into the unreal world of computer memory and creative accounting.

Since I work a full day on Saturdays, I don't work on Friday nights: the best TV night of the week with *The Tom Jones Show*. Dorothy laughs when I complain that he's only filmed from the waist up as he wiggles a dance routine during a song. Dorothy and Harold have a color TV, but most shows are still in black and white. The *TV Guide* has a (C) listed by the title if it'll be broadcast in color, and Tom Jones has it!

Shortly after I started working, I wrote Mom, telling her where I'm living and that I'd like to send her and Stevie a bus ticket to attend my graduation the following spring. We had such a good visit when Dean and I showed up I thought she might actually want to come. After a long time, I receive an envelope postmarked from Zig Zag, Oregon, and immediately know the answer.

I learn over time *he* had beaten Mom so viciously after Dean and I visited that she finally called the police. They hauled *him* to jail because it was plain what *he'd* done to her, but she still didn't try to leave *him*. When *he* was released three days later, they sold almost everything and moved to Oregon about the same time I was moving to Indianapolis. I wonder why I keep trying. I don't understand why I care.

I work at Block's with Dorothy's great-niece Judy. When I tell her about the scenic beauty of the West, she's interested in seeing it. Since she has a car, we plan a trip for the following summer after my graduation. During the school year, the trip evolves into a move for me—after the rain and humidity in the summer and the freezing rain and snow in the winter. I'm a desert rat and can't wait to get back. Saving money for the trip, I also give Dorothy money every payday to pay back the cost of the guardianship. I'll never be able to pay back all I owe them. The debt goes far beyond money.

After roaming through seventeen moves with my mother then wandering through eighteen moves without her, I'm eighteen when I finally graduate with honors from high school. Crying and hugging Dorothy and Harold, I try to thank them again for everything they've done for me. I know I never would have finished grade school, let alone high school, if it hadn't been for them, and I tell them I'll never forget.

As an adult, I've often wondered what would have happened to me without Dorothy, Dorothy and Harold. I don't think I was brave enough as a kid to be really bad—probably just brave enough to get into really bad trouble. They rescued me in every way.

A few days after graduation, I head back to Vegas with Judy by way of national parks, historic places, the Pacific Ocean, marijuana haunts, and naked men. We visit Mt. Rushmore in South Dakota, followed by Yellowstone National Park, where we watch Old Faithful erupt. We stand with one foot in Montana and the other in Wyoming. In Virginia City, Nevada, I find myself still looking for the silver dollar I'd lost under the wood-planked sidewalks while chasing my brothers around town. I find the old Opera House but can't find the loose boards Dean and I pulled up to snoop around in that grand old place.

My oldest brother, Ronnie, and his family are in Livermore, California, not far from San Francisco, so I call him when we arrive in that part of the world. The next day, we picnic at the ocean with Ronnie and his kids. In all my travels, this is the first time I've seen an ocean. Ronnie warns me to keep my mouth shut when I run into the water, but I'm laughing from the beauty of it all and promptly gulp a mouthful of liquid fishy salt.

After leaving Ronnie's town, sporting black and blue from trying to surf, we drive to San Francisco to walk around Haight-Ashbury, seeing long-haired hippies stoned on marijuana. When we find Carson in Ventura, California, he gives us a ride on his Harley-Davidson Sportster motorcycle.

It's good to see Ronnie and Carson, although it didn't happen often after the turmoil of the Tucson years. I think because of my graduation visit with them both, I'll see much more of them over time, and I'm glad when I do.

The graduation trip continues heading to Los Angeles, California, to walk up and down Hollywood and Vine and attend the Aquarius Theater's production of *Hair*. We haven't had much sleep in the last several days, and I nod off during the performance. The performers wake me, dashing and singing through the audience with some jumping from seat to seat over the heads of the audience. And the cast had disrobed during my nap. My first glimpse of a grown male's penis dangles above my head for a split second, then I'm wide awake. After we hit Las Vegas, Judy spends the night at Aunt Ruth's before heading home to Indianapolis.

Back at Aunt Ruth and Uncle Woody's, I barely survive the pain of finally being old enough but too broke to be independent. I find a job as a service dispatcher at a Chevrolet dealership, where I clear next to nothing working ten hours a day, five days a week. I start off hitchhiking the long way to and from work before an employee lets me catch rides with him. Watching Neil Armstrong, I figure I should be able to buy a car if someone can walk on the moon.

After I save up a small down payment, Uncle Woody helps me find a dependable car I can afford and cosigns the loan so I can qualify. I finally have what I've wanted for so long: a car and freedom, although it doesn't take long to realize I'm a slave to car payments. But for now, I'm so excited and have such a stomachache, Uncle Woody has to drive the car home for me. My first road trip is to Tucson for a weekend visit with Dorothy and Harold. They moved back shortly after I graduated and moved to Vegas. They were over freezing winters too.

After a few months, I come down from the dispatch tower at the dealership to be a service secretary and receive a ten-cents-an-hour raise. Soon after, I find out the guy who walked up the tower to do the exact same job started at fifty cents an hour more than I made when I walked down—just because he's a man. That's my initiation into sex-related job discrimination that they now say is controlled by laws but has existed to some degree in every job I've ever had. The choice has always been clear: complain or keep my job until I find a new one.

A transmission mechanic at work asks me out, and we date for several months. I am secretly hoping he'll ask me to marry him because I'm infatuated with him and I think it's reciprocated. He even takes me to his mother's house for introductions and dinner, which I think goes very well, although I have nothing to compare it with.

One Monday morning, the service manager makes a strange comment.

"You should start dating the body shop tech," he says. "I think he likes you."

"Why? You know who I'm dating."

"He just married the front office manager."

I'm stunned and hurt. We had a date the previous week; apparently, the last one. He hadn't said a word about dating anyone else or getting engaged. I guess the dinner with his mother had been an audition, and I hadn't done as well as I thought.

I find a better-paying job at Central Telephone Company on Fifth and Fremont Streets as an information, then long-distance, then rate-and-route operator. Lunchtime's great because just a short walk to Fremont Street puts me in Woolworth's for fun shopping.

Everyone except me calls their mother on Mother's Day, so no one's allowed the day off. The huge room is packed with operators at every station, constantly lit up with calls. We rotate frequently so the employees can visit a large buffet table stacked high with every kind of meat, side dish, and dessert.

When you call information or dial zero for an operator, a live person in the same vicinity you're calling from answers. A human being is on the other end of your phone to answer questions, and oh! the questions I'm asked.

"Which zero do I use? The one after the nine or next to the N?" "What day is it?" "Is it morning or night?" "What's Maxine's number?"

Maxine's is a gay bar on Nellis Boulevard that doesn't have a telephone. I receive dozens of calls for the number, and no one ever believes me when I say they don't have a phone. I'm cussed out, cried to, and bribed for Maxine's telephone number.

At this time, long-distance calls can't be placed from Las Vegas hotels. A hotel operator patches the guest through to a Centel operator to complete the call but first provides pertinent information: name of guest, number to be called, and payment method. She tells me (if the guest's an entertainer or celebrity) what their condition is (drunk or sober) and what their mood is, relative to their level of sobriety. One time, I'm warned with a "Watch out!" then royally cussed out by a male entertainer for no reason other than he's obnoxious whether he's drunk or sober. On another occasion, I'm asked what being a telephone operator is like with genuine interest by a female singer.

I'm working at Centel when the *Jerry Lewis Labor Day Telethon* is televised live jointly between New York City and Las Vegas for the first time. Jerry Lewis is in New York, and Frank Sinatra is in Vegas. The hotel petitions Centel for operators to work the phones during the telethon. We'll work for free, of course, but the bait is we'll be on national television during the Vegas segments. Tables and chairs are just being delivered when I arrive, and Ed Sullivan often comes in to check on the progress and talk with us. When I mention to a man who is hooking up phones that I can't wait to see Sinatra sing, he starts laughing.

"You won't see him tonight. And if you do, you'll wish you hadn't," he adds with a chuckle.

"Why? He's supposed to host this."

"You've been sitting here too long. Frankie got drunk and threw a cart through the front door when security tried to calm him down. He won't be hosting anything."

When Jerry Lewis starts talking up Vegas from New York, our phones start ringing and don't stop. Hotel honchos walk around, telling us to answer calls and get information faster so we'll look good on national television. After about an hour, a honcho tells us to take a quick break. We had just left our seats when a few barely-dressed-to-the-hilt showgirls walk in to take them. As cameras pan the showgirls making a pretense of answering phones, I watch an overhead screen with Jerry telling the audience that unfortunately, Frank came down with a flu bug and won't be able to appear tonight in fabulous Las

Vegas. I don't know who finished taking calls for the telethon after most of us decide we don't need this abuse and leave.

I'm happy to go water skiing again with Aunt Ruth and Uncle Woody, but now that I'm nineteen going on twenty-one, I can get away with other activities like going out to dance. I never meet anyone who can dance half as good as Dad, but it's fun trying. Aunt Ruth and Uncle Woody like to dance, too, so we regularly go to the Saddle Club on Boulder Highway or the Nashville Nevada Club or the Silver Dollar on East Fremont to dance until the wee hours.

When Dean visits, Aunt Ruth puts a stack of albums on the record player, and we drink, dance, and cut up on the patio. For dinner, Uncle Woody yells, "I'll buy if you'll fly!" then Dean's on his way to Taco Bell for tacos and McDonald's for french fries because their fries are the best anywhere.

I have a job and a car, and I've waited nearly half my life to be on my own. It's time, so I move into a tiny apartment with a girlfriend. Even though I can barely make the rent and car payment, I'm on my own where I want to be. One of the first things I do is invite Aunt Ruth and Uncle Woody to dinner, even though I haven't had any practice cooking any kind of meal. By the time they arrive, I'm a mess.

"Oh! Calm down, kid! I'm your Ant Root, after all!"

The cheap wine I serve helps make the meal taste better, although they both say it's a wonderful dinner. Good food or not, we have a great time during my very first dinner party, and afterward, we're off to Nashville Nevada for dancing until the wee hours.

Shortly after the dinner party, my roommate Donna and I are on our way across town to celebrate her birthday at her parents' house. A police officer is standing in the middle of Owens, stopping traffic from continuing west to Vegas Drive. He's pointing his rifle toward J Street, indicating we have to make a right turn. Seeing flames against the night sky up ahead, we figure that's the reason for the detour. I turn onto J Street as directed, and very soon, all hell breaks loose. I don't know where the cars ahead of me or behind me go, but they're gone. Just half a block off the main drag puts us in a different world. It's ominously quiet, yet the area is teeming with black people. As I slow down to turn right and work my way back to Owens, Donna screams.

"Here they come!"

Dozens of black kids on my left are running toward us.

"Oh, they're just little kids."

I turn the steering wheel to the right with one hand and roll up my door window with the other. That's my last clear thought for several hours. Luckily, the baseball-size rock that smashes the window and my forehead makes me fall to the right as I hold the steering wheel, which completes the right-hand turn. I momentarily black out, but Donna's screams bring me back. I floor the gas pedal and yell for her to steer because I can't see a thing from the dripping blood and dizziness. It sounds like bombs are dropping on my car, and glass is flying everywhere.

Somehow, we make it out of there as I work the pedals and Donna steers. She tells me to slow down because she's going to pull into a driveway where she sees a white police officer. Wiping blood from my eyes for the umpteenth time with a piece of Donna's slip she tore off, I make out a black man through my squinted eyes. Flooring the gas pedal, I yell for Donna to turn the car around. In screaming confusion and fear, she steps on the brake pedal, grinding the car to a stop before I run over the black man who's standing beside a white police officer I didn't see.

The policeman calls for an ambulance while the man listens as Donna explains what happened. I need out of the car. When I open my door, tinkling glass falls to the ground around me. I lean against the car door and cry. I've only had my car for three months, and now the windows are shattered and the body's mangled from dozens of rocks thrown. If I'd been knocked out cold, there's no doubt in my mind we would've been killed by a frenzied mob of little kids.

The man brings out a chair for me and a clean towel for my bleeding face. He talks a long time before I realize he's talking to me. He continues to talk until I can listen, then he says how sorry he is for what happened. He says how ashamed he is for what his neighbors are doing. He talks about how there are good and bad black people, just as there are good and bad white people. He says he'll lock my car in his garage until things calm down and a tow truck can be sent for it. He gives me his phone number on a slip of paper, and the next day, he calls Aunt Ruth to check on me. He's a nice man, and we were fortunate to have found him.

The hospital calls Aunt Ruth because they won't treat me without her consent; I'm not twenty-one or in danger of dying. She tells Uncle Woody to call the police before they attempt a drive to the hospital. Uncle Woody calls to find out a riot on the Westside has been in full swing for two days. It wasn't on the local news or in the newspapers, apparently to preserve Las Vegas's gambling and entertainment image.

The confrontations between police and Westside residents lasted over a three-day period with more than fifty people injured and almost two hundred arrests. The area was finally cordoned off by police and the military from Nellis AFB, although what caused the *unrest* has always been in dispute. Obviously, racial prejudice was a large part of the problem. Considering the fact that black entertainers could perform on the Strip but had to eat and sleep on the Westside, just imagine how the black community must have been treated. But Las Vegas had to preserve its image.

That thinking didn't preserve my head. If I'd known about it, I wouldn't have been anywhere near it. Uncle Woody asks the police what route to take then drives Aunt Ruth and a loaded gun to the hospital to bring me home.

The next day, Mom calls Aunt Ruth. She says she's been thinking about me and wants to know if I'm all right. I guess I'm finally old enough for Mom's uncanny knack of calling at the right time, but I won't talk to her because I'm trying not to need her anymore. Aunt Ruth keeps her updated.

My car's repaired and my forehead heals, even though glass works its way out for months. It's a long time before I can close my eyes and not see rocks and glass flying at me. I give up my apartment and stay with Aunt Ruth for several months until I'm brave enough to venture out on my own again.

Eventually, Dean graduates from Officers Candidate School as a second lieutenant and will soon be on his way to Germany. He's on leave now and drives to Vegas in a brand-new Pontiac GTO. It's a powerful convertible with a five-speed stick shift, and the color is army green.

Dean takes me out on the town. He dresses in his officer's uniform, and I borrow one of Aunt Ruth's cocktail dresses. He's twenty-one but I'm nineteen, so I truthfully assure him I'm never carded on dates. But as the night progresses, I realize the reason I haven't been carded is because my dates don't have Dean's babyface. And if they don't card the guy, they certainly aren't going to card his date. Dean's mustache is lighter than his black hair, so he darkens it with black shoe polish. Apparently, that still doesn't add enough years because we're both carded after ordering drinks before dinner at The Flame on the Strip.

"Won't you take my word as an officer and gentleman that the lady's twenty-one?" Dean asks the waitress while showing his ID.

She visibly caves in and smiles sympathetically. She must have thought she couldn't possibly stand in the way of true love—not knowing we're brother and sister—and returns with two drinks she serves to Dean.

"I can't serve the lady, but after I leave, you can," she whispers to Dean.

Dean leaves his GTO with the understanding I'll take care of it and pay the insurance payments while he makes the loan payments. I sell my car and now have the extra money I need for an apartment. I do take care of Dean's car and end up keeping it for a decade. When Dean returns from Germany three years later, he signs it over to me.

"I don't want to drive around in an old car," he says, grinning at me.

I can finally make ends meet with no car payments after Dean left his car, so a coworker and I rent an apartment together. It's a converted motel on Main Street with two rows of single-story apartments and parking in the middle, and it's conveniently located near downtown where we work for Centel on Fifth and Fremont.

Several months later when someone knocks on my door much too late for company, I wait, making sure I don't hear anything unusual. When I hear a second knock, I figure it's safe to open the door.

The Old
Lady

20

"Ace in the Hole"

ROBERTA SHERWOOD

Dad's smiling in the doorway, fanning a fistful of $100 bills that would choke a horse.

"Wow! Dad!"

Dad's been in Vegas for over a year, but I rarely see him because I have no desire to see Claribel. He's alone now, and I'm really glad he's here. He continues smiling, making his way to the kitchen table, then asks for a beer.

"The tables were hot tonight, and I couldn't do anything wrong. Best night I've had in months," Dad says calmly, sipping his beer. His steady smile is the only telltale sign of his excitement. I, on the other hand, am about to bust.

"Oh Dad, please take me back with you. If I can just watch, then I'll get the hang of it!"

"No."

"But—"

"I've told you why before."

"I know, I know."

"Besides, I won't be going back tonight. I know when to quit. I won enough to cover bills for several months, buy some extras, and put some back."

Dad's been earning a living playing craps and takes a $400 stake to Binion's Horseshoe Club on Fremont five evenings a week. He roams around the tables, waiting for whatever sense he has that sometimes tells him even before a table turns hot.

The dealers know and like Dad because he's a good player and a good tipper. A craps table is truly hot for only a short period of time, and in that short period, all hell breaks loose, making it hard to follow the action. A good dealer makes sure you keep track of your bets because they remember what you like to do and remind you about odds.

"I promise you won't even know I'm there if you'll let me go one time."

Smiling, he doesn't answer. Dad doesn't let anyone go—not even Claribel. He says it ruins his concentration, and he might as well flush his stake down the drain. Dad's a smart man with character and self-control. And to Dad, it's not a game; it's his livelihood. He knows what nights to gamble: When there are just enough people but not too crowded. He knows when to walk away and sip a beer at the bar. He knows he has two chances out of three for a bad night, depending on whether the tables are hot, chopping, or cold, which translates to win, break even, or lose. He knows that gamblers really don't count their money at the table because they don't have time, and they don't want to affect their judgment. And he knows the game takes intense concentration.

I've heard the cocktail-waitress-story several times. Dad was engrossed at a hot craps table when a new cocktail waitress touched his arm, asking if he wanted a drink. Without thinking, he flung his arm out, hitting the waitress and spilling her tray. Dad was sorry and embarrassed but also upset because his concentration was shot and his nerves rattled. His chance of winning any money that night evaporated.

Dad says it's the hardest job he's ever had, and that's saying something with all the physically demanding jobs he's done.

"There's nothing more frustrating than working all night only to get home and see you barely broke even or you're just a few dollars ahead."

I know I don't have much hope talking Dad into letting me go, but I usually try anyway.

Pass, don't pass, come, don't come, hard numbers, point numbers, field numbers: a man must have invented the game. Seven is heaven on a come-out roll and a hell of a note when you're going for a point. Go figure. If I can't watch Dad, I may never know what they all mean.

The odds are stacked in favor of the house, of course. For instance, if your point is five and you roll a five before you roll a seven, the house will pay you six for every four of whatever you've bet. The reason: In this situation, there are six ways to lose and only four ways to win. In every craps situation, there are more ways for the shooter to lose than there are to win. Obviously, over a period of a year, the house will come out considerably ahead. However, in any given period during that year, and for no reason at all, a table will run hot or cold. The hot times, usually all too brief, are what crapshooters live for. That's why Dad likes Binion's best, with all those tables in one place and more opportunities for one to get hot.

Dad contentedly finishes his beer and stands to hug me. I'll have to live many more years before I come close to understanding him. I have no idea our thoughts originate at opposite sides of the universe. Dad's a quiet man and comfortable with himself; I'm a young woman now who's uncomfortable with a quiet man.

Dad would have done anything I wanted that night, I know now, except take me gambling. He was waiting for a suggestion because he had long since learned not to put himself in a position of deciding what to do. Since that only invites the female to gripe about the decision, he won't "I-pick-you-bitch." Had I asked to go to a late dinner or even dancing, Dad would have gladly taken me. We would have gotten away with dancing, too, because Claribel wouldn't find out. We wouldn't tell her, and that wasn't being dishonest from Dad's point of view. It was only avoiding an unpleasant situation for something as harmless as dancing with his own daughter.

I never faulted Dad for staying with Claribel. His broken heart after Mom left was palpable, and he still loved Mom on the day he died—just like George Jones's "He Stopped Loving Her Today," the truest song I've ever heard. And I understood he didn't want to be alone. I also understood that Claribel would always dislike me and would never return any offer of peace, so I tolerate only so much of her. Ultimately, Dad's and my relationship suffers. I know he loves me, but we miss opportunities to share things, understand each other, and of course, dance—which we both love to do together. I've learned to accept *the way it is* because I'm grateful that Dad is not alone.

So tonight, and for the millionth time, I misread Dad's quiet for boredom with me instead of what it is: contentment with my company in a typically male manner for a quiet man waiting for the female's suggestion. Then we wait for each other and once again miss another opportunity to know each other.

21

"I Only Want a Buddy Not a Sweetheart"

GENE AUTRY

Mercury, Nevada, is the gateway to the most destructive power known to man or woman: nuclear weapons testing at the Nevada Test Site. The test site reminds me more of TV reruns of *Peyton Place*, the first prime-time soap opera, than of a terrible threat to humanity.

I went to work at the test site after Uncle Woody arranged an interview for me with his employer. My addresses for the past fifteen years have to be listed on a security questionnaire form during the hiring process. Because I've had about thirty-five addresses during those fifteen years, the woman typing the information becomes grimmer with each one.

"You can say you were too young to remember anymore," she hints.

"I can remember more."

When she looks as though she might cry, I ask if leaving off the rest will affect my security clearance. With a resounding no and a sigh of relief, she finishes typing the document. I'm officially hired as a clerk typist pending the outcome of the security investigation, which takes almost a year because new employees are thoroughly investigated.

I'm restricted from the more interesting places and have to stay in Mercury until my clearance is granted. Mercury's a buzzing community of several thousand people during the workday and boasts a swimming pool, tennis courts, bowling alley, movie theater, cafeteria, steak house, and DOD housing for those wanting to live in Mercury.

Alcoholic beverages are available during work as soon as it's generally known you can be trusted not to snitch. Bottles of liquor are hidden in certain bins in a certain warehouse, and by mid-afternoon on Fridays, even bosses are mingling with employees during cocktail hour.

Males outnumber females, and with most of their homes more than seventy-five miles away in Las Vegas, Mercury is the perfect setting for a soap opera with all the ingredients: alcohol, opportunity, sex. It's there at twenty years old that I learn a female's most unassailable reason in response to a male's inevitable question: "Why don't you want to?" "Because."

The road to Mercury, US Highway 95, is known as "The Widow Maker." It's a heavily traveled two-lane highway with a history of serious accidents. I start off taking a bus to and from work. The best way to endure an hour and forty-five minutes of rush hour traffic is to sleep through it, and that's what I try to do; however, rattling newspapers and chatty workers make sleep impossible. So, I join the ultimate carpool. We don't have to take turns driving because the same woman prefers to drive every day. She trusts her driving—not ours. She picks up three women at our doorsteps each morning and delivers us back each evening. Month after month, we contentedly sleep as she safely drives without even a near miss on the highway while drinking several cans of cold beer morning and night. She keeps the beer concealed in a cooler within easy reach beneath cans of Coke.

Wackenhut Security guards stop all arriving vehicles to check each person's color-coded badge. If your badge isn't the correct color for the month, you must visit the guard shack for a new one before entering Mercury. The badge also has a little round circle of film-like material that changes color with radioactive exposure. The guards check the film color, too, and that supposedly ensures our safety in a dangerous environment.

Occasionally on weekends, I throw my badge on top of the TV, hoping its small amount of radiation will change the film color. That, at least, would change Monday morning's monotony on the way into Mercury. I like my job, but it's hard getting into gear on Mondays.

The security guards also spot-check employees' personal belongings on the way in and out. I've been told if a black government pen is found in your purse, you can be fired. I heard the story of a janitor who was fired for having a roll of toilet paper in his lunchbox on the way out of Mercury.

There are whispers of Area 51—the place so secret we can't admit it exists, even though I know people who work there. The first Lunar Rover is tested here because the forbidding landscape resembles the moon's surface, although I don't know it at the time. Secrecy surrounds everything.

After my security clearance is finally granted, fellow employees take me on a tour of the test site. The first stop is Doom Town, where buildings have been constructed from various materials to see how each type will withstand an atomic blast. By the looks of the ghost town, none of them did very well. I see realistic-looking mannequins in odd positions around a dinner table. They didn't fare well either.

We tour The Farm where crops are given controlled amounts of radiation, and I see the animals that eat those same deadly crops. I nearly gag looking at a cow with a large piece of hard plastic in its side, serving as a window to watch its organs at work. I listen to stories of plumbing equipment so hot with radiation after clearing a clogged drain it must be forever buried on The Farm.

I stand close to the rim of the massive Sedan Crater that was blown into existence by an above-ground atomic blast. I wonder what keeps adults—whom I still don't like much even though I'm now one of them—from blowing up the entire world with their weapons. After the tour, we stop at the warehouse to drink a few rum and cokes until it's time for the drive home.

I don't like my boss, and especially so after word gets out that he was caught in the supply closet, banging his secretary. One morning, several armed Wackenhut guards walk by my desk as they escort my boss—and his boss—out of the building. I sit quietly, petrified and wondering if I'm next because I have no idea what's happening.

The news explodes and covers Mercury like a mushroom cloud before lunch. Scrap material at the test site is sold to the highest bidder, usually scrap dealers from Vegas, then large trucks haul the material out of Mercury. My chain of command was caught receiving kickbacks from scrap dealers for putting perfectly good equipment on the trucks, hidden beneath a layer of legitimate scrap. I think about the government pen I leave at home because I'm scared to bring it back to Mercury with the random searches. I think about the janitor with a roll of toilet paper and listen while the bigwigs say the scrap deals may have been going on for years.

Several trades go out on strike, one at a time, several months later. Eventually, the strikes cause office staff layoffs based on seniority. I'm bumped from my job three days in a row by employees with more seniority. The first two times, I'm able to bump someone else with less seniority, but the third time, I'm at the bottom of the barrel and laid off.

For the first and only time in my working career, I apply for unemployment benefits. Many people are in line waiting to apply because of layoffs at the test site, so I settle in to wait as long as necessary. Glancing behind me to see how many came in after me, I'm looking at my boss's boss who'd been fired and escorted out.

"Let this be a lesson. There are consequences for behavior." His voice is quiet, but his tone arrogant.

"I already knew that," I reply before turning back around.

Several weeks later, I'm called back to work. But with another job finally lined up, my three-year employment ends at Peyton Place.

I've had many types of jobs: office work, dealership service writer, telephone operator, bank teller, bartender, and blackjack dealer. My favorite was bartending at a neighborhood bar. I made sure the jukebox was fired up and the customers' drinks never empty. Trouble was, when the boss could tell I was pregnant, he laid me off. Then no one would hire me because I was pregnant. Finally, a bank rehired me as a teller but wouldn't sign me up for health insurance because I was pregnant. Oh, the joy of being female in the workforce!

Like so many women, I've been ridiculed by male bosses so unsure of their own self-worth they demeaned me to prove they were the boss. I was called into my boss's office to find him holding a small gun pointed directly at me; I learned fast how to run backward. He was probably high on coke, even though it was only seven in the morning. I've watched a boss spend afternoons swishing mouthwash and swallowing it—not to freshen his breath but for the alcohol content in the mouthwash. I stood on a chair to move a clock hand ahead one hour on an office wall clock then saw the boss tap his wristwatch, looking puzzled, as the office staff left for the day one hour early.

I've never been fired. With security and survival always first and foremost, I played the game well. I learned early on to withstand rudeness, sarcasm, poor judgment, and discrimination. I refrained from laughing at ludicrous male posturing and laughed at unfunny jokes. I've always worked hard, looking up at the glass ceiling before I even knew the term or what it meant. Except for two layoffs, each time I left my position it was on my terms, not theirs, when I was ready.

Trouble was, I never got very far up the ladder—I was still working on finding my self-worth. I thought I was better than all the crap that happened to me as a kid, and I didn't have to lie or steal to protect myself because I protected me. I still had to work to reinforce what I thought. Eventually, each piece of self-worth I fought for stuck when I finally believed what I had thought to be true.

22

"Oh, Lonesome Me"

DON GIBSON

Over three years after I moved back to Vegas from Indianapolis, Aunt Ruth and Uncle Woody decide to move to El Dorado Springs, Missouri, where he had been born and raised. They tell me I can go, too, if I want. Although I hate the thought of them leaving, I have no intention of ever stepping foot in Missouri again.

Dean's still somewhere else in the army, Dad's moved, Carson's in California, and with Aunt Ruth and Uncle Woody gone, it's just me again, so I decide to marry my karate instructor when he asks. Somehow, I knew I shouldn't, but I did anyway. I have him for a little while until I find out he likes girls much younger than me. I leave after receiving a phone call from the sister of a fourteen-year-old he recently got pregnant. Then I find an apartment.

Several days later, I call to arrange a time to pick up my motorcycle in the garage. When he doesn't answer the door, I pound on it some more. Finally, it dawns on me that he must have another girl in there with him. So I break the dining room window. After I break the bedroom window, he finally opens the door. Grabbing an afghan from the couch, I glance around and open the broom closet door to put the afghan over a fourteen- or fifteen-year-old naked girl huddled there.

"You should get out of here and never see that bastard again," I tell her.

I pass him on my way to the garage, where I start my motorcycle and roar to the nearest bar, completely disgusted.

My disgust didn't help the girl, and what I didn't know at barely twenty-one filled volumes. It never occurred to me that what he was doing was illegal while I reeled in what must have been my failures for this situation. Because of my ignorance, I harmed her, and probably more, for not reporting him. I still regret that.

Soon after I found my latest apartment, Dorothy phones from Tucson one Sunday afternoon, and I immediately know by the sound of her voice that something's very wrong.

"I have to tell you …" Dorothy says. "I have to tell you Ponchita just died."

Dorothy and Harold kept Ponchita all the years I roamed the country, trying to catch up to Mom, and they still have her. She's over ten now, and she's been sick for several days. Dorothy had taken her to the vet again that morning. When he said nothing more could be done, Dorothy brought her home. Ponchita laid under the kitchen table with Dorothy and Harold close by. Soon Harold crawled under the table to sit with Ponchita and cradled her in his arms while she died.

Suddenly, I'm flying on my bike again down my desert path to Hooligan's with Ponchita in the basket. She's waiting for me when I open the door to whichever crummy house I'm living in, and she flies into my arms. Ponchita's slip-sliding on Dorothy's kitchen floor, trying to make traction and come to me. Then I die inside and cry like a baby.

I'm not a needy kid anymore. I work, provide for myself, and don't want or expect anything from anyone. I think that's why *he* doesn't object when, in my early twenties, I initiate a relationship with Mom. Part of me is still missing: that hole in my heart. There must be a reason, something I've missed, something I still can't figure out, but I need her to love me, and I still don't understand why she doesn't consistently want me around. Of course, I have to visit her in Oregon first—*he'll* never bring her to Vegas if I don't—where I spend a few days with them.

Stevie's nine years old now and a talented bundle of energy. After I admire Mom's antique wooden butter paddle, Stevie takes me into the forest, chops down a little tree, strips bark from a pretty chunk, and carves me a replica butter paddle.

Then they spend three days with me in Vegas.

"After three days, fish and company go bad," *he* says.

I think three days is *his* limit for behaving *himself*, so they always leave on the fourth morning. These first two trips lead to regular visits with Mom, Stevie, and *him*: some good, some not so. But *he* never beats her in front of me again. I know it still happens because Mom mentions it sometimes, but I think they began to see how isolated they were by driving everyone away. And I never witnessed another crying jag like the ones before she left us. It seems she's over them.

They quit drinking one time just before I arrived.

"I have to see if we can quit," Mom says.

The night before I return to Vegas, Mom and I are watching television with *him*, who's drunk and talkative. After proving *he* could quit for a few days, *he's* back at it.

"I can't stand *him* unless I'm drinking too," Mom whispers.

She never tries to stop again after that.

He still slugs Mom's drink after they finish the first drink or two. I finally tell her in such a way I hope won't cause an argument between them, and Mom starts refilling glasses instead of *him*. But it's already too late because she mixes them almost as strong as *he* does. It's still years, though, before Mom starts rubbing her temples repeatedly with her fingertips while she drinks. Later, I read the first brain cells destroyed by alcoholism are ones beneath the temples.

Stevie stays with me twice during his summer vacations. He's ten years old the first time I buy him an airplane ticket.

"What's bastard mean?" he asks the first evening.

"It's a cuss word."

"You know what I mean," he says, fighting tears.

"Why do you ask?"

"They called me that again last night."

"You know they say things they don't mean when they're drinking. I've told you that before."

"Am I a bastard?" he asks as tears roll down his cheeks.

"Absolutely not. You're my little brother!" I tickle-torture him until he forgets about being called a bastard.

I teach Stevie how to swim and take him shopping, bowling, and to the movies. We spend two glorious days at Disneyland—it'll never lose its magical hold on me. Before he leaves, I teach Stevie how to make a long-distance telephone call from home and from a pay phone. I tape several coins to a small piece of paper and tuck it away in his wallet, along with my telephone number.

"If you ever need me, call, and I'll come get you. You can live with me anytime you want, Stevie. Don't ever forget that."

I don't think Stevie realized how bad his life was because it was all he'd ever known. Stevie loved Mom, which I understood completely. And he loved his *dad*, which I also could understand. But that meant I was never able to convince him to live with me. I wish I had because his life might have turned out differently.

A few months after Stevie's visit, I'm on my way to meet Mom, Stevie, and *him* in California for a visit with my oldest brother, Ronnie. Ronnie's kids and Stevie are just the right ages to enlist in schemes to annoy Ronnie. On the last day, we tie all of his clean socks, underwear, and tee shirts into as many knots as possible—tight knots. I'm long gone before Ronnie discovers them. A year later, Ronnie gets even when Stevie's at my place for a visit. Ronnie had paid him five dollars to tie my panty hose, underwear, and bras into knots—really tight knots. Tight knots are very hard to undo in female things. I start making plans to retaliate, but I don't hurry because I have plenty of time.

At twenty-four, I'm happily in love and remarried. I met him through a mutual friend, and at last, I'm living a regular life doing what normal people do. I love my husband, and the marriage should last forever. But a couple has to get out of bed sometime, and when we do after the first year, I'm faced with the reality that I can never compete with my father-in-law, who's a successful doctor and partner in a Vegas hospital. To make matters worse, I won't be intimidated by his wealth or his hateful behavior toward me. It's evident he'll never accept me. It's also painfully evident my husband won't attempt to protect me from his father's peculiar attitude.

My husband has an air ambulance business flying a six-seat, turbo-charged Cessna airplane. It's subsidized by his father, who also pays him a monthly retainer to fly him anywhere anytime he wants to go. Occasionally, I'm invited too.

Late one Friday afternoon, my husband takes off from North Las Vegas airport with his parents and me aboard. We're flying to a Reno casino to see Hank Thompson perform. The old-son-of-a-bitch, as I refer to my father-in-law in my mind, is being unusually courteous to his wife, son, and even me. I vow to myself not to think of him as the old-son-of-a-bitch the rest of the night.

When we arrive at the showroom, I'm in a state of barely controlled excitement. I hope with all my heart that Hank Thompson sings "Bummin' Around" tonight. I can see the old record twirling on Mom's record player with sheets hooked up out of the way as she dances me then each of the boys up and down the length of the Chicken Coop.

Hank Thompson does sing "Bummin' Around" along with his other hits, and I thoroughly enjoy the show. I'm excited again when we're invited backstage to meet him. When my father-in-law introduces himself, Hank Thompson and each member of the band shake his hand. The warm hand-shakes and small talk continue as he introduces his wife and son. When Hank Thompson turns to me, as I'm the next and last to be introduced, you can hear a pin drop in the total silence. I glance at my father-in-law, who's staring at me with a toothy grin, obviously enjoying the moment, and I turn to my husband, who's staring at the tops of his shoes. Looks like he's seen this little skit before. I look up just as Hank Thompson takes a step toward me with his arm outstretched.

"Hi, I'm Hank Thompson. I'm sorry but I didn't catch your name, pretty lady."

"Hi, I'm Sherrie." Then each band member shakes my hand as they introduce themselves. I'm glad the room's dimly lit so maybe they won't notice the bright-red shame on my face.

Before the shame leaves my face, I leave my husband in heart and spirit. When we later divorce, I unknowingly take my unborn baby with me. And I never think of the old-son-of-a-bitch as anything other than the old-son-of-a-bitch again.

After seven years in the army with the rank of Captain, Dean's forced to leave his command after he's arrested by military police. His crime? Sipping a drink in a bar. Sipping a drink in a gay bar, to be exact. Dean's relieved of his command and given an honorable discharge because of his rank. He moves to Las Vegas and buys a doublewide mobile home. At the time, I didn't know the reason he left the army.

After I decide my marriage will never work, I call Dean, asking if I can move in with him.

"Of course, but there's something you should know first," he says.

"I already know, Dean."

"I have to tell you something first, then you can decide."

"I already know."

"You don't understand! Will you listen to me?"

"Dean, I've always known, okay? Now, can I move in with you or not?"

"But how can you know? I've never told anyone—"

"I just know, damnit! Now back to my original question. Can I move in with you or not?"

Dean's utterly relieved someone knows his secret and still loves and accepts him. It was years before I read about such things, but I always knew Dean could no more help being homosexual than he could being tall and handsome. People don't just wake up and decide they're going to be gay. This is what he is; this is who he is. He was born this way, and somehow I had known it—whatever *it* was—since we were kids.

We go out on the town to celebrate his relief. We dance, laugh, drink, and talk. We end up in a gay bar in the wee hours, where Dean bores the bartender with stories of his remarkable sister who knows his deepest secret without him knowing that she knows.

"Isn't it amazing?" Dean asks over and over.

After a woman in a man's suit tries to pick me up and Dean nearly falls off his barstool laughing, we decide it's time to go. We make it home, still talking and laughing. We're finally best friends again and always will be.

Shortly after I move in, Dean begins managing a McDonald's restaurant. He works odd shifts, but he's usually there in the evenings. After work, I sometimes stop by to see him and pick up a free dinner. The teenagers working the front counter are unusually quiet when I arrive early one evening.

"What's wrong with you guys?" I ask.

"Your brother's really irritable," one replies.

"Yeah. He yelled because a couple kids didn't show up for work," another says.

"He told me I'd be fired if I show up late one more time," another chimed in. "I tried to explain I had to finish my homework, but he wouldn't listen."

I already knew irresponsible teenagers were driving Dean crazy. I figured we might as well finish the job.

"You guys don't have to put up with that crap. You should go out on strike!"

From their smiles, I know they're game for my plan. I jump up on the counter to organize them into a mutiny just as Dean walks out of his small office. He stands there sputtering as I jump to the floor, and the entire teenage staff follows me out the front door while customers applaud. Dean follows us outside and orders me off his property or he'll call the police. I ask if I can have a cheeseburger first, and he says I can if the kids will go back inside to cook and serve it. I'm 86'd from Dean's restaurant for several days until he finally calms down. Then he makes me promise I'll behave myself before he allows me in his restaurant again.

I still haven't been living with Dean long when our brother Carson is in a terrible motorcycle accident in California. His right leg is amputated just below the knee, and nearly everything else is pretty well mangled. He spends almost a month in the hospital, and I spend most of the month with him. He's an amazingly tough guy and lives through the ordeal.

During his first day home from the hospital, I watch him cut wire that's holding his broken jaw shut and drink the first beer he's had in many weeks.

The next day, Carson spends the afternoon teaching himself how to jump kick-start his Harley-Davidson Sportster with his left foot while maintaining his balance with half of his right leg missing. To further complicate things, he has to compensate for the missing big toe on his left foot, which had been amputated years earlier after the oil rig accident. When I mention that it was really poor planning to have the leg cut off with a full set of toes attached, he says he's luckier than I am because he only has four toenails to cut. He's going to be just fine.

Knowing Carson, I'm not surprised by his actions. Through the course of his life, I think he had broken almost every bone in his body at one time or another. His straight, narrow, Romanesque nose now has a noticeable curve, and he has to shave his lower lip because the whiskers below were forced upward to grow through his lip as the result of some accident or fight. But he's still one of the handsomest men I know, and his smile is never far away.

Throughout the month I'm with Carson, the whole family comes to see him. During the visits, everyone's able to see Ronnie too. That becomes more important to us all when less than a year later, Ronnie's killed.

After I return home from Carson's is when I find out I'm pregnant and get laid off at the bar because I start showing.

The following summer, *he* drives Mom and Stevie down for a surprise visit.

"It's more fun making them than having them," Mom laughingly replies when I ask what labor's like.

It's June in Las Vegas and sizzling hot. I'm eight months pregnant, and with each degree over one hundred, it seems another pound of water's added to my ankles. I waddle when I walk, and the baby has a stranglehold on my bladder, making Mom follow me into the bathroom to complete most conversations.

"The first time you hold your baby in your arms, you'll forget all about the labor," Mom assures me.

While they're visiting, it's decided that after the baby's born, Dean will drive to Oregon and bring Mom back to teach me newborn baby things. I'm so relieved she'll be with me for a while. For the millionth time, I pat my stomach and wonder if I'm patting head or butt. I can't wait to see if it's a boy or girl, and I'm scared to death.

"Don't worry. A baby's more fun than having a puppy around," Dean says.

He's hunched over the kitchen counter, cutting noodles, when Mom shakes her head as she watches him lay a carpenter's square on the homemade, rolled-out dough. He's using the tool as a straightedge to cut perfect-size noodles to drop into simmering chicken broth.

"I hope he washed that thing first!" Mom loudly whispers to me.

"Probably not," I loudly whisper back.

"I have to cook dinner and be insulted too?" he says. It's obvious he loves every minute of it.

I'm fortunate living with Dean while pregnant because he's not charging rent. Now I can buy baby things and save up what I can to get the baby out of hock after birth since the bank where I'm working wouldn't give me medical insurance because I was pregnant when I was hired. I won't have any paid time off after the birth either, so I make sure to drag myself to work until the day I go to the hospital. It'll be a long time before the baby's mine free and clear.

Dean leaves for Oregon the second day we're home. I'm still tired from the ordeal—I went in at 11 a.m. and was home at noon the next day—and my seven-pound, eight-ounce bundle of baby man is wearing me out. Stacey is a beautiful baby, and I love him completely.

"Every crow thinks theirs is the blackest," Gramma would have said.

"Hurry, Dean. I'm so tired I don't think I'll last much longer."

"I'll have your mother back in no time," Dean says.

Only one dream and one comment stain Mom's two-week visit—the best time I've ever spent with her. One morning, she starts crying over a dream, saying she's had the same one many times.

"I'm surrounded by dark, swirling water in the dream. I can't get away from it, and I'm so scared because I don't know what to do."

She tells me dreaming of clear, pretty water means good luck, but dark water means bad luck—a bad omen. In the coming years, she'll mention the same dream to me several more times. After she finishes crying over the dream, she asks if I ever cry.

"Sure I do. Not when anyone's around though."

"What good does it do to cry if no one sees you?" Mom asks.

I think about that comment and wonder if I'd only been an audience all those times I ached for her when she cried. I still love her, but thinking about her comment over time, I don't think I like her as much as before.

Ronnie's killed—along with his boss and secretary—in a private airplane crash three months after Stacey's born. A likely explanation is the boss suffered a heart attack at the controls. At thirty-eight, Ronnie leaves six kids behind: the oldest nearly sixteen and the youngest fifteen months. His kids had a dad who adored them and always wanted them close, and for Ronnie not to be able to raise them is unspeakably sad.

We gather at a little motel in Livermore, California, a couple of days before the funeral. Mom, Stevie, the baby, and I have a room together, and Dad, Carson, Craig, and Dean have rooms close by. The boys come over soon after they arrive to see Mom. Before Dean leaves, he takes me aside to say he's bringing Dad over in a few minutes.

"Oh, Dean. Are you sure?" I ask.

"It's been a long time, Sherrie. Besides, Dad wants to see her. Ask Mom and see what she says."

I'm not so sure Dad knows. By the look on Dean's face, I think he's hatching this plan on the fly.

"C'mon, Sherrie. Everyone's adults. I want them to see each other again."

I don't ask Mom but rather quietly tell her Dean's bringing Dad over in a few minutes. She's silent for several seconds and stands to straighten up suitcases and such.

"Okay?" I ask.

"Yes," Mom replies.

Mom walks to the bedroom where Stacey's sleeping to gather up his soiled clothes. She's standing at the kitchenette sink washing out baby undershirts when Dean and Dad lightly knock then walk in.

"Hello," Dad says, sitting down comfortably in a chair by the door.

"Hello," Mom says as she sits down on the couch beside Stevie and me.

"How have you been?" Dad asks.

"Oh, okay, I guess. Just washing out the baby's things." She looks at the wet undershirts in her hands. When she hangs them over the shower curtain rod, Dad never takes his eyes off her. Dean's grinning from ear to ear.

"I'm sure sorry about Ronnie," Dad says when she sits down.

"I know. Me too. It's such a waste." Mom wipes her eyes with a tissue.

"You look good," Dad says.

"Thank you. So do you."

And so it goes. Time's stopped in a little motel room in Livermore, California, for a few short minutes.

"Well, I guess it's time to go," Dad says calmly, standing up. "I'll see you at the funeral."

"Yes. Thank you," Mom says. Then Dad and Dean are gone.

23

"I'm Moving On"

HANK SNOW

When Dean plans to sell his mobile home to buy a house, I decide to move back to Tucson. I need to be around another woman who isn't afraid of months-old babies and knows what to do when all else fails. Dad's retired in Marana, north of Tucson, so I know I'll see Dad and Dean regularly.

Staying with Dorothy and Harold, they allow me the time to find a job—with medical insurance this time—and get on my feet. I find myself still, and yet again, in awe of Dorothy. She can manhandle Stacey and get him in a good mood before he even knows he's heading for a bad one. I learn how to be a mother from watching the *consummate mother*.

Dad calls frequently, saying it's time to bring Stacey out for a weekend visit with Grampa. Stacey's just learning to walk, and he's a bundle of energy. Dad follows him everywhere outside to explore the garden, the pigpen for one little pig, and everything in between.

"You made a beautiful baby," Dad tells me as he follows Stacey for the millionth time to the pigpen. "Now you have to play with your doll," Dad chuckles.

Amazingly, Claribel seems fond of Stacey and never shows the slightest indication of mistreating him in any way. I know because I watch for it.

Humankind is the most powerful force the world has known: brilliant and dangerous. Yet newborn babies are the most helpless babies in the world—completely dependent but durable enough to flourish when loved. It really takes so little to make a child happy—just love and care. Why is that so hard for many adults to understand?

I buy the old lady—my mobile home—from a coworker who kept it as a rental. She's old, but I don't care; she's mine. I don't have much and scrounge only enough furniture so the place won't echo with Stacey's chatter. Dorothy sorts through her kitchen and picks out odds and ends so I have enough to get by. The kitchen sink and appliance colors are horribly mismatched, and white sheets hang as drapes in the front room. But I see it as it can be and clean until the little place sparkles.

Everything's ready when we arrive on a Saturday morning in January. I give Stacey a tour of our new home, and we explore every nook and cranny together. At almost a year and a half old, he becomes an extension of my hip when we're home together. Because he's an extension of my heart, I don't mind. I desperately want to build a life worth living. I'm blissfully boring, taking care of my home, working, and watching my baby grow. I finally have a family and a permanent home.

I have a houseful for my first Thanksgiving holiday. Dad and Claribel come a few days before Thanksgiving. The day before, Dean and a friend drive down from Vegas, Carson and a friend ride their motorcycles over from California, and Craig comes from somewhere too. We're stacked like cordwood for sleeping arrangements, but no one minds. The happiness derived from having company that belongs to me for a family holiday outweighs any misgivings about what might happen. But as the days progress, Claribel's testier by the hour for no reason I can figure out and just glares if I try to talk to her.

Putting trash in a bag after Thanksgiving dinner, I head for the door. Dad follows me out to take the bag then walks beside me to the trash bin.

"I don't know why she's mad at me, Dad."

"Oh, don't worry about it. She just gets this way sometimes."

Walking back home, Dad quietly says, "I don't want to be alone."

"I know." I've always known that.

"It was a wonderful meal," Dad says, hugging me before we return to Claribel's frostiness.

It wasn't a terrible meal like my first dinner party for Aunt Ruth and Uncle Woody, but Dad was being gracious to say it was wonderful. Stacey and I still have a couple of years to eat really bad gravy before it begins to taste like Mom's or Dorothy's. And the same goes for homemade noodles. My biscuits may never make the grade: they smell good baking but still look and taste like hockey pucks.

Back inside, Dean once again comes to my rescue and diverts Claribel's attention to save the day while everyone just stays out of Craig's way—even Dad.

"Craig's just like your mother," Dad tells me. "You never know when he's going to blow."

I know Dad's seen much more than me, but based on my perspective, Craig's blow is always violent behavior followed by remorse, while Mom's is terrible tears and withdrawal, rejecting those who love her, with no remorse afterward. She couldn't even offer "I'm sorry," which is violence in its own way, I think. And that could go on for a long time.

I think Craig inherited every bit of meanness there was on Mom's side from her dad and oldest sister, Anna. That wasn't his fault, but he was also thin-skinned and never tried to accept or forgive or forget. So Mom's behavior during our early years was even worse for Craig.

After the years roaming with Mom, Craig continued roaming to bum off those he knew until he finally took the suggestion to leave, then the cycle continued at the next place he landed. I knew he worked construction, at least sometimes, but I also knew he lived under the radar and didn't follow normal rules. And I knew he was miserable.

As our holiday comes to an end, I hope the passing years are calming for Craig and he'll find some peace from his tortured life. Things happen; people change. I just don't want to be around him to find he didn't.

Christmas is a wonderful time to make a little boy happy, and in so doing, myself too. This is our first Christmas together in our little home, and we're both busting with excitement. There's wide-eyed wonder from an almost-two-and-a-half-year-old boy talking to Santa for the first time.

I love this time of year and have planned for it since summer. Christmas shopping's finished before the first day of autumn, with Stacey sitting in a shopping cart facing me and oblivious to the toys piling up behind him. Months of scrimping more than usual and eating scrambled eggs with cut-up hotdogs for dinner helped pay the layaway bill, and now the toys are mine and Santa's to give. I had his first tricycle out of hock in time for Dad and Dean to put it together over the Thanksgiving holiday.

We share special moments each evening when he carries a worn copy of *The Night Before Christmas* onto my lap and nestles in for another reading. I take in the awe on his face and in his voice Christmas morning when he shouts that Santa "even oozed a nackin" after finishing the cookies and milk we put out for him. And the breakneck speed of tiny fingers tearing wrapping paper off presents under the twinkling Christmas tree. And finally, relative quiet while he plays with boxes and materials from the toys' packaging.

My present came in the mail after Christmas. A letter from the Arizona Department of Economic Security (DES) in Phoenix began: "Effective Feb. 1, your child will no longer be eligible for subsidized daycare services." I'm in the working-poor bracket at the same time Arizona's economy is in the sewer. I have a few resumes still in circulation, but I've given up hope of finding a better job. The only thing keeping me afloat is the subsidized daycare Stacey qualifies for because his mother's next to dirt poor. Now that's going to stop.

The letter knocks the wind out of me then makes me fighting mad. If I'm going to lose all I've worked so hard for and have to go on welfare, the politicians in Phoenix are going to hear about it. Surely there must be more mothers like me. All I have to do is find them—and find them I did.

It begins with one telephone call. An inquiry leading to another call and then another and another. During a week of working my phone half the night, I have a growing network of mothers who, like me, will be forced onto welfare and hate the thought of it.

An early conversation introduces me to Julie, a young married mother who works a part-time, minimum-wage job by day and takes college classes at night. Her husband goes to a union hall daily to see if he'll be picked up for work, and their child's in DES-subsidized daycare. Julie's schedule allows some flexibility during the day, so we're a perfect combination; I plan and coordinate activities, and Julie carries them out. I find a printer who donates time and materials to print several hundred flyers, petitioning DES not to force working-poor mothers onto welfare. Julie picks them up and delivers them to mothers, who plaster them on every available surface in town. Soon, I'm invited to meet with a lady at the Tucson Chamber of Commerce. I'm running headlong into my first taste of politics that, in the end, leaves me feeling sick but also amazes me because of the people I meet along the way: some in politics, some not.

I meet Sharon at the Tucson Chamber of Commerce early one evening while she's entertaining several businessmen from Egypt. She's very supportive of my stand on the DES decision and offers assistance. She gives me contact names, phone numbers, and, most importantly, encouragement. Then she invites me back the next evening to attend an informal cocktail party and buffet for the Egyptian businessmen.

I spend most of the next evening talking with Ammon. He's dressed in a business suit, and he's an extremely polite, soft-spoken, older Egyptian who's very interested in my cause. It seems he is also delighted with my American ways.

"You are very mad with this DES. Am I right?" Ammon asks.

"I'd gladly shoot them on sight," I laughingly reply.

Ammon laughs, nearly spilling his drink. After asking where I live, he listens with interest while I tell him about my small home and life with my little son.

"Your small home is palace to girls in Egypt," Ammon says. "Girls your age live with parents if not married and no freedom and privilege such as you."

"It's a good thing I wasn't born in Egypt then. I wouldn't be able to live that way, and I'd get in trouble."

"Yes, yes," Ammon laughs. "Very good so Egypt doesn't get shot up."

Ammon's impressed that a young woman can voice her opinion in America and have it heard and considered. He hopes his daughters will someday have that right too. He tells me about his country's present troubles and his high hopes for the future with Anwar Sadat finally leading Egypt into the twentieth century because his country is far behind others in today's world.

We speak several more times before he returns to Egypt, and each time, he encourages me to continue the great fight, saying with hard work victory will follow. We correspond for months after he returns to Egypt. Ammon writes shortly after Anwar Sadat is murdered and says he is heartsick and fears for his country. I reply, but I never hear from him again.

The great fight's on. I continually try to figure out ways to lean on Arizona's politicians to show them we aren't ignorant; we're just in the working-poor bracket. We know welfare and other programs will be far more expensive to the state in the long run compared to subsidized daycare. The days and nights merge into one long blur—composing letters to be copied then individually signed by networked mothers; drafting petitions; begging poor, single mothers to register to vote so they can legally sign the petitions; and constantly making sure everything I do is legal. And I still have to work eight hours a day too. I'm tired, but we're fighting back and people are beginning to listen. My home phone never stops ringing.

Plans for a rally begin to materialize and grow. After a hall is donated that can hold several hundred people, I invite every political figure in the state, as well as local newspapers and television stations. Of course, the opposing political party never shows. I figure if we can fill the hall at least half full, it'll be a success.

People begin filing into the hall shortly after I arrive. I'm hiding in the wings, studying my opening comments one last time with Julie taking care of any last-minute details. I have a list of politicians and guest speakers who confirmed their attendance and keep the list handy for reference during introductions. I look at my watch for the umpteenth time, but it's still fifteen minutes before the scheduled start. Suddenly, Julie appears flustered and out of breath.

"You better come have a look," she says.

Fearing failure, stage fright, and wondering why in the hell I thought I could do this, I walk out onstage and nearly faint. The joint's packed. The invited speakers are filling the chairs. All the local television stations' news crews are here, as well as both local newspapers. By the time I give the opening dialogue, the hall is standing room only, with people lining the walls and doorways. The speakers all pledge their support, backing our resolve to remain taxpayers. The politicians promise to take our fight to Phoenix. Instead, the mothers are summoned to the state capitol a few days later to defend our stand on the Senate floor.

Mothers take buses to Phoenix, where we fill the Senate chamber. A few of us have been invited to speak, and when called, we stand to read our speeches then sit down. The presiding officer, a woman with a gavel, makes various comments after each speech. Our reaction to one comment makes her pound the gavel repeatedly and threaten to clear the chamber if we don't stop stomping our feet in unison to protest her observation.

"Many of you may be better off on welfare" is not something we want to hear.

"Why don't you go on welfare and tell us how you like it," someone shouts.

"Ladies, ladies, don't make me clear the room!" the woman admonishes, pounding her gavel some more.

I'm the last one called to speak, and when I begin, the gray-haired committee chair immediately interrupts me. He's now standing in front of a microphone, wearing a three-piece suit, and looking over the top of his glasses and down his nose at me. I'm caught off guard and stammer a jumbled answer when he asks me a question.

Then he asks, "Don't you find it odd your assistant Julie attends college and yet qualifies for subsidized daycare?"

Julie's not here, and I find it odd that he even knows about her, which helps me regain some composure.

"I admire anyone who continues their education."

The chamber's alive again with stomping feet. The woman's pounding her gavel, telling us to be quiet. The committee chair watches me as he silently twirls his glasses.

After reading my speech, I'm wishing I could sink through my chair when a lady pats my shoulder from behind. She's a nun and an Arizona congresswoman from Tucson. And she's one of the sweetest people I've ever met.

"You did fine," she tells me.

"He made me look pretty dumb."

"On the contrary, you did just right," she says with a laugh.

She goes on to say that the resolution to continue funding daycare at current levels will go to committee for a vote the next day. She tells me how each committee member will vote, and the resolution will pass. We will win tomorrow, and the old guy in the three-piece suit already knows it. *Why, then, did we have to go through this?* I wonder. Why did they jerk us around and demean us? I'm relieved and happy but somehow demoralized.

A lifetime later, I'm still amazed at politics, politicians, and the public in general. My kids graduated from high school without learning, among other things, about women's struggle for the right to vote—the same right white men have had from the beginning. They never learned about Elizabeth Cady Stanton in school, and they thought Susan B. Anthony was nothing more than a funny-looking coin.

Gramma was thirty years old before she could vote. And during those years and before, a married woman didn't have the right to own or inherit property or keep the wages she earned. A single woman who owned property was made to pay taxes on that property to a government that wouldn't recognize her as a citizen. When the same woman married, her property automatically became her husband's. If that woman later divorced because her husband was a wife beater, an alcoholic, or worse, all of her property—including her children—became his property alone because it was the law in most states. Armies of women worked nearly their entire adult lives to change that travesty.

Many women today still don't register to vote, and many who are registered don't vote. How can so many of those who do choose to vote for platforms that condone absurd recommendations demanding that women submit graciously to their husbands and single women with children should get married? No matter that the one we might marry and submit to graciously could be abusive, unfaithful, or just a jerk in general. The message: Stay married no matter the circumstances, and be happy about earning seventy-five cents for every dollar a male earns doing the exact same job. Better yet, just stay barefoot and pregnant, then you won't be able to challenge any male.

But during that day in Phoenix, a bunch of poor, scared mothers took the politicians on and won their fight by saving their self-respect. We were proud of that.

Although the outcome is favorable, I give up hope of finding a decent-paying job. After the great fight's over, I decide to move the old lady to Vegas, where I usually earned a decent living. We move into the same mobile home park where I previously lived with Dean.

24

"Once a Day"

CONNIE SMITH

Time rolls on. From well before kindergarten to high school graduation, Stacey has the same address. I'm proud of that fact; he hates it. He bugs me to move somewhere, to go someplace different. I try to explain that moving around and being the new kid on the block isn't much fun. If you constantly move, where's "back home"? Stacey doesn't understand, and I don't expect him to, so I weather his storms and watch him grow. And I wonder how any mother could leave her child at such a wonderful age.

"Kids step on your toes when they're little and on your heart when they're big," Dorothy says. I know it's worth it even though mine's not big yet.

I'm working at a Chevy dealership, making good money as a service writer now that we're back in Vegas. Trouble is, working ten-hour days leaves little time to spend it and even less time to raise my little son. I'm worn out, so I quit my job and find office work at another dealership for half the money. I spend years a step away from poverty, making sure to manage without being subsidized from anyone while I pay more for monthly daycare than I pay on lot rent for the old lady. All the while, I look for a better-paying job with hours that'll allow me to be a mother too.

After I put Stacey in bed the night before his third birthday, I bake and frost a thirteen-by-nine-inch chocolate cake and decorate it with a miniature plastic fort, complete with cowboys, Indians, and horses. Three candles top off the decorations. Afterward, I assemble a spring horse he can ride in the front room. For the final touch, I hook a belt with a plastic six-shooter and a cowboy hat to the saddle horn. Then I'm in bed asleep.

Sometime in the wee hours, I feel a little face close to mine, smelling like chocolate Ding Dongs. Stacey recently started eating a Ding Dong at night before crawling into bed with me—habits I'm trying to break.

"Mommy! Dares a horsy out dare!" Stacey whispers.

"Oh, there is, huh? It'll still be there in the morning, so go to sleep." I hook my arm around him to flip him into bed—so much for breaking habits.

"But Mommy!"

"Hush and go to sleep now."

I fleetingly hope my bed won't be covered in chocolate Ding Dong crumbs before I fall back to sleep.

Stacey's still asleep when I stumble out of bed and head to the kitchen. I brew a cup of tea and open the refrigerator to take the cake out so he'll see it when he gets up. But the cake isn't there. I close the refrigerator door and open it again. It still isn't there. The cake isn't on the counter or the kitchen table or in the refrigerator. Where the hell did I put it? Toying with the idea that I've finally gone nuts, I wonder how fast I can put together another cake. *At least the horse is still here*, I consider. I make sure the nuts and bolts are tight and the springs fastened properly. At this point, I don't trust what I did the night before.

After everything checks out okay on the horse, something catches my eye underneath the bar that separates the front room and kitchen. The cake decorations are in a neat pile with the cake a few inches away. I can almost see Stacey's butt print in the carpet between them. He'd taken the heavy cake out of the fridge without dropping it and carried it to the front room, where he took off each small decoration to lick off the frosting without harming the cake at all. It wasn't Ding Dongs I smelled the previous night: it was chocolate frosting. I put the decorations back on the cake. Damn, I love that kid. And I'm so glad I'm still sane.

During these years, my dream is to pick up Stacey from daycare after work then stop at a hamburger joint for dinner without budgeting for a month. I manage to keep the lot rent and daycare paid, and Stacey fed, clothed, and supplied with the latest "He-Man" toy, but I rack up a ton of debt on charge cards that control my life for over twenty years. I do what I must to take care of the little boy I love so no one else has to do it for me. And I do have help along the way.

Carson makes several trips from California with materials to put up a chain-link fence for me. On the next trip, he brought Stacey a puppy. Craig shows up and rebuilds a used wood porch to fit alongside my little home. The visit turns into a fiasco, of course, when he breaks the front-door glass with his fist after I ask him to save the rest of the peanut butter for school lunches because I can't afford any more until payday. When I start sweeping up glass, he grabs the broom and breaks it over his knee. Then he smashes Stacey's Saturday morning breakfast donuts on the kitchen floor, daring me to do something about it as he grinds them with the heel of his boot. Finally, he grabs his stuff and storms out, leaving another mess for me to clean up. I make up my mind if he comes back, I'll call the cops on him myself. But he never shows up again. Just because you're related to someone doesn't mean you have to like them.

Dad and Dean complete a remodeling or repair project for me every time Dad visits. When Mom comes, she stocks me up on groceries, and *he* even catches up the yardwork. When Dorothy and Harold visit, they fill up my freezer with meat. During one visit, Dorothy and Harold take us to Walmart to buy Stacey a gift. Harold heads directly to the sporting goods section and the bicycle aisle, where Stacey's eyes light up.

"There doesn't seem to be one quite the right size for you, Stacey," Harold says after a few minutes.

"That's okay. Thanks for trying, Papa."

Nanny and Papa both look like they could cry, and Stacey's bravely fighting back tears. Watching them is one of the sweetest sights I've seen. Suddenly, that day from long ago runs through my mind. The day when a little lost girl walks home to a run-down house on Buckeye Lane to see a brand-new, sparkling-clean bicycle with a basket and colorful streamers waiting for her.

"I'm not through looking yet, Stacey," Harold says.

While Harold continues searching, Dorothy beckons me to follow her.

"Dad will find him a wheel if we have to hit every store in Vegas," Dorothy says.

I follow her to the electronics section and the television aisle, where *my* eyes light up. We've been watching a tiny, eight-inch, black-and-white TV for so long I've forgotten what color looks like. Harold drives home with Stacey's first bicycle in the back of the station wagon next to an eighteen-inch color television.

And Uncle Dean's always a regular and welcome sight. At least twice a year, and usually more, he whisks us out of town for a visit with Mom in Oregon or Dorothy and Harold in Arizona.

"You don't have to be perfect," Dean says on one trip, after I've made sure Stacey's comfortably sprawled out on the back seat.

"Yes I do," I reply without thinking.

"No, no you don't. He's fine. You need to calm down."

"He's not going to grow up like you and I did, Dean."

"He won't. Not with you. So stop worrying."

That's the best compliment anyone's ever given me. But I still make sure Stacey learns how to cut his fingernails and toenails and bathe himself by the time he's six years old—just in case.

I have a few boyfriends along the way. I want male companionship but never wanted—and always feared—the power a woman can hold over her family after living it firsthand with Mom, so I cheat myself out of a lifetime companion or two by dating safe males—immature men-boys—who are fun but wouldn't make a wart on a man's butt. I don't develop any lasting relationships, but I do make a disastrous miscalculation and get pregnant.

Roe v. Wade protects my legal right to an abortion, but even if it didn't, I'd still have one. No politician can decide what I will or will not do with my body. What they should be doing with their time and energy is finding solutions for thousands of unwanted, abandoned, and unadoptable children already here, but a pregnant female is easier to tackle than throngs of unwanted children. It's my body, my responsibility, and my choice. And I'm the one who'll live with the decision.

After the abortion, I see a gynecologist for a diaphragm. The doctor inserts it while he explains how it works.

"You're all set," he says. "You can leave as soon as you remove it." Then he walks out.

Twenty minutes later, I'm still trying to get the damn thing out. If the doctor had returned, I would've gladly broken his nose. I decide I'll find a female gynecologist who, I'm sure, will never leave a woman alone that long with something completely foreign and very small stuffed inside her for the first time. I know a female gynecologist will be more humane to another female. And I find I was right the next time I visit one.

During this time, I've started drinking more than I should because it takes the edge off all the things I don't want to think about anymore. When I have a free evening during a Stacey sleepover, I'm irritated I can't have a drink in a bar—let alone play a game of pool—without at least one male who can't take a friendly no for an answer. *Let'um go screw a knot-hole*, I think. So, cleaning house and taking care of the corners so the center will take care of itself, doing laundry, drinking, listening to sad-ass songs, and watching end-happy movies fill my nights.

Months after the abortion, Dad's annoyed with me when I stop to visit on my way to Dorothy and Harold's in Tucson. As I'm leaving, Dad says I should visit longer before heading out. Claribel's obviously enjoying Dad's irritation with me; it shows in her half-smile and steady stare. I kiss Dad and leave.

Dad has a heart attack and dies a few months later. I'm cooking Sunday dinner when Dean calls. Craig's in Marana, so he's making funeral arrangements. Evidently, Dean called Mom, too, because she calls to say she wants to go to the funeral.

"Why?" I ask.

"I want to be there for you kids."

I want to believe her, though I don't. I don't know what to think, but I can't dwell on it. And yet, I feel Dad would like Mom being there. The first time Mom left *him*, I drove to Oregon, rented and filled a U-Haul, and headed back to Vegas with her and Stevie.

On the way, we stop in California to visit Ronnie and his kids. Dad doesn't live far from Ronnie, so I visit Dad too. Claribel's cooking dinner, leaving us alone, and Dad tips back in his easy chair with his pipe while we talk.

"What brings you here?" he asks, glad to see me.

"I'm moving Mom and Stevie to Vegas, and she wants to see Ronnie."

Electric silence fills the room. Suddenly, Dad's leg shoots up and his foot slams the recliner into an upright position as his hands grip the armrests.

"She left him!?"

The look on his face breaks my heart. I have to look away to avoid the hope I see. After so long, she can still do this to him.

"She won't stay, Dad. She'll go back to *him*," I quietly reply.

I continue inspecting the carpet until Dad regains his composure, tips back, and relights his pipe. Then we talk about other things.

Mom flies to Vegas, and Dean drives us to Marana for the funeral after attaching a small flag at half-mast to the car antenna. When we arrive at Dad's house, Carson's already there, with Craig sitting in Dad's easy chair tipped back and feet up when we walk in. I'm about to die from anxiety over Mom and Claribel meeting for the first time, which doesn't bother Dean at all and turns out completely non-eventful; however, Dean nearly explodes when he sees Craig in Dad's chair.

"How can he show so little respect for Dad?" Dean fumed later.

When Craig's eyes meet mine, he rubs his fingers and thumb together, indicating he needs money for Dad's funeral. I call the funeral home in Tucson, only to find out we can't see Dad because Craig told them not to embalm him.

"We would have paid for the embalming," I snarl at him. That's the last time I ever intend to speak to him.

We stay a short time at Dad's before heading to Dorothy and Harold's in Tucson, where we'll stay through the funeral.

I think Dad would have been mad over the flag incident like I was. We were told that because of the cost, Dad would not receive an American flag from the government in acknowledgment of his military service. Reagan had cut taxes during his first term, which caused the economy to tank, and he raised taxes only on the middle class, of course. Many programs were then underfunded, and the practice of giving an American flag to the family of a deceased veteran as a token of respect was discontinued for a time. Dad was a decorated WWII veteran, yet we had to purchase an American flag to honor him because his country and his state wouldn't.

We know Craig intends to take Dad's ashes, and there's no way that's going to happen. Dean walks to the pulpit immediately after the service, with me right on his heels. He picks up Dad's ashes and keeps them until we return to Dorothy and Harold's. Dean and I will decide where and when to scatter them. Later in bed, Mom reaches to turn off the light and rests her hand on Dad's ashes until she whispers "goodnight."

The next morning, Dad comes back to Vegas with us as the antenna flag flies at half-mast.

Dean knew how much Claribel disliked me because she told him at every opportunity. Even so, some months later, he talks me into stopping in Marana on our way to Tucson.

"She took good care of our dad, so you can manage an hour's visit with her."

Our pace slows then stops as we walk up the driveway to the sidewalk. We look at each other without saying a word. The desert sand has drifted to reclaim the sidewalk and first porch step. The place is dead without Dad. It takes a minute to realize Claribel doesn't live here anymore either. Walking back to the car, I know Dean wishes as much as I do that we hadn't stopped for one last sense of Dad.

Dad's death seemed to be the precursor to more changes.

Dorothy didn't leave Harold's side when he was dying the following year. She fussed over him and took care of him like she'd done nearly her entire life.

"I love you, and I'll see you again," she tells him. "I will see you again."

In my mind, I see Dad as clear as day. He's smiling, handing Harold a beer. They both contentedly drink and talk as they'd done so many times before, sitting at Dorothy's kitchen table.

In the years following Harold's death, Dorothy and her sister Juanita visit a couple of times a year. Stopping occasionally so I don't get too far ahead of them, I carry their matching carry-on bags as they follow me through the endless walkways of the airport. Walking together holding hands, they look like two little girls on an outing. I see now what I'll always miss because, for the first time in my life, I regret not having a sister.

Both widows are elderly now: shorter, rounder, and more beautiful. Dorothy and Juanita have the same hairstyle and could be mistaken for twins. Sweet little old ladies who can still rack my butt in a New York second playing euchre as they smile sweetly and take my last quarter.

Over the years, Mom left *him* a couple more times to move in with me. She wasn't happy with *him*, but she wouldn't be happy without *him*. I knew she wouldn't stay. After only a short time, she was on her way back. The last time she called to say she wanted to leave *him* and move in with me, I told her no.

"You know you won't stay, so why put me through it?"

She was mad at me for quite some time. Even so, I felt good finally standing up to her. She can't do any more damage to me than she already has.

Before Stevie turned sixteen, *he* kicked him out. I couldn't understand why Mom let *him* do it. A few years later, Stevie had a son who died at six weeks old from spinal meningitis. Not long after, and just a month after Harold died, Stevie was killed in a logging accident on a job in Oregon. He was only twenty-three years old. Every physical piece of evidence that *he* and Mom had been together was gone.

25

"The Prisoner's Song"

VERNON DALHART

It's September and over a hundred degrees in the shade when I park in my driveway with a pickup bed full of groceries. Stacey watches for me and hops in the bed to carry groceries inside but first tears through sacks to see if there are any goodies. "Oh boy! I love these! And these too!"

Even though I'm in the house waiting for a delivery of sacks from him, I can still hear sacks rustling and Stacey rummaging. I'm sure the neighbors think I starve him by the way he acts on grocery-shopping nights. I love that eight-year-old towheaded bundle of energy. As he carries in an armful, I go out to help. Gathering up sacks, I feel a tap on my shoulder.

"Are you Sherrie Lancaster?" a sleazy-looking guy asks.

"Yes."

"You've officially been served," he says, shoving an envelope in my hand.

"What? What's this?"

"A subpoena."

"A subpoena? I haven't done anything …" my voice trails off in confusion.

"That's not what they think," he says, tapping the envelope before he walks away.

"What do I do with this? You can't do this then just leave, damnit!"

But the cocky man's opening his car door.

"What's wrong?" Stacey asks.

"I'm not sure, and he won't tell me," I say, motioning to the man.

"There are directions, a phone number. Call Monday," the man calls back.

"Monday!" I yell. "This is only Friday! Can't you tell me what it's about?"

"All I can say is it's drug-related. You're wanted in Denver." Then he drives away.

"Drugs? Denver? Mom! What have you been up to?" Stacey's eyes are like saucers. Was that a flicker of amazement? Maybe I'm not so dull after all. "Wow, Mom, drugs?"

"Oh, stop it. Get the groceries in the house. I gotta call Uncle Dean."

"Wow, Sherrie! Drugs? What have you been up to?" Dean asks after I stumble through the story.

"Stop kidding around!"

After Dean stops laughing, I ask what I should do.

"Well, first you better get rid of all your drugs …"

"Dean, that sleazeball was serious."

"I know, I know. Read it to me."

There isn't a lot of information in the subpoena—only a phone number, directions to go to the Federal Marshal's office to arrange for an airplane ticket, and the need to respond promptly. I'm being subpoenaed to appear before a grand jury in Denver, Colorado.

"A grand jury? You're really in trouble." Dean chuckles.

"Dean!"

"Okay, okay. You could be met at the plane, handcuffed, and put in jail. I'm being serious now," he adds.

"But I haven't done anything, damnit!"

"I know, but they don't. You may have to get a lawyer to prove it."

Now I am worried, but there's nothing to be worried about. I haven't smoked pot in years, and I don't do other drugs. What could Denver want with me?

I'm in my boss's office bright and early Monday to show her the subpoena and ask for a day off. When I mention I want to talk to a lawyer before I go and why, she makes an immediate appointment with our company attorney. He advises me to go, but afterward, I wish he'd warned me what it would be like. Back in my boss's office, she grabs her purse and heads for the door.

"Come on, let's find the Marshal's office to arrange your flight!"

A male boss has never been this helpful.

By the end of the day, I have a round-trip ticket to Denver for the following morning and arrangements for Stacey in case I don't make it back the same day.

It's snowing when I land in Denver. This is frigging terrific. I'm scared to death, sweating bullets, and freezing now too. Making my way off the plane, with every step I take, I expect someone to stop me. Breathing a sigh of relief, I lean back in a taxicab that arrives downtown much sooner than I want.

After waiting only a minute in the reception area, I'm whisked into another room that I soon learn is only a door away from the grand jury. I sit down at a small conference table littered with file folders and a bright light shining from above. The room's messy with boxes piled over the floor and around the table. The only thing on the wall in front of me is a large clock ticking away seconds.

How many times have I seen this movie? I nearly laugh when a scene runs through my mind with a cop pacing and then propping a foot up on a chair. His shirt sleeves are rolled up with his arms resting on his knee. A cigarette dangles from his mouth as he hammers away at an obviously guilty man profusely sweating under a solitary bright light.

I turn to see if the wall behind me is a two-way mirror just as two men in suits walk in. One's short with light hair, and the other tall with dark hair. *They're pleasant, reasonable-looking men*, I'm thinking. After brief introductions, the short man keeps a reassuring smile as he sits down behind piles of folders across from me. The tall man immediately starts to pace, studying the contents of a folder. I barely have time to think, *Oh crap, it is like the movies*, when the tall man starts asking questions. Soon he's firing them at me, giving little time for answers.

"How long have you been at your present address?"

"About eight years."

"How long have you owned the mobile home?"

"About nine years."

"What's your phone number and area code?"

I reply with the number.

"Have you ever changed your phone number?"

"No."

"Do you own a black Cadillac with gold rims?"

"No."

"Do you know someone who does?"

"No."

I'm intimidated and confused: intimidated because I know they think I've done something wrong, and confused because I try to figure out why he asks what he does as I answer and he's already firing the next question at me.

"Have you ever ridden in a black Cadillac with gold rims?"

"No."

"What do you drive and what color?"

"A white GMC baby pickup."

"When was the last time you rode in the black Cadillac?"

"I told you I don't—"

"Have you ever changed your phone number?"

"I thought about it once, but I don't think I did."

Fired questions go on and on, then the tall man's quiet for a minute. The small man never takes his eyes off me, even when he flips through folders, and he still hasn't said a word. I glance at the wall clock. I've been sitting here for over an hour. The tall man takes off his suit jacket, throws it over a chair, and thrusts his face in mine.

"The grand jury's in session just beyond that door," he hisses and points. "I can have you in there in two seconds and have you sworn in just as quick. If you lie to them, you will go to jail! Who do you date?"

"No one now."

"When's the last time you went out with Angel Romero?" He's pacing again.

"I don't know A—"

"Do you sleep with him?"

"No, I don't know—"

"Have you ever avoided going to jail for drugs because you cut a deal?"

"No."

"When was the last time you did drugs?"

"It's been years since I smoked pot."

"You make a lot of money selling drugs."

"I don't—"

"How long since you went out with Angel?"

"I don't—"

"Do you do drugs with Angel when you're balling him!?"

He's in my face again with his hands gripping my chair. He's yelling as spit flies into my face.

"I can put you before the grand jury right now! You'll have to tell the truth or go to jail!"

I don't remember when I started to cry or when the small man pushed a box of tissues toward me, but used ones are rolled up in balls in front of me.

The tall man knocks them off with a swipe of his hand. My hands are shaking, but I can't feel them shake. It's like they belong to someone else. My face is burning hot, and my ears feel like they're melting. I must look really guilty.

"When's the last time besides today you flew out of Vegas?"

"Two weeks ago."

"Where did you go and why?"

"Albuquerque. My company sent me."

"The last time before that and why?"

"Last February. Reno or Albuquerque, I'm not sure. My company sent me."

"Who do you call here in Denver?"

"No one."

The small man hands the tall one a thick wad of papers that he waves in my face.

"I have months of your phone bills. There are dozens of calls to Denver. Why do you call here so often?"

"I don't call, and I don't know—"

"You're the best goddamned liar I've seen in a long time! I think I'll put you in front of the grand jury." He's in my face spitting again.

"Go ahead!" I scream at him. "Stop spitting on me! What do you want?"

"The truth!"

"I'm telling you the truth!"

It goes on and on. I think it'll never end when suddenly it does. The small man leaves. The tall man puts his suit jacket back on and paces. He doesn't look at me or talk. I sit very still, afraid he'll start again. After several minutes, the small man returns with yet another folder. Both of them look at it then briefly at each other.

"What's your phone number?" The small man speaks for the first time.

I repeat it again.

"Okay, thank you for your time. You're free to go," the tall man says.

"What? What!! How can you do what you've done and then say I can go?"

"Well, apparently you're not the person we're looking for," he dryly concedes.

"I told you that!"

"Well, you got to understand, little lady, that I deal with the scum of the earth. Drug dealers, pimps, murderers—"

"Everyone's not like that!" I'm interrupting him for a change.

"Well, you got to understand, little lady, that the vast majority of people who sit where you are end up in there," he says, motioning toward the grand jury. "Then they go to jail."

I can't believe it. He asked if I balled Angel, and now he's condescendingly calling me a little lady.

"You really got to understand the scum I deal with."

"You understand everyone's not like that, you bastard!" I yell at him.

He leaves and doesn't come back.

As I wipe my face with a tissue in a haze of rage, fear, and tears, the small man says my name, pats my hand, and sits down beside me.

"You've never changed your phone number since you've lived at your present address," he says matter-of-factly. "You've lived at your present address seven years, not eight. The last time you flew out was three weeks ago, not two, and you went to Reno last March, not February."

"How do you know all that?" I'm eerily amazed. This is creepier than the intense questioning.

"We know everything about you. Your place is very well kept. I loved your yard and flowers."

"You were at my house! When? Why didn't you talk to me then?"

"Three weeks ago. It would've saved a lot of confusion had you been home. We didn't realize you were out of town when we arrived."

"If you know so much about me, why did you think I'm a drug dealer?"

"Well, not only did we have copies of all phone bills proving regular calls to drug connections here, but also you absolutely fit the physical description of the female we're looking for: tall, slim, short blond hair, blue eyes, attractive."

"But I don't call anyone here …"

"We know that now. We have the correct phone number, just the wrong name. We called the phone company in Vegas, gave them the number of the woman we're looking for, and asked for the name on the account. We were given your name. But your number is one digit off from the number we gave them to check. They made a mistake, and we didn't catch it until now. We were sure you're the one we're looking for because of the physical description, but after you continued to answer questions basically the same way and didn't crack open, we began to have doubts."

"Crack? I feel like I've been hit by a Mack truck. One damn digit! Which one?"

"Oh, I can't tell you that," he laughs. "You're free to go. What time's your flight?"

"Not until five." The wall clock ticks off seconds past 12:30 p.m.

"I'll fix that for you." He returns and says, "You've got a 2 p.m. flight now."

My flight's the last one allowed to take off before the airport closes due to a snowstorm. And I'm going back to a hundred-plus degrees. I lean back in my seat and close my eyes as relief is slowly replaced with excitement. I'm on my way home—back to the rhythm of my life. Boring never sounded so good. But as usual, it didn't stay that way for long.

26

"My Buddy"

DORIS DAY

What am I doing walking down a hospital hallway to the AIDS ward? What nightmare have I stumbled into? Dean's best friend, Millie, called to say she's taking him to another doctor because his flu is worse. In her next call, she tells me he's being admitted.

Dean's lying on a hospital bed with his eyes closed. Another man's thrashing on a second bed in the room. When I kiss his cheek, Dean opens his eyes in a panic.

"I have AIDS," he whispers. "I'm a statistic."

He covers his eyes with one hand and quietly cries. He turned thirty-nine the previous week, but we didn't celebrate because he was sick with the flu.

Millie's sitting in a waiting room, talking to a woman. The man sharing Dean's room lives next door to the woman. He'd told her he had AIDS and asked her to drive him to the hospital. She didn't know him but without hesitation, drove him here and waited for him to be admitted. In the first minutes of my exposure to this terrible world of AIDS, I meet this woman: the first of many who try to make this nightmare bearable by being there for those who are sick and those who love them.

Millie tells me about the second doctor visit. He had taken one look at Dean and said, "You have AIDS. You also have PCP, pneumocystis carinii pneumonia." Then he told Millie to take Dean directly to the hospital.

We walk back to Dean's room, and Millie kisses his cheek and leaves. I stay while nurses prepare him for the first of many lengthy battles against the horror of AIDS. We talk very little, and when I do, it's with a confidence I don't feel. Dean's replies are quiet but resolved. I won't see him cry again during the next twenty months.

"I'll be back as soon as I fix dinner for Stacey," I tell him. As his grip on my hand tightens, I add, "I'll be back after I feed the kid."

Up to now, I have left nine-year-old Stacey alone only for short periods and never at night. I agonize over how to be in two places at the same time. I know I'll be spending most of my evenings with Dean, and I can't afford a babysitter every night. After Stacey's fed and asleep, I head back to the hospital and stay several hours. Stacey never knows I've been gone.

I quickly fall into a routine. The hospital's a short distance from where I work, so I walk there every day during lunch. After work, I come home to be a mom. As soon as Stacey's asleep, I head back to the hospital. Somehow, I know I won't let Dean die alone: I'll be with him. I tramped a million miles behind him exploring when we were kids, and I'll tramp behind him now as far as I can go.

The nurses in the AIDS ward take nearly as good care of me as they do Dean. They tell me how to enter the hospital after visiting hours. They find a comfortable rocking chair and haul it into Dean's room for me. They tell me things I should know about AIDS and comfort me after a session when a doctor reduced me to a crying baby because of his forceful explanation of what Dean has yet to face.

I can't believe anyone can be so sick with thrashing and horrible fevers hitting 105 degrees regularly and soaring to 108. A special mattress makes a loud noise and provides freezing cold to break the fevers. Dean's so hot one night, my fingers burn when I touch him. He begs me not to let the loud noise start because it's so cold. His body shakes and his teeth chatter from fever. He begins to shake more violently from the ice mattress that freezes him. Eventually his fever breaks again, and he restlessly sleeps.

They tell me he'll probably die soon. They tell me if he does live, he may have dementia from the fevers. They tell me he'll never be free from pneumonia, and they tell me to get a power of attorney. Then they tell me I'd better call our mother. My head's spinning, and I'm so tired. I think I'll scream if they tell me one more thing about his condition or what I need to do. *Just make him well*, I think. That's all I want.

I explain to Mom that Dean's pneumonia is getting worse. "You better come if you want to see him." I expect them to arrive the following evening. How am I going to tell her that Dean has AIDS? How am I going to tell her he's gay? Am I going to tell her he's gay?

"Oh, Dean. What do you want me to say to our mom?" I ask.

But he can't talk for me this time. I have to do it myself.

When they arrive at my home, I calmly explain Dean's pneumonia is a result of AIDS, and he's dying.

"How did he get it?" Mom asks.

"Who knows. There are many ways to get it. The important thing is you can't get it by holding his hand or kissing his cheek."

"Oh! I know that!" Mom searches for an ever-ready tissue. She cries, and *he* doesn't say a word.

I'm relieved they don't ask if Dean's gay. Whatever their reasons, they don't ask. I'm glad I don't see any aversion in their eyes so I don't have to say they have no right to judge him. I don't have to tell her to just be a mother for once and love him unconditionally like he's loved her his whole life.

"I knew Dean wasn't rough and tough like the other boys," she says.

It's late when we finish talking and they go to bed. I head to the hospital to tell Dean that Mom will be here in the morning, though I know he can't hear me. They stay for a week.

I arrive at the hospital to find the curtain around Dean's bed drawn shut. I can tell from Dean's sounds that he's scared, and I can tell from the nurse's sounds that she's changing his bedsheets. This nurse is one of my favorites. She's an older lady with a caring grandmother aura. Her legs are so swollen they look like tree trunks. She's been nursing a long time and spent long hours walking from room to room during her night shift. The skin around her ankles flows over the tops of broken-down shoes with the soles worn to a dangerous slant.

Her kind voice murmurs soothing sounds, and after a few minutes, she opens the curtain to stiffly walk away on wooden, swollen legs.

"You're wonderful," I tell her.

"It's easy. He's a nice man."

Later that night, the man sharing Dean's room dies. Early the next morning, Dean's fevers stop, and he slowly gets better.

"Dean, do you know who I am? What are you doing loafing around? Talk to me!"

Dean briefly looks at me then closes his eyes to go back to sleep. He's lost over fifty pounds, and he's very weak.

"Give him a few days, and he should be more responsive," the nurses say. "But keep trying to get him talking!"

This is as agonizing as watching him nearly die. He's getting better, but will he know me? Twice a day, I start talking as soon as I hit the door. I'd be so happy to hear him tell me to shut up.

"Do you know who I am, Dean?"

"You're my sister," he weakly replies.

I fly around the room, acting like a happy idiot. Kissing his cheek, I tell him to keep right on talking.

"I will if you stop asking stupid questions."

Dean's back!

The next time I hit the door talking, Dean says things that don't make any sense. That stops me cold. There is something wrong with him. He keeps talking weird, but he can't keep the familiar smirk off his face. If he weren't so weak, I'd pound him. And I tell him so.

After several more days, Dean is discharged. He's been there for nearly a month. But before the week is out, he's back in the hospital, sicker than before.

They tell me again that he'll probably die soon. I call Mom in Oregon again, and they drive down. We have the same routine: they go to the hospital during the day and stay with Stacey at night. They stay another week.

The nurses couldn't find my overstuffed rocker, so I sit in an uncomfortable, straight-back chair. Dean's losing more weight. His already salt-and-pepper hair is turning saltier by the day, and he isn't fighting the fevers. AIDS, that four-letter word, is consuming him. I hold his hand and daydream us both back to our exploring days when I tramped a million miles behind him while he looked for our next adventure.

We race down a shale hill on our butts, causing an avalanche of shale to slide too. Then we crawl back up on hands and knees, trying to knock the other back down. We slide down and crawl up again and again.

We tramp through a cornfield where the corn's harvested, but the stalks haven't been plowed under. With little effort, I can pull a stalk from the ground, with dirt clinging to the root ball. After a good swing, I launch it to fall like an arrow on the head of an unsuspecting brother. The battle's on with cornstalks flying until we've annihilated each other.

Afterward, I think about that amazing tree in Missouri. We're standing on a bluff, overlooking a beautiful meadow with only one tree in the center. It's a huge, ominous, evil-looking tree: a thorn tree with thorns on the trunk and every branch. Like AIDS, it's living but looks dead.

When sitting becomes unbearable, I walk up and down the AIDS ward, only to witness other unbearable scenes. I hear a mother's keening when she learns her child is dying. I see panic in a father's eyes: panic from seeing his son dying or from just learning his son is gay. I witness an occasional round of applause when someone manages a few steps, and the choruses of "good luck" when someone gets to go home for a while. I observe the silent bedside vigil and the empty bed that doesn't stay empty for very long.

It's been nearly another month when my heart skips a beat as I walk into Dean's room. His eyes are open.

"Dean! You're awake! How are you?"

A garbled slur is all he can manage, and I see panic in his eyes. When I check him over, his wrists and ankles are tied to the bed.

"Ah, claustrophobia attack, huh?"

After I quickly untie him, he immediately starts to relax, so I find a nurse to ask why he's tied.

"He won't stay in bed and keeps falling. I can't watch him every second!"

I tell Dean they'll tie him up again if he doesn't stay in bed, and he must buzz for the nurse if he needs help. But he can't press the buzzer when I put it in his hand. When I ask how he's getting out of bed, he shows me how he does it: by twisting his shoulders and lurching over the side rail. I catch him before he falls on his head.

Dean tries but can't talk. When I get a pad and pen from my purse, he can't press hard enough to write. I try a pencil with the same result. His eyes are flashing blue fire. I instinctively know now that he wasn't just trying to get out of bed: he was trying to leave.

"Good! Get mad! Get really pissed, damnit! Then you'll start getting better, and that's the only way you're gonna get outta here! You can't leave until then, so you better stop trying, or they'll keep you tied up forever!"

I can't believe this. For two months he's been near death, and now I'm yelling at him. Damn! It feels good! I untie him later that night and again the next day.

"Will you promise you won't try to leave, Dean?"

He nods yes. The claustrophobia attacks are harder to bear than his desire to leave, so he'll cooperate. When Dr. Crook walks in, I promise her, on Dean's behalf, that he'll obey the rules. I press a pencil into his hand and help him make an "X" beneath a statement saying he won't try to leave.

"I'll believe you this time, but you must stay in bed and not hurt yourself," she says.

Dean nods in agreement, and Dr. Crook attaches the paper with Dean's "X" to his chart, pats his arm, and continues her rounds. That night he's not tied to the bed.

"If Dr. Crook comes in, don't help me," Dean says a few days later.

Shortly, I push my chair out of the way for Dr. Crook to check his chart. Dean sits up, swings his long legs over the side, and stands up. He steadies himself for just a second then takes two steps away from the bed to turn and face Dr. Crook. He dances, or rather shuffles, a little two-step dance and smiles.

"See, I'm better. Will you be my personal physician?" Dean asks.

Dr. Crook looks up at him with tears in her eyes.

"I didn't realize you're this tall, Dean. I also never thought I'd be looking at you standing here like this. And yes, of course, I'll be your personal physician."

"Help me now," Dean says after she leaves.

I help him sit and swing his legs up as he lies down.

"I have to get back to work," I tell him.

Then I leave so he won't see me cry.

27

Still "My Buddy"

DORIS DAY

Dean quickly improves, and Dr. Crook discharges him. The following weekend, he walks through my door slightly stooped, dangerously thin, and in control. His eyes are snapping happy as he sets Easter presents on the kitchen table for Stacey and me.

Dean's Ford Thunderbird is his pride and joy. I've started off all previous road trips at his bidding by dusting the dash and controls before we get outside the city limits. If he's in the middle of nowhere on his way to Mom's, he's happy.

He's soon heading there on his own, to be followed by Idaho, visiting places again where we lived as kids. He travels to Rock Creek Canyon to find the treasure can the boys buried thirty-three years ago. He finds the house and drives around, trying to find where they buried the treasure. He asks a rancher, who recognizes the meadow Dean describes. The rancher tells him how to find it. Dean spends hours digging for the treasure but never finds the can. I wish it had still been there for Dean to find.

By summer, Dean has regained a lot of weight he'd lost, and Millie decides it's time to celebrate by providing Dean, Stacey, and me an expense-paid vacation to Southern California. She takes us on a car tour of Balboa Island and a ship tour of the surrounding coastal area. Then we visit Disneyland and Knotts Berry Farm. It's a wonderful vacation, with everyone acting their shoe size instead of their age.

Sunday dinners are at my house, whether or not I want to cook. By midweek, our nightly telephone conversation consists of Dean talking about food.

"Homemade noodles and mashed potatoes sound good. How about fried chicken, mashed potatoes, and gravy?"

When Saturday rolls around, I'm so hungry for Dean's latest suggestion I'm already preparing for the next day's dinner. If I haven't called yet to invite him and Millie, he's calling asking what time's dinner.

Dean plays the organ while I cook and clean up. He plays by ear and has many songs memorized, so when I call out a title, he plays it. Irish tunes are favorites, along with the old songs Mom likes to sing; however, the most beautiful are religious songs. We didn't remain religious after our faithful time as kids in Tucson, but we still love the music. The organ has a built-in recorder, so I record many of his songs that I'll play during his memorial service.

The following summer, Dean gives Mom things he wants her to have, and he gives me things he wants me to have. Among them are the little black Bible I gave him for Christmas in Tucson when we knew Mom would come back, his little wooden treasure box that still has a locket with Mom's picture, Dad's ashes, and *The Little Shepherd of Kingdom Come* book. He tells me that when the book disappears from my bookshelf, I'll know he has stolen it from me again.

Dean starts working on me to go with him to Mom's for her sixty-fifth birthday. He's already arranged for Stacey to stay with Millie. For the first time, Dean doesn't want him to go. He says it's time for just us to have a vacation.

I know there's more to it than that because he's losing weight again, but I let him talk me into it anyway.

"What if you get sick on the trip, Dean?"

"Then you'll drive me home."

I agree and the deal's sealed. I try to renege one time but finally do what I know he wants me to do.

We make the trip in the usual sixteen hours. Dean's at his best, and we talk and laugh the entire way. Among many topics we discuss, I remind Dean of the bra incident years ago when he told me, "Don't worry, I'll tell you when it's time to wear one."

"I'll still tell you when it's time to wear one so don't worry," he immediately replies with his deadpan, perfect timing.

Mom makes her big breakfast the following morning and says she'll fatten Dean up in no time. The next morning's a repeat of the previous one. After he kisses Mom's cheek and thanks her for the meal, he lies down. An hour later, Dean calls for me, and every bit of happiness evaporates. I know he's sick. Dean is shaking so hard the bed's rattling. I sit with him until the shaking stops and the fever starts.

I call Dr. Crook to tell her I'm going to drive him home. She says that if we leave soon, he should be okay.

"However, if his fever reaches one hundred and five, get him to a hospital."

"I better go to town for a thermometer, Dean."

"Don't bother," Dean replies, lying comfortably on the couch.

"You're really hot. I'll call the hospital."

"No thermometer, no hospital," he tells me. "We'll celebrate Mom's birthday today when they get back from the store, and we'll leave for Vegas first thing in the morning."

"If you die on me, Dean, I'll kill ya."

"We'll be fine," he says and chuckles.

They decide to drive halfway back with us to McDermitt on the

Oregon-Nevada border, and we leave the next morning on Mom's birthday. Dean slept little the night before, and I haven't slept at all. I tried to keep him on his medication schedule of every two hours, but by early morning, I couldn't get him to take any pills—he's too sick.

We rent two motel rooms in McDermitt. I get Dean into bed and go to Mom's room for takeout burgers. We take turns eating and sitting with Dean. By 11 p.m., I attempt to get him comfortable before I plop down on my bed. He tries to be quiet so I can sleep, but he's restless and can't stay still.

"Do you want me to throw you in the car and head home?"

"Do you really want to?" he asks.

I know that's exactly what he wants. While he dresses, I knock on Mom's door to tell them we are leaving.

"We'll go with you, but I can't until morning," *he* says.

"I have to leave now."

I start the car to warm it up, pack our things in the trunk, and spread a blanket on the back seat for Dean. As I'm finishing up, they walk over, dressed and ready to go. I'm relieved *he* changed *his* mind. Just then, Dean steps out, dressed and ready to go too.

"Get back inside. It's thirty degrees out here!" I tell him.

He and Mom had just bought coffee in the office, where they learned we can get a "Flight for Life" to have Dean in Vegas in just a couple of hours, but it's very expensive.

"I'll pay for it if he'll go," I tell them and then head inside to discuss it with Dean.

"No."

"I'll stay with you the whole time, Dean."

"No. You said you'd drive," he reminds me.

We're on the road just past midnight, heading home, following *him* and Mom. Dean sits in the back and dozes. I position the rearview mirror so I can see his face. We stop often, but as the night wears on, he can't get out of the car anymore. I buy cold Pepsi at the last stop, and when Dean asks for a drink, I pass an open can back to him. He takes a sip and says, "Ummm, that tastes good." And he keeps it down.

It's still dark at 6:30 a.m. when Dean has a heart attack. His torso forcibly lunges forward and back twice, but he remains sitting upright. I reach back for his hand, and his fingers are icy. I can barely see to drive as tears soak me. An eternity later, Dean leans up in the seat so he can see out the windshield.

"Mom's still up ahead, Dean."

But Dean isn't looking at the car ahead. He's hunched down so he can look through the windshield at a higher angle. He intently stares for a long time while I watch his face in the rearview mirror.

"Who do you see, Dean? Is it Dad? Is Dad helping you?"

But Dean can't answer. He sits back and deeply exhales a long, final breath. It's 7:20 a.m. when Dean goes exploring without me.

We're several miles from Tonopah, Nevada, where I have to explain what happened to the mortician and the sheriff. Then I call Dr. Crook to tell her I should have put Dean on that plane. She's a compassionate lady.

"You know how Dean hated the hospital. You let him die with dignity doing what he loved to do," she tells me.

I still hold on to that today.

After spending two nights, *he* decides to leave the following morning. I don't understand why they won't stay for the memorial, but whatever. Mom's lost three sons—Ronnie, Stevie, and now Dean—and however she handles it is up to her. When the memorial's over, I bring Dean's ashes home and place them beside Dad's on the organ.

The following spring, Millie calls to say it's time to scatter their ashes. She had promised Dean she'd help me do it. I originally wanted to take them to Idaho and scatter their ashes when sagebrush is blooming with the sweet smell in the air. But Dean had told Millie of a closer place where he and Dad had been happy.

I attach Dad's small flag to my car's antenna at half-mast. My rosebush is in full bloom, so I cut an armload. We drive to a spot by a big, beautiful Joshua tree close to Mountain Pass, California, and scatter their ashes and roses. I'm glad they're together.

28

"On the Front Porch"

BURL IVES

A profile catches my attention as I walk down a hallway at work. I don't know why, but I'm drawn to stop and glance in that direction. A few cubicles away, a man is completely engrossed at his keyboard.

I still don't know what caused the need to look. I couldn't see his handsome face: only a partial profile. I couldn't see the lively blue eyes under barely controlled eyebrows; a straight, masculine nose; a strong, square chin; or dimpled cheeks that were deeply grooved from his wonderful smile—a smile I would soon be lost in for years.

"Who's that?" I ask a coworker.

"New employee. Just started a few days ago."

This is my first week back from our last trip to Oregon. I'm still numb from all that happened and barely functioning on autopilot.

"Oh," I mumble and continue on to wherever I'm headed, completely unaware my life just changed again for forever and a day.

Later, I take an elevator down to the break area. I don't feel like talking, but someone always wants to. A female coworker asks if I've been to Wet 'n' Wild—a water park on the Strip. Yes, I tell her, and I launch into a Stacey story that's consistently safe ground—I can get through it without crying. I notice the man standing not far away; I'm partway through my story about Dean convincing me to go down a huge waterslide after he and Stacey had taken the plunge.

"Okay, chicken," Dean says. "Your little boy can do it …"

"We just walked up a million stairs. I'm resting."

While we spar, Stacey climbs onto the slide.

"See ya at the bottom!" he yells, and he's gone. Later, I hear a faint splash.

"You go, then I will."

"Oh sure, chicken."

Well, two chickens are enough. I step onto the slide and lie back, crossing my ankles then my arms over my chest. When the attendant gives me a small push, I have time to say, "Oh, shit!" just once before I hit the water in what amounts to an eighty-mile-an-hour douche.

When the coworker laughs, a male chuckle joins in. I look up to see the man standing just feet away. He's neatly dressed, and his total presence is warm, friendly, and handsome.

"I'm not fond of rides like that anymore either," he says. "Hi, I'm the new kid, Bill."

"Hi, I'm Sherrie," I stammer through embarrassment.

I can't believe I just finished talking about a douche in front of a male—and a stranger, at that. I know my face is burning red. After a couple minutes of small talk, I leave as graciously as possible and fly back to my desk.

I spend the next couple of days walking the parking garage on breaks so I won't have to talk to anyone. But it's not long before I see Bill sauntering toward me.

"What's that young man of yours been up to these days?" he asks.

In what I soon learn are Bill's thoughtful and considerate ways, he starts the conversation on my safe ground and keeps it there until I'm ready for a change. As time goes on, his broad knowledge and sense of humor make any subject a delightful adventure.

There is such a thing as love at first sight, and it's much more than a person's appearance or demeanor. Something caused me to stop and look in Bill's direction the first time we were in the same vicinity. Something caused him to gravitate toward me. We loved each other from the beginning, and though we didn't realize it at the time, we knew we genuinely enjoyed each other's company. We spend more than a year being best friends.

Getting to know Bill is the best journey I've taken. We spend hours talking. I'm fascinated by his perception, the way he simplifies the most difficult problem to make perfect sense of it, and the gentle way he guides me to an understanding after I've been out in left field. His voice, mannerisms, strength, and manliness burrow into my mind and heart. Someone in this vast, indifferent world actually cares for me. It matters to someone how I feel. I matter to him. Bill's interested in me—in my opinions, likes, and dislikes. He likes me for what I am, and I like what I am when I'm with him.

"This is a lovely home," Bill says the first time he visits.

"It's small and a bit cluttered, but it's mine. And my world fits here."

"Ah! but it's organized clutter. I see you everywhere in here."

We're interested in each other. As time passes, we acknowledge our interest in us.

"There can't *not* be an us," he says. "And I can't hit and run. I love you *all that I am.*"

And I couldn't agree more.

Bill wants to be near me, and I need him there. A man wants a woman; a woman needs a man. When we're together, we're silly teenagers or sage adults or irresponsible kids. But first and foremost, we're always best friends. Best friends become best lovers, and for the first time in my life, I know what it is to love and be loved unconditionally. At forty years old, I finally know what it feels like to be a woman. And it's especially nice to really like someone you love.

Bill's alternating boyish charm, playfulness, and sophisticated gentleman-liness cushion me and keeps me safe from things that still rankle close to the surface. In the safe circle of his presence on my porch, watching a magnificent sunset, I can finally talk to someone about the years I chased Mom in my attempts to be where I thought I belonged. He helps put my past in perspective and teaches me many things, but the most precious is trust. And I trust him completely.

29

"Walking the Floor over You"

ERNEST TUBB

The last time I drove to Oregon to see Mom, I told her I wanted another baby before I'm too old.

"You probably think I'm crazy."

"No, I don't. I understand perfectly," Mom says.

She links her arm in mine to walk back to the kitchen. We continue the baby conversation and change the subject when *he* comes back inside.

A month later, Bill's happy when I tell him I'm pregnant, and I can't wait to tell Stacey. I'd never meant to raise him as an only child. I'd always wanted enough kids for a decent-sized baseball team.

Stacey's ecstatic at the news. He just turned thirteen years old: what a wonderful age. His skin's as soft as a baby's butt, and he still has a hint of dimples where his knuckles will soon be. I often wonder how any mother could leave her child at this magical age—there doesn't seem to be any age that isn't magical.

Samuel's another beautiful bundle of baby man. He sleeps in my arms, swaddled in a receiving blanket, when Bill brings Stacey in to check out his brother. Stacey gently rubs Samuel's hand with his finger, then the tiny fist opens to clutch that finger. Stacey doesn't move until the baby lets go.

At home, Stacey carries Samuel all around the house. Wherever one is, there's the other.

"When you're big enough, I'll teach you how to throw a football and a baseball. I'll teach you all that stuff. Don't worry about girls, either, 'cause I'll tell you about them too!" Stacey promises the baby.

Bill chuckles, sitting at the kitchen table and whispering to me, "I'll sure be glad when Samuel's ready for girl stuff. Then Stacey will tell him, and I'll listen, then maybe I'll finally understand girls too!"

$\backsim$

He stopped speaking to me after *he* learned I was pregnant. I'm pregnant but not married, so it's beneath *him* to talk to me. I don't talk to Mom much anymore, either, because I know it's stressful for her when I do call. And she never calls me—she's not allowed to.

Several weeks after Samuel's first birthday, Mom calls, happy and talkative for the first time in ages. After a few minutes, *he* takes the phone and chats like *he's* been talking to me once a week for the last two years. When Mom's back on, I ask why *he* decided to talk to me.

"Oh, it's okay now."

"Well, it's not okay, and I don't want to talk to *him*."

Mom immediately cries and hangs up the phone. Just before the line goes dead, I hear her say, "Well that's it, it's over!"

When the phone rings a couple of hours later, I know it's *him*. I ask Stacey to take the baby to my bedroom and stay there. I'm finally going to tell *him* off after thirty-two years, and I don't want my babies to hear.

"Hello."

"Oh, now, I just don't understand why you're mad at me," *he drunkenly gushes.*

"*You* haven't spoken to me for two years. Why start now?"

"Well, you know how it is. You're not married and all and have a baby."

"How dare *you* judge me, *you son-of-a-bitch*! After all *you've* done to my mother! And *you* didn't marry her until after Stevie died. *You* didn't raise one of *your* kids! Not even Stevie. *You* kicked him out before he was grown. Don't *you* dare judge me after how *you* treated *your* own kids!"

"Oh, so that's what this is about," *he says,* suddenly sober, referring to the long-ago abandonment.

"No, actually, this is about *you. You are pitiful!*" Then I slam down the phone.

I know Mom will never speak to me now. I briefly wonder if *he'll* beat the hell out of her again tonight, but I put it out of my mind and silently talk to Mom one last time.

I guess I'm the one who'll finally say goodbye, Mom. I never wanted to. You always said, "so long," never "goodbye." To you, goodbye was final: over and done. "So long" meant you knew you'd see that person again. Even that long-ago Saturday in the park, you said so long and not goodbye. That had been the source of my hope: the reason I always knew I'd see you again. Now I suppose I never will. I love you, Mom. Goodbye.

I finally let her go from me as I watch Stacey play with Samuel on my bed. Stacey nearing his fourteenth year and Samuel in his second—both are so achingly innocent. And I wonder for the millionth time how any mother could leave her children at such wonderful ages.

Time marches on. Two beautiful boys: one nearly grown, one starting school. There are hopes and dreams with shadows and worries.

Dorothy told me all you can do is your very best and love and guide them then cross your fingers, hope, and pray. If you know you've tried your best, you won't have thorns in your pillow at night. But sometimes your best will never be good enough. Remember, they step on your toes then on your heart.

One boy cares only for himself; one boy adores the other. One is increasingly belligerent; the other gentle and calm. I probably give too much leeway in the hope that maturity and time will smooth over the struggle of a boy growing up. I learn the hard way that patience isn't the best way to teach character.

One calculates what's in it for him; the other will gladly give you anything. One constantly breaks the heart of the other who has the sweetest heart I've ever known. The oldest lies when the truth is easier. The youngest could never conceive of lying, and he's the one soon to be diagnosed with autism.

I used to know what the oldest was thinking before he knew—then I didn't. I didn't understand him anymore. Then I did—another emotionally destructive tug-of-war with me, just like how it was with my mother. How could this have happened? When? Why? Not a day goes by that I don't try to understand it. What did I do wrong? Will I ever know? I have to keep it together. And I will because I have to.

Within seven months, the only ones who loved me unconditionally are both gone.

I miss seeing Dorothy's beautiful, warm-brown eyes again when I fly to Tucson. She's leaving quickly, having slipped into a coma before I arrived. Dorothy's sister, both daughters, and her two oldest granddaughters are walking, sitting, crying, and keeping Dorothy's sons informed by phone. It's heartbreaking. I cry for Dorothy and myself and them as I sit beside her, holding her hand. Much later, I realize I can feel Dorothy's heartbeat against my arm while I hold her hand. It's a beautiful, comforting feeling—full of Dorothy's love, strength, and caring. Dorothy's heart continues talking to mine for a full minute after someone says she is gone.

Several months later, Samuel is admitted to a pediatric hospital for five days with pneumonia. Bill is seeing doctors and having tests while I stay with Samuel in the hospital. Thankfully, Samuel fully recovers … but Bill can't.

Now I have to break the sweetest little heart and tell him his dad couldn't get well.

When each of my babies was born, I promised myself and them that they would always have a mother and a home to come back to for as long as I live. But things have their own way of turning out because if someone has always had something, he might not have a need for it. The oldest left home, and I haven't heard from him in years. When I could finally think about it without crying, I realized it's probably best because I couldn't absorb much more hurt—for myself or for Samuel.

Samuel and I still climb autism together. He's made fantastic progress, sometimes by leaps and bounds and sometimes by baby steps, but it's still all progress. I'm so proud of his courage, which is something he has to have, given the world he must live in. A world unwelcoming to anyone who doesn't fit into its acceptable mold for any reason.

I do know the curse stopped, at least for one generation, with me. My kids will leave me when they're ready and not the other way around. I can only hope that the oldest has the will to keep trouble away, and I will remain able to continue helping the youngest find his way.

30

"Driftwood on the River"

ERNEST TUBB

NEVADA, MISSOURI
TWENTY MILES FROM EL DORADO SPRINGS

I did see her one last time—after her recurring dream about dark, swirling water came true.

The woman looks uncomfortable. "I don't know if you can see her. I have to ask the coroner."

"I told him yesterday I was flying in today," I reply. "He said we could see her."

Aunt Ruth, Mom's only surviving sister, is with me. The coroner told me that he embalmed them both, even though *his* brother said they were to be cremated. They will be, but I'll be able to see her first.

I had learned only the day before that Mom was dead. I also learned that they had moved back to Missouri from Oregon. I called Mom's neighbor

Rod in Oregon to see if it was true. Rod's wife confirmed that they'd recently moved. Then she asked if my dad's name was Ralph. I said, "Yes, why?" She wanted me to know what Mom said when they were fishing just days before they moved. Rod's wife sat with Mom to keep her from wandering away while the men fished. Unexpectedly, Mom turned to her and spoke.

"Ralph was a good man," Mom said.

Rod's wife questioned Mom, but Mom hushed her and retreated again to her silent world when she saw *him* returning.

Rod was surprised when I told him I'd be staying with my aunt in El Dorado Springs. Rod said *he'd* told Mom many times that all her sisters were dead. *He* moved Mom to a house close to El Dorado Springs, where she spent one night before she died. The two sisters didn't know they were only twelve miles apart.

The woman opens a door and waits for me to enter, but I freeze in the doorway. The room smells like chemicals. I face a counter with sinks and crane-neck faucets with plastic hoses attached. I know they've been used on her. Two narrow tables sit side by side with less than two feet between them and perpendicular to the counter. A body lies on each with feet closest to the counter.

I can see Mom's beautiful silver hair. A rumpled, stained sheet covers her with a piece of rough two-by-four sticking out near her shoulder. *It must make her lay right,* I think, touching her hair. She's so pale. I hope she'll open her sparkling-blue eyes and be glad I'm here. Maybe she'll finally know how much I've loved and missed her all my life. At last, maybe she'll be sorry for the pain she and *he* caused so many people.

I always thought *he'd* kill her in a drunken rage someday, but I never imagined they would die together because alcoholism prevented them from helping each other out of their van. Apparently, they had both been drinking when *he* swerved to avoid hitting a downed tree, skidded off the narrow country road, and ended up stuck in the mud. A river close by, swollen from spring rains, continued overflowing its banks while they sat there. The dark, swirling water crept into the van and was chest high on her before it began to recede. They probably died from hypothermia.

I was sure I'd know somehow when Mom died. Somehow, she'd come to me in a dream like Gramma had done. But I didn't know. Three days passed before they were found. And I never imagined it would end in Missouri where it all started thirty-eight years earlier when she left us to go with *him*.

I turn to look at *him* under *his* rumpled, stained sheet. I look only long enough to make sure *he's* dead then turn back to Mom.

I wish I could fix her hair and put on her makeup like she'd done for Gramma. But *his* brother won't let me into her house to gather what I could use or keep because the brother came from the same mold as *him*. Sadly, I won't be able to do what I know she'd want me to do. But I've already missed her for so long, so how can this be any different? I kiss her goodbye.

Aunt Ruth and I arrange a memorial service. Afterward, I scatter her ashes and flower petals on a bluff by a river in a beautiful spot with trees, a gnarled tree stump, and yellow and blue wildflowers—close to where *his* family will later scatter *his* ashes. There's no reason to bring her home with me. Each time she moved in, she always went back to *him*. I know she'll want to stay with *him* this time too. Maybe now she'll finally be content and not cry anymore.

EPILOGUE

"Back in Your Own Backyard"

EDDIE FISHER, WINTER GARDEN THEATRE, OCTOBER 1962

LAS VEGAS, NEVADA

I still can't get over how well sunsets are done just off my porch. Yet even now, I occasionally have a familiar urge to wander. A bit of homelessness will remain, I guess, because of that last walk from town years ago, which seems like just yesterday. I sometimes still find myself stuck between the life I'm living and the one to where I can't return. I see the twinkling, friendly lights of Burley from the outskirts, but I'll remain just there: on the outskirts. I see a lost kid trying to belong somewhere and a dirty face filled with determination and stubbornness—a mix that served me well. *I'm still sane,* I think.

At some point, we have to decide to hell with what's gone before. Learn from it so we won't make the same mistakes, and move on even if we have to start out on our knees to get a sense of direction. My mistake was twofold: taking way too long to figure out I had to move on without Mom then taking too many years to do it successfully. It was hard. But we already know life's hard. We have to be gentle with ourselves then do what we know is right for us.

I don't know what adventures are waiting, but life goes on for those willing to live it. How we live comes from within, and if we try, we'll find responsibility and tolerance there. Then we can take care of those we love so no one else has to do it for us. Indifference is a cold-blooded soul killer.

I suppose if I move from the old lady someday, it'll be one of the hardest things I've ever done. Bill gave me love and life here, and I raised two sons here. Mom and Stevie stayed many times. Carson visited and teased and smiled that smile I still see even after he was killed in a California firestorm. Dad and Dean cared for and improved my home and life. I look at the well-traveled copy of *The Little Shepherd of Kingdom Come* on the bookshelf and hope to see it gone one day, then I'll know Dean stopped by again. And Dorothy, Dorothy and Harold ... So many have graced my doorway and never will again, but I see them here.

Aunt Ruth told me one time that people usually end up doing what they like. Samuel's laughing while playing video games, so I'll take some time to admire one more magnificent sunset and listen to music—songs that take me adventuring with the boys or walking down a lane with Mom or wrapping me up in Dad's wonderful rhythm dancing across a salted floor or showing me Dorothy's beautiful, warm-brown eyes—the songs that lift me and make me whole. No matter what comes next, those songs will carry me through.

I am a fortunate woman. And I'm glad to be a contented one.

Left to right: Craig, Ronnie, Dad holding
me, Carson, Mom, and Dean.

Left to right: Craig, Ronnie, Aunt Ruth holding me,
Carson, and Dean in front of our rock garden.

Me looking through the picture window in Barracks Home.
I'm undoubtedly standing on something I shouldn't be.

Dean with me holding a doll in the front yard of Barracks Home.

Dean holding me in the backyard of Barracks Home.

I really want to turn those TV dials.

Gramma and me.

The cowboy girl.

Left to right: Dean, Craig, Carson, Ronnie, and
me front and center in front of Barracks Home.
Mom made the boys' shirts and my dress.

I want to go with Carson and play ball.

CORVALLIS, MONTANA

Churning that damn, delicious, fresh cream butter.

KIMBERLY, IDAHO

Me by the Chicken Coop. Notice the painted
rock frog below my right hand.

WENDELL, IDAHO

The Rock House at Niagara Springs Ranch.

Dean and the horned owl that had just made a
wet mess down the back of Dean's shirt.

Our New House, with the fireplace at right under
construction. The driveway rocks are petrified wood.

Carson, Trix, and Zip.

Mom and me wearing the matching dresses she
made for a night out dancing with Dad.

Left to right: Me, Dean with our dog, and Craig. Mom took
us on a picnic on Saturday while Dad was at work, and she
snapped this photo. She abandoned us on Monday.

TUCSON, ARIZONA

My fifth-grade school photo when we lived on Buckeye
Lane. My hair hadn't been washed for weeks, and I was
spitting out baby teeth when I walked at night.

INDIANAPOLIS, INDIANA

Left to right: Harold, me, and Dorothy the
day I graduated from high school.

ZIG ZAG, OREGON

Stevie and me at Mom's.

LAS VEGAS, NEVADA

Dorothy and me.

TUCSON, ARIZONA

Dorothy and Harold's fiftieth wedding
anniversary with Dad and me.

LAS VEGAS, NEVADA

Juanita and Dorothy in jammies, celebrating their
latest euchre trouncing at my old lady home.

Dean and me on his thirty-eighth birthday.

AUTHOR'S NOTE

The Health of Children website states more than seven thousand children are abandoned in the United States each year.[2] This means that approximately 136 more kids are abandoned—each and every week. Many of them are overlooked, underfed, and terrified. Every year, thousands of throwaway kids reach maturity without the slightest idea of how to navigate their trauma, let alone the world in which they are expected to live.

I've depicted a throwaway's silent fight for somewhere to belong, to survive, and to find self-worth through my eyes and experiences. I've attempted to show the waste of generational indifference that shatters families and creates far-reaching consequences.

When I first heard the term "dysfunctional family" in my thirties, I thought how sad that must be. As the term played around in my mind, I came to realize that was my family. How could this have happened? Why us?

When I started putting my story on paper from many yellow sticky notes

---

2   Health of Children. "Abandonment." Accessed Nov. 13, 2021, http://www.healthofchildren.com/A/Abandonment.html.

I'd compiled, listing data points for the immense hurt I carried around, I originally thought I'd be able to figure out Mom—to understand her more. I thought I'd finally get to the why. Why was she filled with emptiness in a family of seven who loved her? Why did she leave us? Was she just selfish? Was it because sex was better after she left? Why did she accept brutal beatings? Was it because she couldn't or wouldn't say "I'm sorry" and felt she had to endure them to pay for what she did to us? Did she accept them because of the childhood rape or the violence she had seen from her dad and oldest sister? Was it a combination? Probably, but I'll never know for certain.

I do know for certain that Dad did the very best he was able to do for me during those times as he carved his way through his own suffocating loss. I came to understand him more during the adventure of writing about him. But I always knew he was a decent, fair man with character. A good man—just like Mom always knew too. And he was one helluva dancer.

Music became a reprieve from the pain of my childhood. It became the salve and the glue at various times, especially in my youth. Throughout my life, it has been my connection to family and the conduit for understanding and remembering. But how could I capture all the music I'd been moved by and listened to through the years? There were so many songs to choose from!

I considered: Do I stick with classic country from the 1950s through the early 1980s or traditional pop or that rock-and-roll golden era from the early fifties to the early sixties? I had listened to them all on my little transistor radio and loved every song. Ultimately, I picked mostly classic country, which I intensely hope will come back someday—the songs that led me to recall a piece of my young life while I listened to them.

I've listened to many artists singing the songs I chose for chapter headings—artists from Mom's generation and even earlier, along with artists from my own. I selected the artist for a particular song because that's who I still hear when the song travels through my mind.

I have to say, with all the references to songs and singing, I can't carry a tune in a bucket, and neither could Mom. But many times, we had a great time trying.

All events in this book have been relayed honestly, according to my memory of them. Some are out of order for continuity's sake, especially during my never-ending eleventh year and some of the later chapters. A few names have been changed. Yet, the essence of the people and experiences has been left intact. As hard as it has been to again drag out and reflect on many of these experiences, they did actually happen.

Most recently, after writing my story, *Roe v. Wade* was overturned—which leaves me disillusioned about society's future. White, male Republican politicians, and those who support them, keep issues like abortion, health insurance, equal rights, civil rights, and women's rights in flux on purpose, holding back women and other minorities so white men can keep control over them. They intend for the majority of people in this country—women—to not pay attention to what politicians do and don't do. It's just a game for them to stay in power and do much of nothing on behalf of those who need support, while saying all the right things to make sure nothing changes in favor of minorities. In this way, white men's authority over women, and all who don't look like them, continues. I believe it would be a much better country when women start running it.

During my life, I have met other "adult abandoned children," who were either abused or neglected. When the conversation turns to childhood, they use the same veil I've used. I see the same fleeting, furtive look with a side-step then a pivot to safer topics. They use my honed defenses to hide shame, no matter how long ago trouble found them.

By sharing my story, I hope to reach other "adult abandoned children" of all ethnicities or classes, those women who still cannot handle the shame, who fear everything because they believe they are worth nothing. My hope is that my experiences will show these women that they are not alone, and it didn't happen to "just them."

I believe it is possible to find a way through the soul-killing indifference of childhood. We cannot change an indifferent, selfish parent, but we can survive one to have a meaningful life.

Finally, I hope to reach those mothers who contemplate leaving their children behind. I hope that by reading my story, you will find a way to keep your children with you. If you have to leave a relationship for any reason, please take your kids too. They need their mom much more than they need anything else.

ACKNOWLEDGMENTS

Even though Bill's gone, I love him even more for giving me the courage to think I could, and should, write a book. "You should write that down. These things just don't happen to most people. I don't think you understand how unusual your life's been." Thank you, Bill.

I also need to thank those who read early versions and gave me the courage to keep going but had to leave my life before I finished: Dorothy, Juanita, Aunt Ruth, Donna Faye, Donna Woody, Pat, Theron, and BK. My thanks to Mary, Val, Judy, and Lisa for their readings too.

And many thanks to my Samuel, who has the patience of a saint and the wisdom to be out of his mother's reach when he tells me I'm singing out of tune again. If he were able to edit this for me, he would do a wonderful job because he understands verbs way better than I do. What he's done is understand my need to bury myself in this project because he has projects of his own as he grows into a wonderful young man with still the sweetest heart I've ever known.

This book couldn't have been born without Donna Mazzitelli, content and editor extraordinaire (writingwithdonna.com) and publisher of Merry

Dissonance Press (merrydissonancepress.com). With polish, patience, and humility, she has weathered meltdowns, given insightful suggestions, and entered my mind to know when there was more to say. Donna encouraged me and showed me the way to dip into something I have no experience in—a desire to publish my story. Without her, it would still just be a dream. I believe "thank you" is said to someone who cared and shared with kindness. Thank you, Donna, with everything I am and still hope to be.

ABOUT THE AUTHOR

After fifty-two years in the workforce, Sherrie Lancaster retired just in time for the COVID-19 lockdown. Although staying home was wonderful, she soon realized she had retired to clean house and not to take her dream vacation. So she dusted off her first dream—the manuscript she needed to turn into a book to reach those who need its message.

From an early age, Sherrie knew she had to write this story because she never stopped thinking about her unusual childhood. It was great to think about the kid-perfect places where she lived back in Idaho, but *those times* kept interfering. She considered that maybe—by writing it all down—she would become the owner of her heart instead of those childhood events continuing to own her.

When Sherrie began writing, she struggled to put together an engaging sentence, but after twenty years of writing and rewriting, she finally learned how to craft and tell her story.

Sherrie Lancaster lives in Las Vegas, Nevada, with her son Samuel. She sincerely hopes that *Cracks of Destruction* will help others as much as it helped her by writing it.

INVITE SHERRIE TO
YOUR BOOK CLUB!

As a special gift to readers of *Cracks of Destruction,* Sherrie would love to visit your book club either via video conferencing or in person.

Please contact Sherrie directly to schedule her appearance at your next book club meeting. To contact Sherrie, go to SherrieLancaster.com.

ABOUT THE PRESS

Merry Dissonance Press is a hybrid indie publisher/book producer of works of transformation, inspiration, exploration, and illumination. MDP takes a holistic approach to bring books into the world that make a little noise and create dissonance within the whole so ALL can be resolved to produce beautiful harmonies.

Merry Dissonance Press works with its authors every step of the way to craft the finest books and help promote them. Dedicated to publishing award-winning books, we strive to support talented writers and assist them to discover, claim, and refine their distinct voices. Merry Dissonance Press is the place where collaboration and facilitation of our shared human experiences join together to make a difference in our world.

For more information, visit merrydissonancepress.com.